Curved
Joinery

techniques
   that will change
   the way you work
   and how your work
   looks.

Marc Lamm

Publisher:
Marc Lamm, LLC
2909 E, 22nd St.
Minneapolis, MN 55406
cubsrmarc@msn.com
marclamm.com

March, 2018

Printed in the United States

ISBN-13: 978-0-692-06747-5

3

In memory of Malinda

Thanks to Josie Winship, my partner, whose advice on this book you can see in many pages and many ways.

Thanks to Kristine Heim, my friend, who spent many hours editing this manuscript.

4

Contents

7   introduction

11   *section 1 – your shop*

13   chapter 1 –   safety first and always

19   chapter 2 –   specialized tools, equipment, jigs and workstations

49   How I Came to Love Woodworking – part 1

55   *section 2 – the techniques*

57   chapter 3   –   the properties of a curved joint

61   chapter 4 –   inserting strips in curved cuts

81   summary of chapter 4

93   chapter 5   –   joining boards along a curve

107   summary of chapter 5

117   How I Came to Love Woodworking – part 2

121   chapter 6   –   patterns of pegs

135   summary of chapter 6

145   chapter 7   –   creating circles of wood

155   summary of chapter 7

163   chapter 8   –   fans

171   summary of chapter 8

177   chapter 9   –   preparing your panel for use

183   summary of chapter 9

187   chapter 10   –   using these panels in a project

199   summary of chapter 10

209   chapter 11   –   curved joints in 3 dimensions

217   summary of chapter 11

223   chapter 12   –   filling voids

229   summary of chapter 12

233   How I Came to Love Woodworking – part 3

239   *section 3 – background information*

241   chapter 13 –   strong straight edge joints

245   summary of chapter 13

247   chapter 14 –   the properties of wood

253   chapter 15 –   how wood goes from tree to shop

257   final notes

258   glossary

260   index

introduction

A recent survey found that approximately 5.5 million Americans actively participate in woodworking as a hobby. Think of that. Millions of people spend hours in windowless, dust covered basements or garages and pay hundreds or even thousands of dollars for tools, equipment and materials to make things they could probably buy – in some form - at a store. Above that, the U. S. Bureau of Labor Statistics says that more than two hundred thousand people listed "woodworker" as their profession on their tax forms. The median income for that group in 2012 was $28,440 while the median income for all workers was $34,750. That means that in order to be a woodworker, people will accept far less than they could make in another profession. I'm fortunate to sell what I make, but I'd make more driving a taxi. So, why do I do it? If you're a woodworker, you know the answer.

Woodworking is seductive. I love the tools, the designs, the planning and the implementation. I love seeing stacks of hardwoods at a lumber yard, the smell of cherry when I cut it, of oak being sanded and the fragrance of sweet maple sawdust on my hands at the end of the day. I love discovering hidden figures in boards when I oil them and the silken feel of wood after it's sanded. I love the work, but most of all, I love the feelings I get when I'm doing it.

I become so involved in the work I forget problems and conflicts. The work absorbs me and I see nothing but wood and tools. Sometimes that's a problem. I've been late for dinner. I forget lunch. I've gone into my shop in the evening just to check on something, decided to do one small operation and find myself still working at one or two in the morning.

When I complete a project and stand back to see what I've made, it's not pride I feel, but the wonder of what I've done.

Why are we woodworkers? It's not just to make things. We are woodworkers for the bliss the work brings us. The dust, the cost and the effort we put into it is a fair price for the act of creation.

Throughout history, highly crafted woodworking could be found only in palaces, cathedrals and the estates of the wealthiest merchants. A very small group of people had the training, experience and access to the tools necessary to do that work. Late in the nineteenth century, the industrial revolution created a class of fabulously wealthy people who could afford to decorate their homes and businesses with highly crafted and elegant woodworking. That required a far larger group of skilled people. By the twentieth century, union apprenticeship programs were producing a steady flow of trained, professional woodworkers to fill that need. But, people who weren't professional woodworkers didn't have access to the knowledge and equipment necessary to make fine furniture.

The rise of the middle class and the introduction of affordable tools and equipment in the 1950s and '60s changed that. Tool companies started producing "home craftsmen" lines of stationary and hand tools. They weren't as sturdy or powerful as their commercial lines but didn't have to be. At the same time, books and magazine articles came out, written by eminent professionals, that showed amateur woodworkers how to make intricate joints and highly finished furniture. Clubs formed in every city and town where people shared information to help each other increase their skills. Collective shops formed where people who didn't have the space or money for stationary tools could work. Today, anyone who is willing to put in the effort can learn to make things only the few skilled artisans in the past could make.

Most woodworkers are students of their craft. How they work is at least as important to them as the things they make. When I visit someone's shop, they may spend a few minutes showing their work, but they'll spend an hour talking about how they made it.

At the moment I'm writing these words, I'm almost sixty-nine years old. I've been using the techniques I describe in this book for twenty-two years. For most of that time, I've been telling people how I do this work. But, there's far too much information to share verbally. One day, I realized that if I didn't do something, these techniques would die with me. So, I wrote this book.

section one

your
shop

chapter 1

safety first
and always

If you're the kind of person who is sometimes impatient or you don't like planning and preparation, then you're part of a club of which I am the President. I had to learn the hard way that taking shortcuts actually makes projects take longer because you make mistakes. Most important, impatience and lack of planning significantly increases the risk of a serious accident.

Years ago, I met a man who had been a woodworker most of his life. We talked about saws, wood and the things we make. When it was time to say good-bye, he held out his hand to shake mine and I noticed a space where his two middle fingers should have been. It might have shocked me once but by that time I'd seen a lot of woodworkers with missing fingers. I've been lucky not to be one of them.

When I was younger, no one could convince me to be careful.
I didn't wear hearing or eye protection and rarely used push
sticks. I took the anti-kick back apparatus off my table saw
and sometimes put my finger right next to the blade. I
believed that people who used safety devices did so because
they weren't quick or smart enough to avoid accidents.

I'm lucky that I never had a serious eye injury or lost a finger
but I've developed tinnitus from the high-pitched whine of
machinery and the pounding of hammers day after day.
Several times, only luck saved my fingers.

In the fall of 2011, I was cutting strips which I use in my art.
(You'll read about that technique later in the book.) Over the
course of a year, I probably cut several hundred of them. Doing
an operation over and over helps you perfect procedures and
improve efficiency. Your jigs get better, you eliminate
unnecessary steps and you reduce wasted motion. But, it also
can put you at risk if your attention wanders and you lose focus
on what you're doing.

That morning, I was working like a machine, moving boards into
position, pushing them through the blade, setting strips aside and
starting on the next cut. Efficiency has its rewards and I was
putting out a lot of work. I keep two push sticks at my table saw
– one to move a board through the blade and the other to press it
against the fence. Sometimes I'd get lazy or thoughtless and push
the board with my right hand and press the board against the fence
with my left. I did that even though I knew it was dangerous. But
when you're doing repetitive work, you can forget that taking
shortcuts and not giving absolute and uninterrupted attention to
what you're doing increases the chances of a serious accident.
Eventually the odds will play out against you. That day, they
played out for me.

I'd been cutting strips for ten or fifteen minutes and was putting
out a lot of work. After a while, my mind wandered. Maybe I
was thinking about finding a machine that makes strips or
maybe I was thinking about the daughter I hadn't seen in a
while. Suddenly, I heard a loud bang like a hammer on a board
and felt my hand get knocked back as if the hammer had hit

my thumb. I looked down and my heart sank. Blood pooled
at the end of my thumb so I couldn't see how much was missing.

"Damn," I said. "I did it. I finally did it."

In forty years of woodworking, I'd cut my fingers a few times
and needed stitches but never this bad. I poured disinfectant
on the wound, tied a clean rag around it and got a friend to
drive me to the hospital.

Fortunately, the blade was dull, and kicked my hand back –
the hammer I heard – but didn't hit the bone. The thumb is
slightly deformed and the nerves are dull but otherwise it
functions normally. If that blade had been sharp, I probably
would have lost most of the thumb. A momentary lapse of
attention nearly changed my life.

———————————

When you're working with tools, especially power tools, you
can't let your attention wander, not for a second. You can't
daydream and you can't look away. You must give full and clear
attention to where your hands are in relation to the blade at every
moment. Tools and machinery are unforgiving and – except for a
Sawstop table saw – don't have the capacity to compensate for
your lapses.

Before starting any operation, do a risk assessment. Check your
environment and think about how you're going to do things safely
before you do them. Stay focused on your work whenever your
hands are anywhere around a blade, sander or lathe.

A table saw may be the most dangerous tool in your shop. The blade
runs at 3450 rpm which is far faster than you could see and react
to a situation because your brain can't register an image at that
speed. That's why you can't see the teeth on your blade when it's
spinning. You can lose a finger before you realize it's happening.

Long sleeve shirts pose a significant risk in a shop. If the blade
catches your sleeve, your arm will be pulled into it before your
brain can register the problem and trigger your muscles to resist.
A one-horse motor on a table saw has more than enough power
to drag your arm into the blade before you realize it's

happening. Of course, it's possible the blade will only rip the fabric, but if your sleeve doesn't tear, the material will pull your arm into the blade like a rope tied to your wrist. To show how strong the material of your shirt is, grab a sleeve at both ends and try to tear it apart. You can't do it because it's actually as strong as a thick rope. A lathe poses the same risk because a sleeve can get caught by a spinning object and wrap around it before you can react.

While there is no lathe or band saw that can compensate for mistakes, a Sawstop table saw can do that. It has a plasma field around its blade and when skin approaches it, the field instantly cuts power to the motor and triggers a brake which slams against the blade so fast you can't be cut. It's an expensive tool, but what's a finger worth?

please consider these points about safety

1. Survey and evaluate all potential dangers before starting an operation.

2. Never wear long sleeve shirts, sweatshirts, gloves, jewelry or anything which could be caught by a saw blade. Rolling up your sleeves is not a solution because your sleeves could roll back down as your arm passes the blade.

You probably know most of this, but if it saves a trip to the hospital, it's worth your time reading it.

3. Long hair presents a similar danger. Hair that gets caught by a blade or a lathe can twist like a rope and be stronger than you can imagine. Tie long hair back behind you. Better yet, keep it tucked inside a hat.

4. Remove jewelry. A ring could be crushed on your finger and a loose fitting bracelet or necklace could be caught by a blade or lathe.

5. Stay focused on your fingers every moment they are working anywhere near a blade and keep them out of the line of cut. If a board splits, the sudden loss of resistance could send your

fingers into the blade. When cutting a curve, there is a much
wider field of danger which must be considered.

6. Never push any tool toward your hand or body. If a drill bit
slips off a board it could drive into your hand. If a knife or
chisel slips off a board, it could cut you.

7. Use a push stick to move a board through a blade and a
feather board or a second push stick to hold it against the fence.

8. Keep floors clear so you won't trip while carrying a load and
make sure boards are stacked securely.

9. Wear a dust mask whenever grinding or sanding.

10. Use a dust collection system. Inhaling wood dust over a long
period can damage sinuses and lungs. Some studies show that
dust from aromatic woods like cedar or exotics can cause sinus
and lung cancer.

11. If possible, use a dedicated sanding room with a dust collector.
That will reduce the amount of dust in your shop.

12. Wear surgical gloves whenever you work with solvents or
finishes, even when doing a quick operation. Solvents like mineral
spirits, acetone, lacquer and shellac easily penetrate the skin, enter
the blood stream and can damage the liver and kidneys.

13. You can get surgical gloves at any paint store and most
hardware stores. Blue nitrate gloves are more resistant to solvents.
Latex gloves can be dissolved by solvents after a short exposure
making them worse than useless since you think you're protected.
I buy gloves in boxes of 50 or 100 so I never run out.

14. The one time you shortcut safety may be the time something
goes wrong and you get hurt. Cuts and scrapes are part of
working in a shop, but if you lose a finger or an eye, you'll have
to live with that the rest of your life.

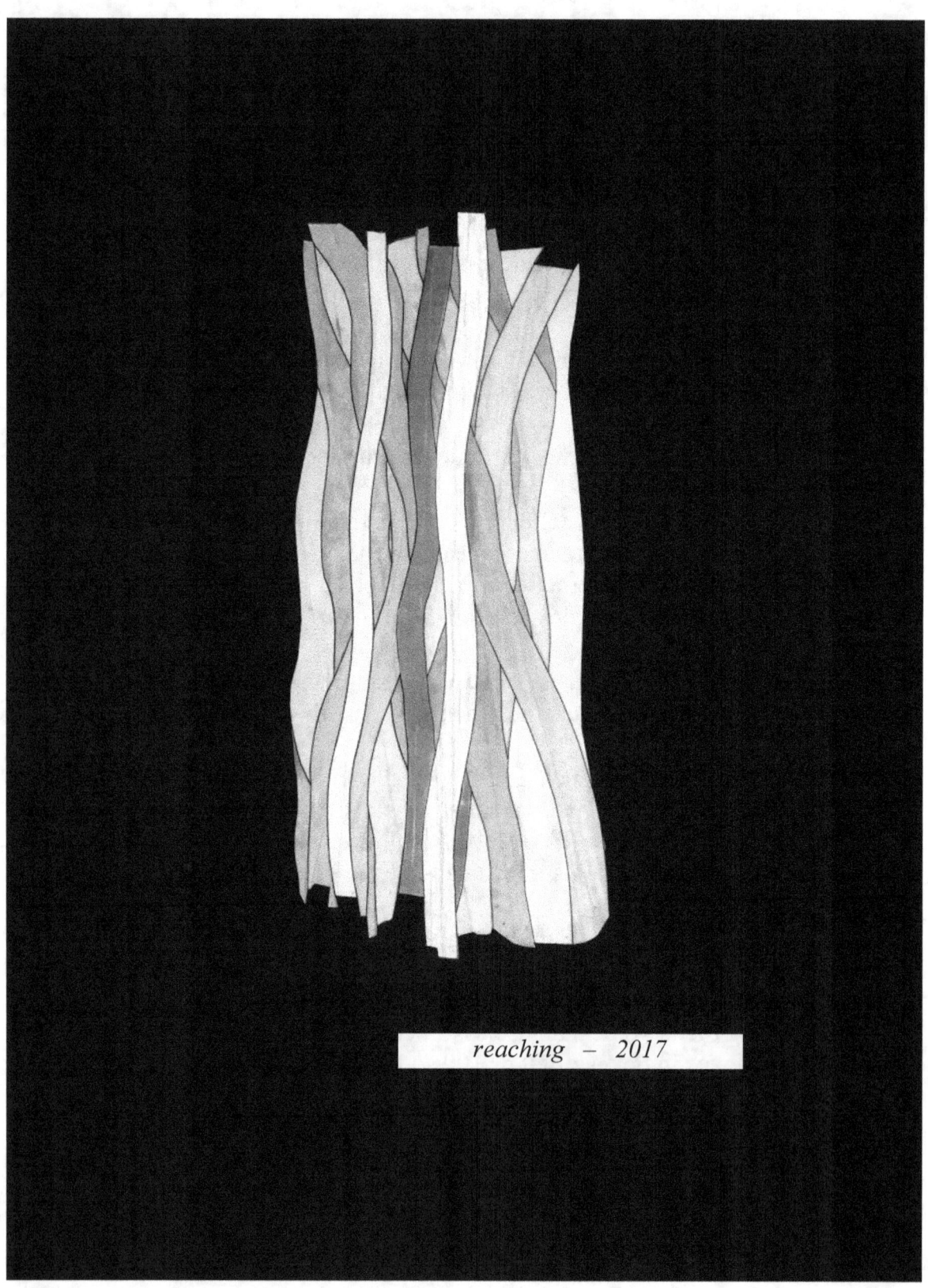

reaching – 2017

chapter 2

specialized tools, equipment, jigs and workstations

For the operations I describe in this book, you'll need 3 large pieces of equipment:

• a table-saw – a one horse or larger motor with a sturdy, properly aligned table and fence are a minimum requirement.

• a band-saw – a one horse or larger motor. If you want to make panels that are 2 feet wide, a 13 inch throw will work. The size of your work should determine the size and power of your saw.

• a drill press – You can't produce holes and pegs that fit precisely with a hand drill. A quarter horse motor will work but with large bits, a half horse motor is nice to have. Sharp bits are more important than a powerful motor.

In this chapter, I describe jigs and workstations that will make your work easier. They will be useful for these techniques but also for all your work.

a suitable work-station

A warped board is difficult to control and can make a cabinet, table or desk wobble on a floor or fit poorly in a corner.

A panel will warp if it's made with warped boards. However, flat boards will make a warped panel if they're glued up on a warped work-station. Panels match the condition of the surface on which they're assembled. If the top of a work-station is warped, the finished panel will be warped in the same way.

You can check the surface of a work-station with one of the following two methods:

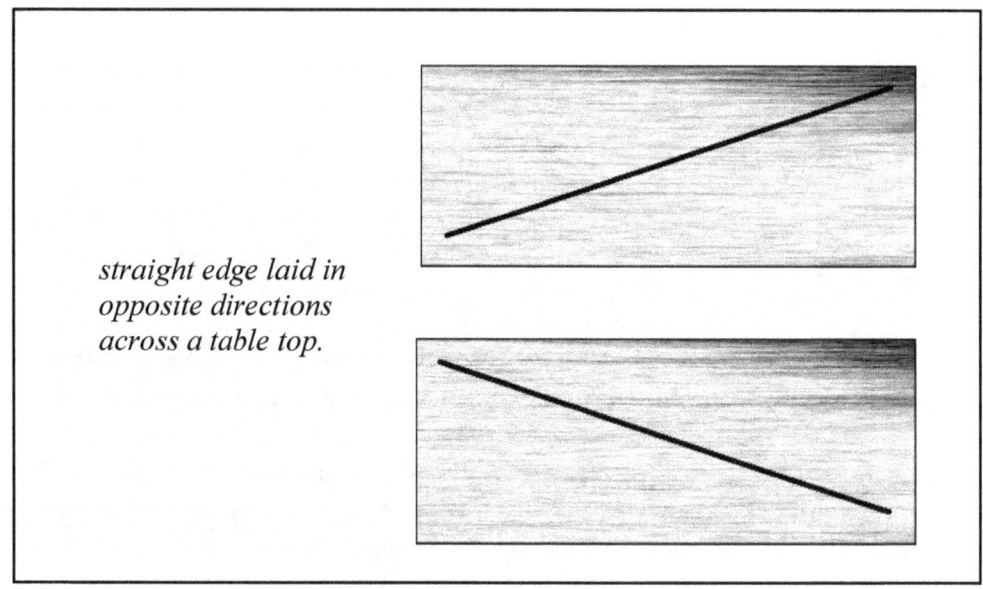

straight edge laid in opposite directions across a table top.

Method 1 – Set a long straight edge on the table diagonally from opposite corners. It should sit flat on the table in both directions. If the straight edge lays flat on the table in both directions, the table is not warped.

Method 2 – I prefer this method because it's quick and easier.

1. Kneel down so your eyes are slightly below the level of the leading edge of the top of the work-station.

2. Rise up until you see the entire length of the back edge above the front edge.

3. Drop down slowly till any part of the back edge disappears.

4. If the top is out of plane, one corner of the back edge will still be visible above the front edge.

5. If the top is in one plane, the entire length of the back edge will disappear at the same time as you drop down. It will take some practice before you can be sure you've got it right but once you master it, it's really fast and accurate.

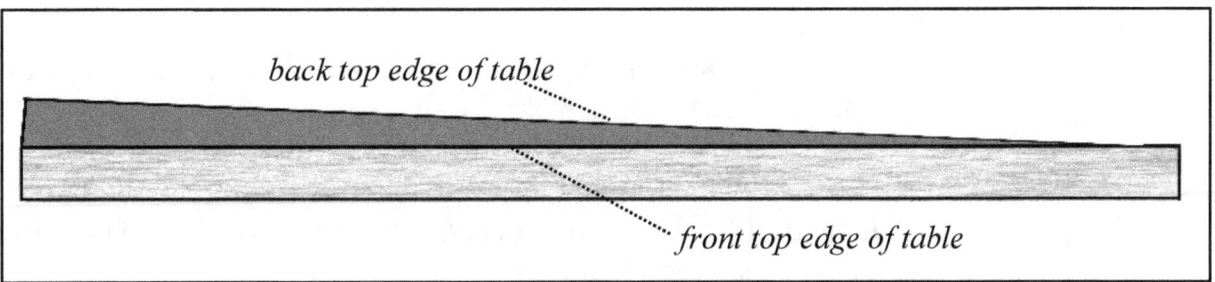

exaggerated edge view of a table top which is out of plane

If you find the table top is out of plane, here's how to fix it.

For free standing tables:

1. Mark the spots on the floor where the legs of the table will sit.

2. Move the work-station out of the way and use method 1 above to determine which of the spots on the floor is lower than the other three. You could also use a level if the floor is flat.

3. Mark that spot. Place a plywood shim on it and test it again. The plywood shim must be larger than the leg so the leg will be fully supported.

4. Set the work-station back in position and check the top again to see if it's in one plane.

Raise or lower one corner to get the table top in a single plane.

5. If the top is still not in one plane, add shims.

6. If you've used more than one shim, glue them together. You may want to attach blocks to the edges of the plywood to prevent the leg from falling off it.

7. Make sure the legs of the work-station are on the marks when you assemble a panel.

If the work-station is attached to the floor or wall, you'll have to plane or sand the top to fix it.

1. Lay a long straight edge on the top of the work-station diagonally from opposite corners. Determine which two corners are higher than the other two.

2. Run a joining plane from one high corner diagonally to the other.

3. Test the surface.

4. Continue planing until the straight edge hits all corners diagonally.

Once the work surface is in one plane, check to see if it has high spots by laying a straight edge on it in several directions.

If it has high spots:

1. Draw a series of lines on the table top with a pencil. They can be random, irregular and in no particular direction but make sure the entire surface is marked.

2. Set a joining plane to take a shallow cut.

3. As you plane, the marks will disappear. The marks which remain are low spots.

Continue till all the marks are gone.

keeping a panel flat and level during assembly

Tightening the clamps on a panel can pull the edges up, especially if it includes several boards. This reduces the contact at the joint and may cause the panel to have a permanent bow.

To prevent this,

1. Lay a set of 2x2s (strong-backs) on the table so they are perpendicular to the line of the joints.

2. Apply glue to the boards then put enough pressure on the clamps to hold the joint together.

3. Use four small clamps to firmly hold both edges of the panel down on the strong-backs.

4. Ensure that the joints line up flush at the surface as well as possible.

5. Apply full pressure to the clamps.

Clamping the panel to the strong-backs prevents the panel from bowing up. The center of the panel won't rise because the clamps exert more pressure on the top edges of the panel and the bars or pipes of the clamps minimize the amount the center of the panel can rise.

The key ingredients for making a good panel are a table which is in one plane, controlling moisture migration and clamping the panel to a set of strong-backs during the assembly.

a mobile and versatile work-station

For years, I glued panels by laying strong-backs on a table. They did the job but they were difficult to use and required storing when not in use. If the panel was narrower than the table, the clamps which held the edges of the panel to the strong-backs couldn't get under theme. I set a second set of boards under and perpendicular to the strong-backs so the small clamps could clear the top of the table.

I designed and built a work-station with removable strong-backs. They're versatile, strong and can be easily moved and stored like saw horses.

The following pages have instructions for how to make them.

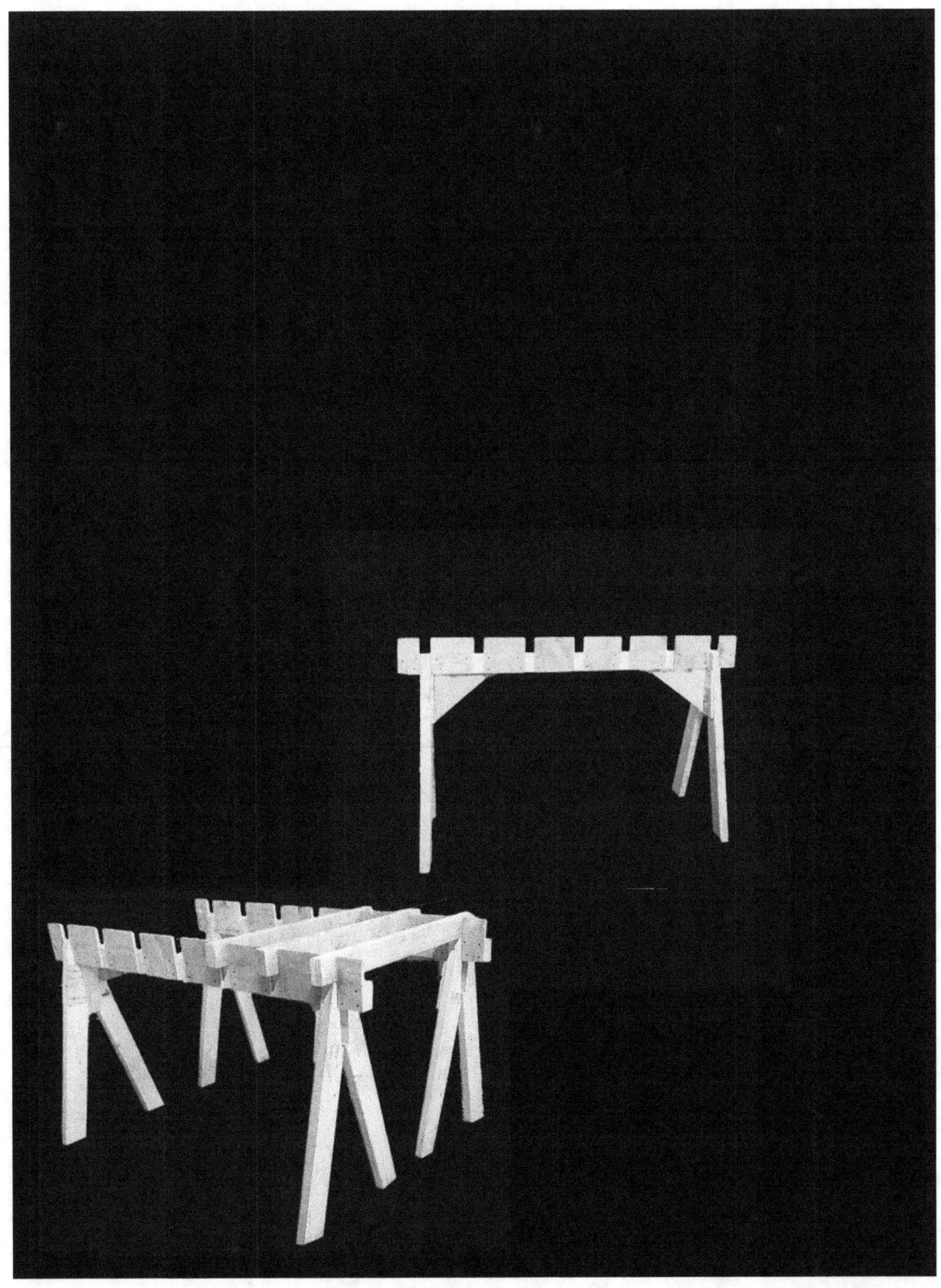

the top rails

For each work-station, you'll need two rails.

Select two clear straight grained 2x4s that are approximately as long as the longest panel you might make.

1. Mark the side of one 2x4 four inches from one end.

2. The second mark will be eight inches from the first one.

3. Continue marking the side of the 2x4 at eight inch intervals.

4. Set the second 2x4 edge to edge against the first.

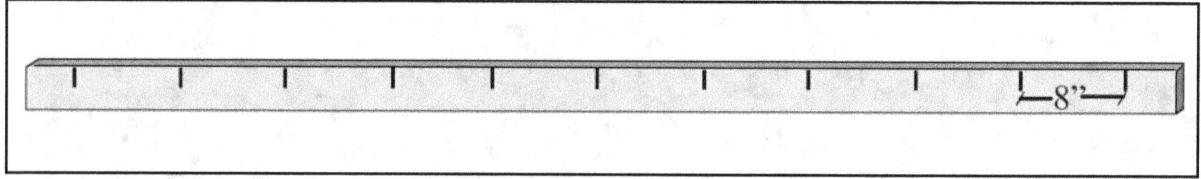

2x4 marked at 8" intervals

5. With a hand square, transfer the marks from the first 2x4 to the second one so you'll have squared lines down the side of both boards.

Plywood is much more durable than OSB for this.

6. Count the number of marks you made on the rails.

7. Cut 1/2 inch plywood into 6-3/8 x 6-3/8 inch squares. Make enough to match the number of marks you made.

8. Set the first full square to the side of the first mark/line (4 inches from the end) so the bottom edge of the square is just above the bottom edge of the rail.

9. Attach the plywood to the 2x4 with four 1-1/4 inch screws.

10. Attach a plywood square on the next line you drew on the rail in the same way. This leaves 1-5/8 inches between the

plywood squares which are 2-7/8 inches above the rail. No square should be more than 3-1/4 inches above the rail so they don't go above a 2x4 strong-backs.

11. Continue adding plywood squares to the rail until you are within 6 inches of the other end.

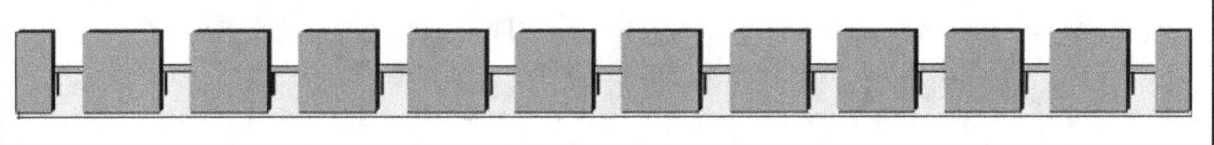

2x4 with 1/2" plywood squares attached to side of marks

12. Mark the 2x4 at 1-5/8 inches from the last square at each end. Use a hand square to draw a line down from the mark. Cut 1/2 inch plywood into 6-3/8 x 4 inch rectangles. Attach one of the 6-3/8 x 4 inch rectangles to the line. Cut the rail to the outside edge of the 4 inch rectangle.

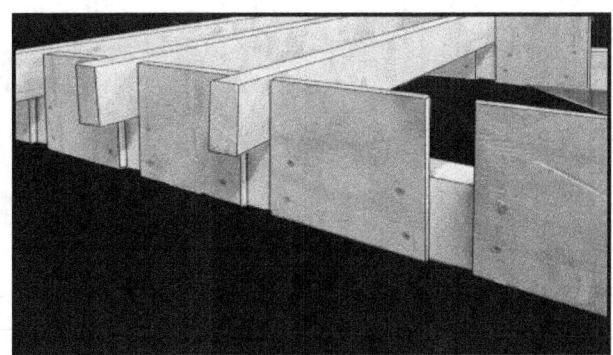

1/2" plywood squares screwed to rail

the legs

Each work-station needs eight legs.

1. Select eight straight grained 2x4s approximately 48 inches long.

2. Draw a line at "X" (image A) with a protractor or framing square at 60 degrees on one end of the 2x4 and cut the line. If

you want the saw horses to have a wider base, use a sharper angle. However, wider legs take more room in a shop.

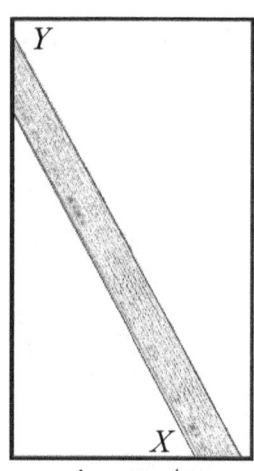

image A
leg cut to size

3. Set that end of the leg on the floor so it sits flat on the cut. Mark the 2x4 at the height you want your work-station to be.

4. Measure down 3-1/2 inches. The strong-backs will make up for the 3-1/2 inches you cut off.

5. Draw a line at "Y" (image A) at 30 degrees on the side of the 2x4 and cut it.

6. If you don't use 60 degrees for the base of the leg, subtract the number of degrees you use from 90 for the angle of the top cut. For example, if X is 40 degrees, then Y will be 50 degrees. When you set the board on the floor, the cut at "Y" will be plumb (perpendicular to the floor). Use this leg as a template to mark and cut the other legs so that all eight legs are identical.

attaching legs to the rail

1. Attach the long cut, "Y", (image A) of two legs to the rail between the last two plywood squares at each end of the rail with construction adhesive and 3-1/2 inch screws. The top of the legs must be flush with the top of the rail. If they are above the rail they will interfere with the strong-backs.

2. With both legs attached to one side, flip the assembly over and attach the third and fourth legs exactly opposite to the first two legs.

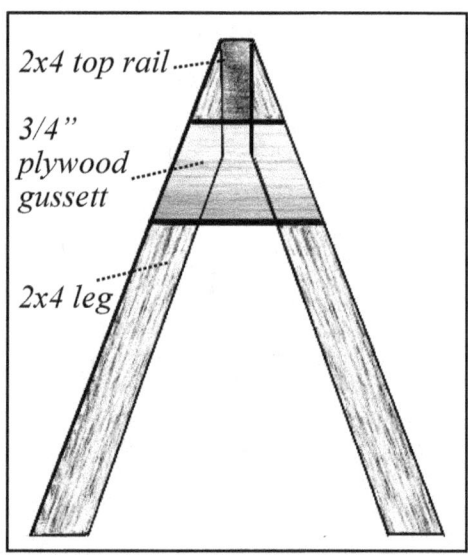

image B – attaching legs to rail

3. Carefully set the assembly upright.

4. Cut four 3/4 inch plywood strips approximately 14 inches wide for gussets. Hold one up across one set of legs and tight under the top rail (image B).

5. Mark one strip along the outer edges of the legs.

6. Cut the plywood 1/2 inch shorter than what you marked. Use that to mark the other three strips plywood. Attach the plywood gussets to the legs and tight to the bottom of the rail with glue and 1-1/4 inch screws.

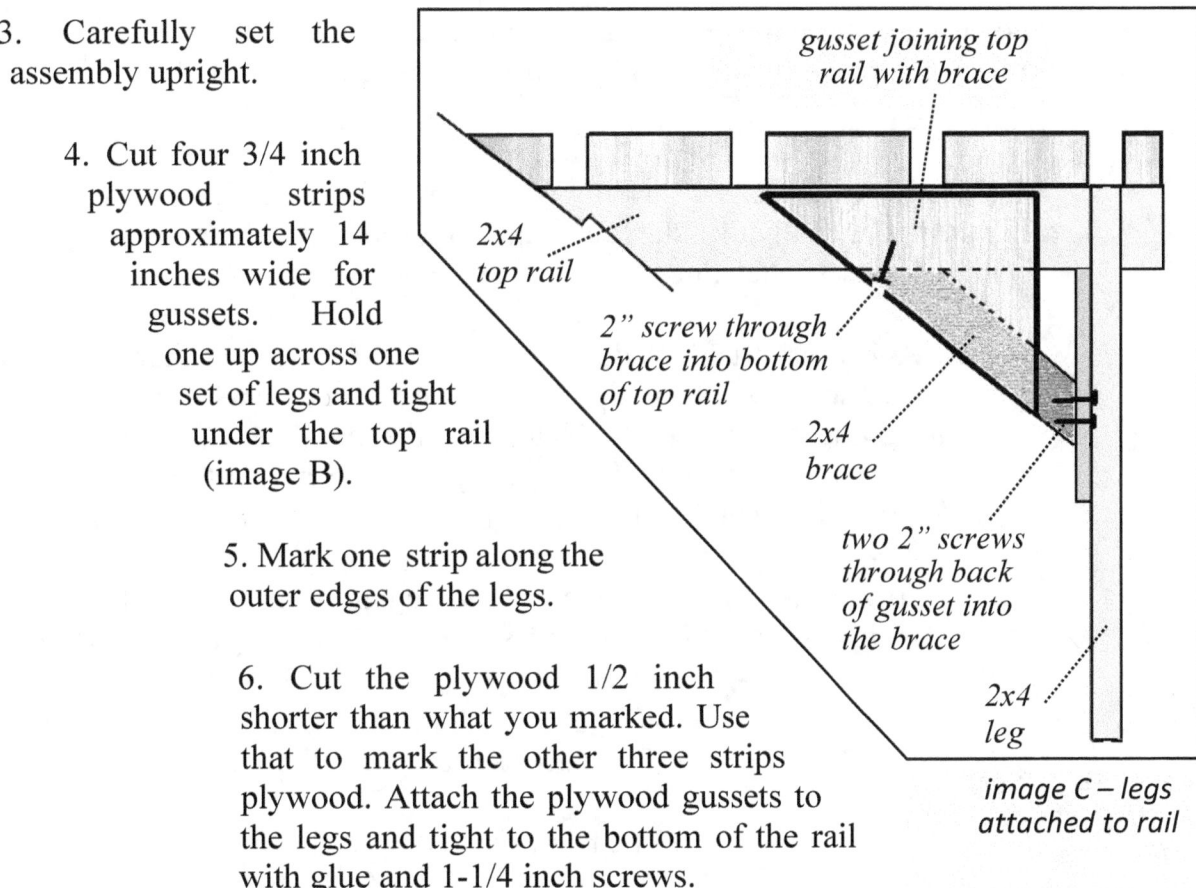

gusset joining top rail with brace

2x4 top rail

2" screw through brace into bottom of top rail

2x4 brace

two 2" screws through back of gusset into the brace

2x4 leg

image C – legs attached to rail

7. Make four 2x4 braces 20 inches long and cut at 45 degrees at both ends with the long points on the same edge (image C).

8. Drill a pilot hole approximately two inches from one end of each brace.

9. Apply construction adhesive to both ends of the brace.

10. Place the brace under the top rail and against the gusset with the pilot hole under the top rail.

11. Use a framing square to ensure that the gusset is square to the top rail.

12. Drive a 2 inch screw through the pilot hole in the brace into the bottom of the top rail.

13. Double check that the gusset and the top rail are square then drive two 2 inch screws through the back of the gusset into the brace.

14. Cut two squares of 1/2 inch plywood 14 x 14 inches then cut them diagonally to make four equilateral triangles. These will be gussets attaching the braces to the top rail.

15. Apply construction adhesive to a gusset and set it against the top rail opposite the side with the plywood squares. Leave the gusset about a quarter inch below the top of the top rail so it doesn't interfere with the strong-backs. Screw it to the top rail with four 1-1/4 inch screws.

16. With a framing square, check again to make sure the top rail is square to the leg gusset. Screw the gusset to the brace with four 1-1/4 inch screws.

I have two sets of horses. One is four feet long and the other is six feet long.

17. Repeat these steps for all the legs.

18. The horses are complete.

2x4s set between the plywood squares support the work and provide an easy way to clamp a panel so it won't buckle under the pressure of the clamps. The 2x4s must be straight without any twist or warp.

The length of the strong-backs will be the width of the work-station. I keep sets of various lengths so I can easily change to the width I need. I usually fill every slot but you could have as few as three on a work-station.

If you won't be using the work-station for a while, you can easily remove the strong-backs and store the horses.

You can make a solid top fot your work-station top by screwing a sheet of plywood onto the strong-backs,

a fence extender

Years ago, I had an accident with a joiner and prefer not to use one. I use a jig which allows me to join boards on my table-saw. The jig doesn't produce an edge as smooth as one produced by a joiner but it has some attributes a joiner doesn't have.

If a board has a severely irregular edge, it will take several passes on a joiner to true it up. I can true up the edge of an extremely irregular board in one or two passes with a fence extender. Since it's 8 feet long, joining the edge of boards that are 7 feet or longer is much easier with a fence extender than a joiner.

Here's how to make a fence extender:

1. Unplug your table-saw, run the blade up to full height and use a hand square on both sides of the blade to make sure the blade is exactly at 90 degrees to the table so the edges of boards you come out square to the surface..

2. Rip 3/4 inch plywood into a 6 inch wide by eight foot strip.

3. Glue and screw a 2 x 2 flush to one of its edges as in image D. The plywood and the 2x2 must sit flat and be in one plane while you're doing this to avoid creating a bow in the assembly.

4. Run the assembly through the saw with the plywood edge against the fence and cut approximately 1/8 inch off the entire length of the edge with the 2x2. This will make that edge flush so it can fit tight against the fence.

5. Sand the edges and bottom of the plywood so the assembly will slide easily against the fence and table.

Here's how to use a fence extender:

1. Clamp the 2 x 2 to the fence of your table-saw with two clamps. The ruler on the table-saw won't work with the fence extender so you'll have to measure the distance from the fence extender to the blade. Moving the fence will be easier if you set the extender so it's evenly balanced on the table.

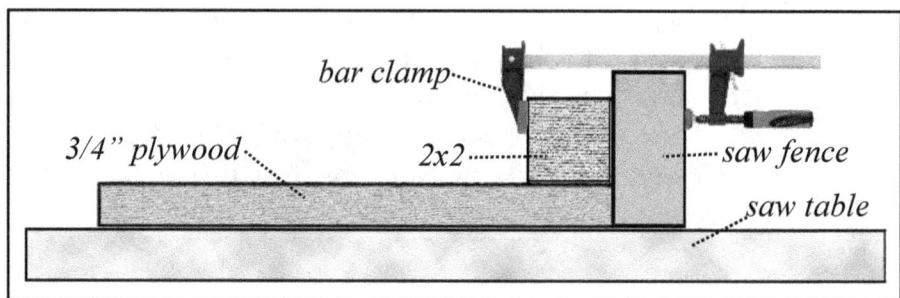

image D - fence extender clamped to table saw fence

2. The extender must be parallel to the miter gauge slot at front and back ends of the table. Double check the distance for the rip before cutting.

3. Run the board you are joining against the extender slowly and carefully. An eighty tooth blade will make an acceptably smooth edge. Try not to stop at any time while you're cutting or the blade may scar the edge of the board.

I have a four foot fence extender for shorter boards.

If the board is so irregular that it can't be joined with an extender, use this simple jig.

1. Rip 3/4 inch plywood 6 to 8 inches wide and at least as long as the board.

2. Lay the plywood on the board and measure from the outer edge of the plywood to the opposite edge of the board so the two ends of the board are the approximately the same distance.

3. Screw the plywood firmly to the board with two 1-1/4 inch screws.

4. Find the shortest distance along the edge of the board to the opposite edge of the plywood and set the fence of the table-saw to 1/8 inch less than that. Run the assembly through the table-saw with the plywood edge against the fence. Remove the plywood and use the cut edge against the fence or fence extender to join the opposite edge of the board.

a simple jig for cutting tapers

Making a clean and straight cut on a panel or board with one edge at an angle to the other edge requires a specialized jig. The jigs I've found on the market don't mechanically attach to the board or panel so the board can move as you push the jig. In some of them, a metal flange on the jig pushes the board through the blade as you push the jig. However, if you need to cut to the inside edge of the board, you'd hit the flange.

1. Establish the difference between the wide and narrow ends of the cut.

2. Rip a sheet of plywood to a width at least two inches wider than the narrow end of the cut - the side that is farthest from the fence - and at least as long as the cut you will make. If you want a panel that goes from twelve inches to six inches along a four

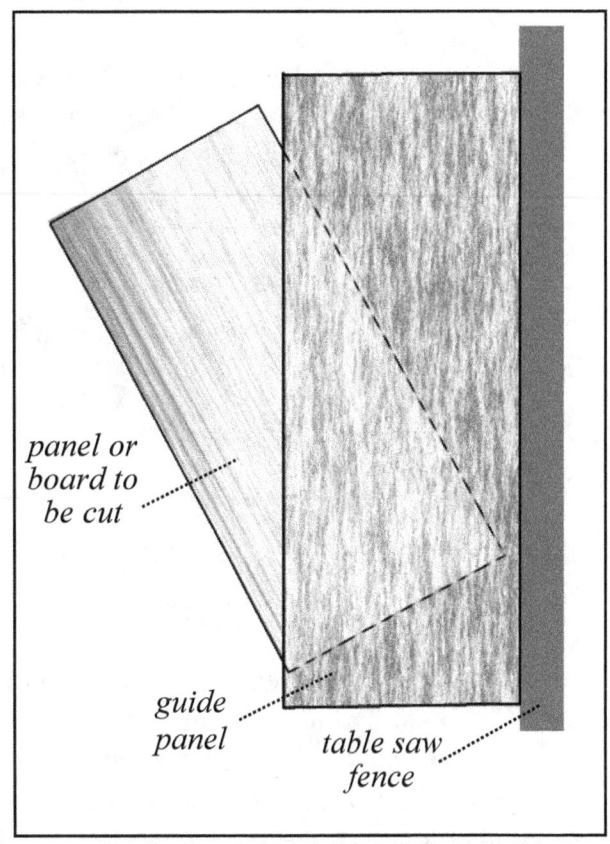

panel or board to be cut

guide panel

table saw fence

jig for cutting tapered panels

foot line, you'll need a plywood at least 6 inches wide and 4 feet long.

3. Draw the line you want to cut on the panel or board and screw the plywood to that line. Put the screws as close to the edge of the board and as far away from the line of cut as possible.

4. Measure the distance from the edge of the plywood to the line and set the fence to that distance.

5. Run the assembly through the saw being sure to keep the plywood flush against the fence. This will give you a straight cut at an angle to the edge of the board or panel.

panel caliper

If you need to know the thickness of a board or panel at any point within it, the simplest and most reliable method of doing that is with a panel caliper.

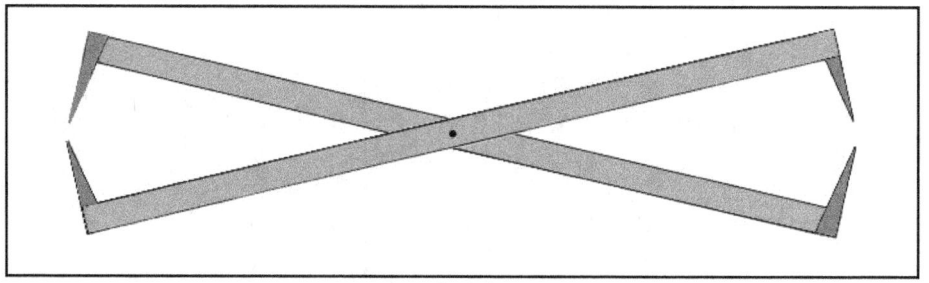

panel caliper

Here's how to make a panel caliper:

1. Cut two pieces of two inch wide and 1/8 inch thick steel bars to exactly the same length. If you'll be working on a panel that's 1 inch thick and thirty-six inches wide, you'll have to reach 18 inches in from each side so the bars should be at least 48 inches long.

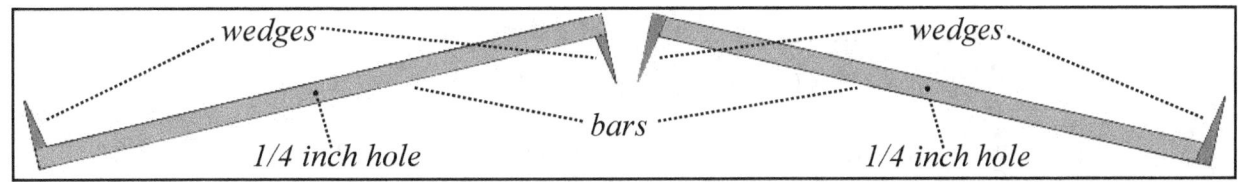

image E – the 2 parts of a panel caliper

2. Find the exact center of one bar in its length and width and mark it with a metal punch.

Whenever drilling metal, oil the bit to avoid burning it.

3. Clamp the bars together and drill a 1/4 inch hole through that mark using a drill press so the holes exactly line up.

4. Cut four wedge shaped pieces of 1/8 inch steel 6 inches long. Clamp them together and grind them to make them all identical.

5. Set a wedge on a bar with a small hand square so the outside edge is square to the bar.

6. Clamp the wedge to the bar using a small C-clamp.

7. Repeat that process till all four wedges are clamped to the bars.

8. As shown in images E, the wedges on each bar must be on the same side of the bar pointing in opposite directions. The second bar will be identical to the first and will be flipped end to end before the final assembly.

9. Measure the distance from the edge of the bar to the tip of each wedge. They must be exactly the same.

10. Weld the wedges to the bar. If you don't have a welder, take your clamped assemblies to a metal fabricator to have it welded.

11. If you can't get the assembly welded, drill 3 holes through the wedge large enough for screws to pass through. Clamp the wedges to the bars as described in operations 5, 6 and 7 above. Drill pilot holes in the bars. Use epoxy and sheetmetal screws

to join the wedges to the bar. File off the tips of screws that stick out the back of the bars.

12. When the welds are cool or the epoxy has set, lay one section over the other. The two must be identical. If they aren't, clamp them together and grind them flush to each other.

13. Flip one bar over and set it on the other to confirm the bars and wedges perfectly match each other. Grind them if necessary.

14. When adjustments are complete, file the tips of the wedges and all sharp edges.

15. Put a 1/4 inch bolt through the center hole of one bar. The wedges must be on same side as the threaded end of the bolt.

16. Place a wide 1/4 inch washer on the bolt.

17. Set the second bar on the bolt so the wedges are on the inside of the caliper. This will make the tips touch each other when the caliper closes.

18. Screw a nut on the bolt until the assembly is snug but not tight.

19. Turn a second nut onto the first nut till it is snug.

20. With two small wrenches, tighten the second nut down onto the first.

21. The bolt should be tight enough that the bars don't move freely so the caliper will hold its position as you use it.

22. Cut and grind the threaded end of the bolt till it's flush with the nut. File off any sharp edges.

Test the caliper.

1. Clamp a board to a table.

2. Measure the thickness of the board.

3. With minimum pressure, grab it with one end of the caliper.

4. Keep the jaws against the block by holding the caliper slightly off center.

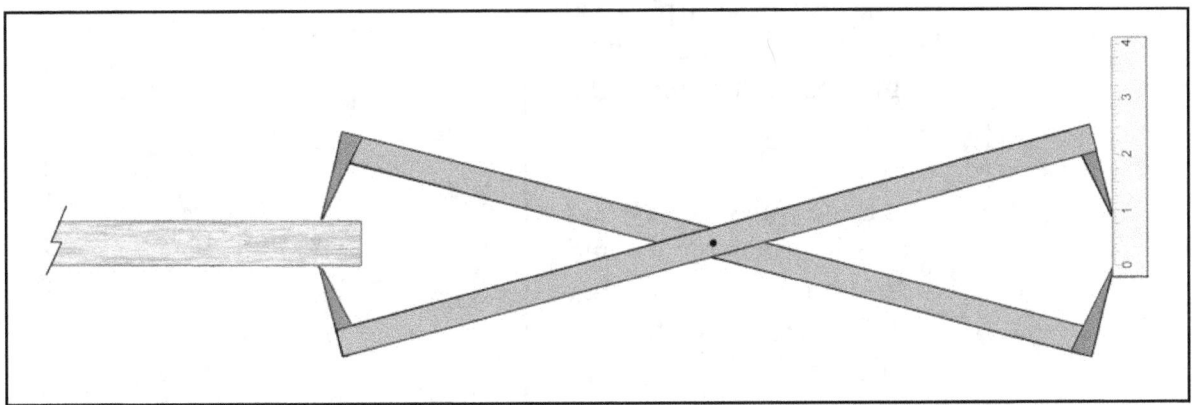

5. Set a small ruler against the open jaw to read the thickness of the board.

6. The measurement should be exactly the same as the thickness of the board.

• If it's not, check that the 1/4 inch bolt is exactly centered in each of the two bars. If it is off center, it will be easier to start over and make a new caliper than fix this one.

• If the bolt is exactly centered, file one of the points to match the measurement at the other jaw.

woodworker's easel

I find it easier to work on a panel when it's near vertical, so
I made an easel that's 4 feet high, 8 feet wide and can handle
a lot of weight and pressure. Here's how to make one.

1. Mark the wall for the top of your easel and draw a level horizontal line from it.

2. Make five identical plywood braces – 4 foot long with an angled edge that runs from 4 to 16 inches.

3. If the wall has plywood or sheetrock on it, find studs and attach 4 foot 2x2s vertically to each of them.

4. Screw a 2x2 to the four foot edge of each brace.

5. Attach each brace to studs or the 2x2s you installed with the narrow ends at the line you drew on the wall. Put one screw at the top and one at the bottom.

6. Set a straight edge against the face of the braces. Adjust them so the top and bottoms of the braces are in line.

7. Add three more screws to each brace.

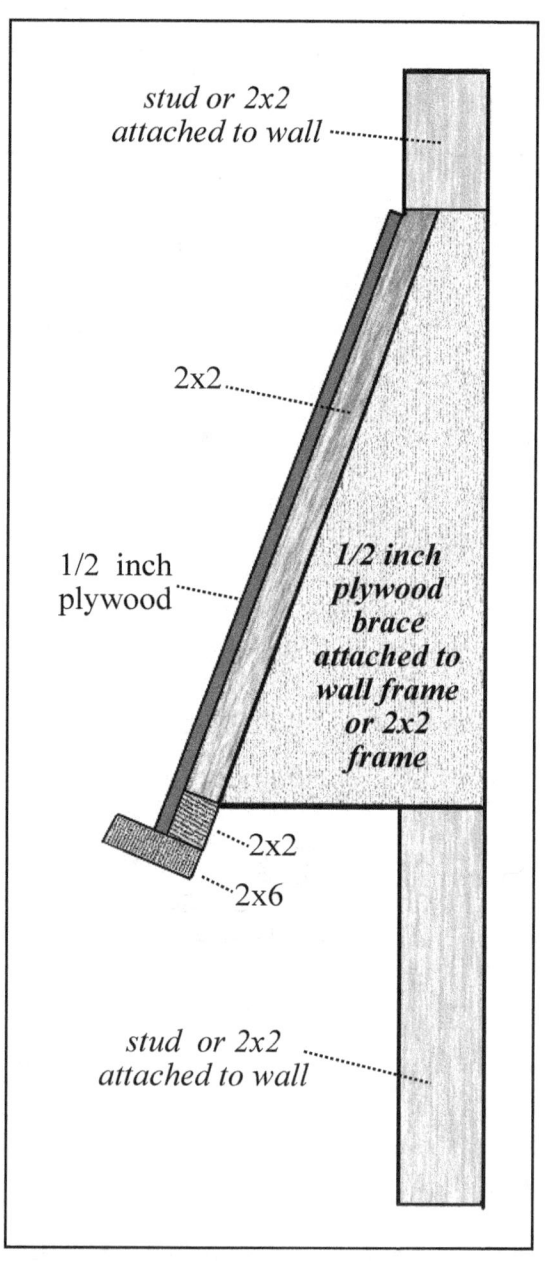

stud or 2x2 attached to wall

2x2

1/2 inch plywood

1/2 inch plywood brace attached to wall frame or 2x2 frame

2x2

2x6

stud or 2x2 attached to wall

woodworking easel

8. Screw the long edge of a sheet of 1/2 inch plywood to an 8 foot 2x2.

9. Mark the top of the sheet to match the layout of the braces. Make sure your marks put the panel in the right position laterally.

10. Square the line down the sheet. This make's it easy to find the 2x2s for your screws.

11. Start a screw on each of the lines.

12. Put two sawhorses or chairs under the braces.

13. Set boards on the sawhorses or chairs till they are approximately two inches below the bottom of the braces.

14. Set the plywood on the sawhorses with the 2x2 at the back and bottom of the sheet.

If you make a portable easel, secure it to something stable so it can resist pressure when you work.

15. Move the plywood laterally till the lines are over the 2x2s.

16. Raise the plywood till the 2x2 hits the bottom of the braces.

17. Drive the five screws you started.

18. Add four screws into each of the braces.

19. Use four small clamps to hold a 2x4 under the 2x2 at the bottom of the sheet. The back of the 2x4 and the back of the 2x2 should be flush. Attach the 2x4 to the 2x2 with six 2-1/2 inch screws. This will be a ledge to set your work on.

20. You can screw boards to the plywood to make ledges at other levels.

a panel sled:

A panel sled will allow you to easily make accurate cuts on long boards or panels. You can buy one or make one yourself. Here's how to make one:

1. Use a hand square to make sure the blade is square to the table.

2. Select a board with absolutely straight grain. There will be lateral pressure on the strips so any cross grain will cause them to crack.

Maple works best because it's extremely smooth when sanded so it will slide easily in the slots.

3. Join the edge of a 4 foot maple board.

4. Run both sides of the board through a planer taking very small cuts until the board fits the slot but is tight enough that it's hard to move.

5. Set the fence to cut the board into strips 1/4 inch thicker than the height of the slot. Cut six strips so you'll have extra.

6. Run all of the strips through the planer until they're 1/32 to 1/16 inch thinner than the height of the slot.

7. Cut any planer snipe from the end of each strip.

8. Secure a strip on a bench with the narrow edge up.

9. Sand one side and both edges of the strip with 220 grit paper.

10. Test the strip in a slot. The entire length of the strip must slide easily in the slot but have no play or wobble. Sand it again if necessary.

11. Repeat the process with a second strip. These two strips are the runners for the sled.

12. Cut 3/4 inch AC plywood into an 8 foot by 2 foot sheet.

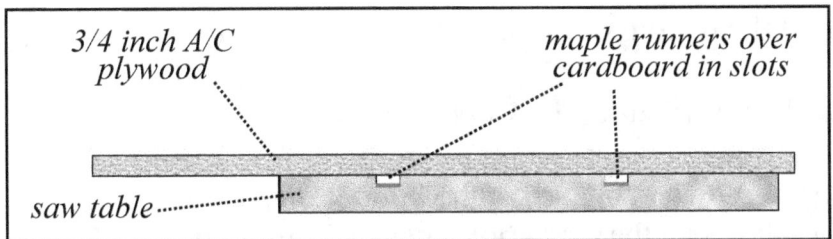

image F – attaching plywood to the strips

13. The plywood will slide easier if you put finish on the bottom. Put a coat on the top as well to balance moisture levels between the two surfaces.

14. Drop the table-saw blade below the surface of the table.

15. Cut two strips of cardboard (such as from a shoe-box) to fit the width and length of the slots in the saw table.

16. Set the cardboard and the maple runners in the slots (image F) so they are flush with front edge of the saw. The top of the runners should be slightly above the surface of the saw. Add a second set of cardboard strips under the maple runners if necessary.

17. Clamp the plywood on the table with the A side down. One end should be five feet to the left of the blade and one edge should be flush to the front of saw table (image G).

18. Mark the edge of the plywood at both sides of the runners.

19. Draw lines on top of the plywood from the marks with a framing square.

20. Drill 4 pilot holes for wood screws with a small bit between the lines into each strip. Use a drill stop or masking tape on the bit to make

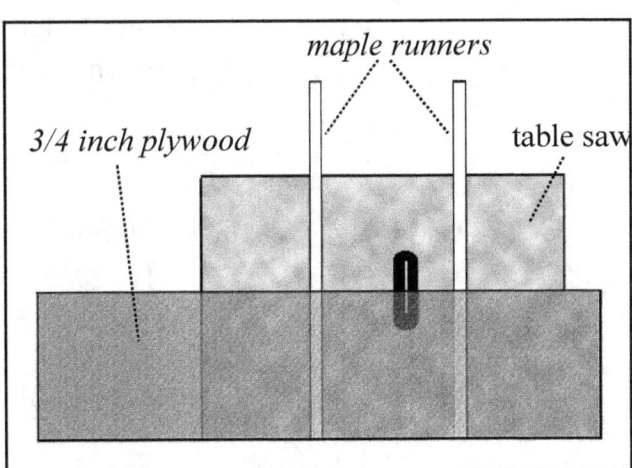

image G

sure the bit doesn't hit the bottom of the slot.

21. Countersink the plywood for the wood screws.

22. Remove the plywood and mark the bottom of the panel slightly to each side of the screw holes with a framing square.

23. Put a small amount of glue on the runners and on the bottom of the plywood inside the lines you drew.

24. Set the plywood on the runners so it is even with the edge of the saw table. Line the edge of the plywood with the runners.

25. Clamp the plywood to the table.

26. Screw the plywood to the runners.

27. Remove the clamps and slide the assembly off the table.

28. Remove any glue which has squeezed out. The runners must be clean and smooth. Use a putty knife then lightly sand if necessary.

29. Clean any glue from the table, the slots and the bottom of the plywood.

30. Put the assembly back in place. It should move freely. If it's tight, apply hard wax to the edges of the runners.

31. Mark the leading edge of the plywood at the saw blade.

32. Remove the plywood.

33. Rip a 2x4 to 2-1/2 inches.

34. Run all sides of the 2x3 through a planer.

35. Turn the assembly over and set it on a table so the edge is off the table.

36. Transfer the mark you made for the blade to the underside of the plywood.

37. Draw a line from that mark to the edge of the plywood with a framing square. That's the line of cut.

38. Mark the edge of the plywood 2 inches on both sides of that line.

39. Glue and clamp the narrow edge of the 2x3 under the plywood so it is absolutely flush with the edge.

40. Drill pilot holes through the plywood into the 2x3 in several spots on each side of the mark but away from the line of cut.

41. Countersink the holes.

42. Screw the plywood to the board.

43. Turn the assembly over and clean any glue which squeezed out from under the board.

44. Glue and screw a 4 foot 1x3 or a 3 inch strip of 3/4 plywood to the top of the 2x3.

45. Unplug the saw and replace the blade with a dado blade.

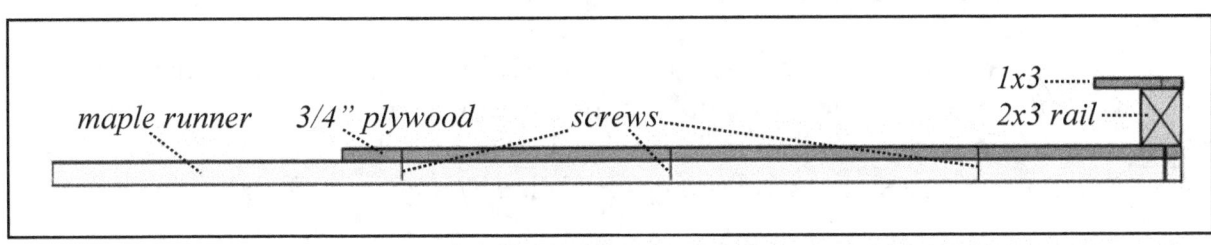

end view of sled

46. Raise the blade to at least 2 inches above the table. Cut as little as possible out of the 2x3 rail.

47. Set the sled on the table.

48. Plug the saw in, turn it on and run the sled through the blade past the 2x3 rail.

49. Cut the ends of the runners so the sled can work with wide panels. For most operations, 3 foot long runners will work well.

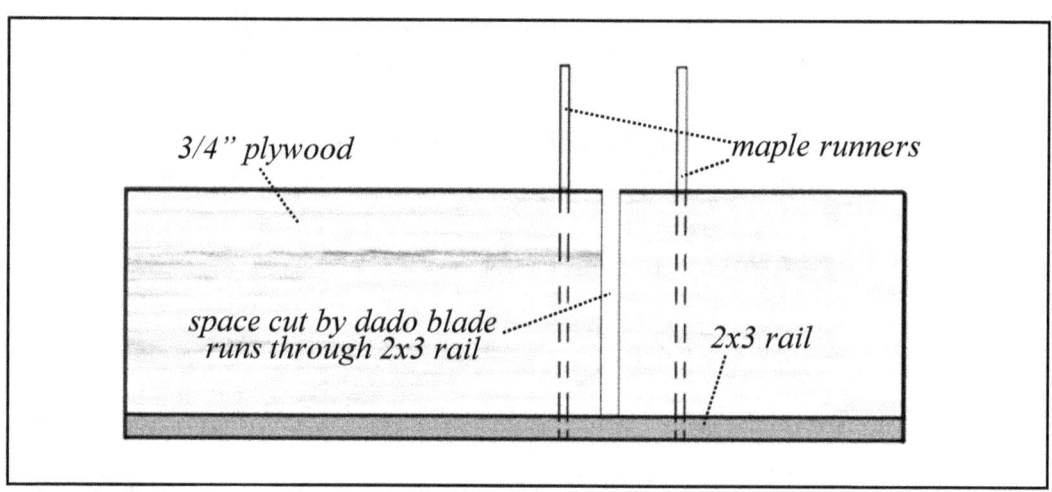

top view of sled

This is your panel sled.

sanding room

Sawdust is a serious health hazard. Even with a dust collector attached to a sander or a downdraft table, dust flies off into the air. I do all my sanding and grinding in a room I built for that purpose. You can make yours any size. Mine is 5 feet by 8 feet.

Attach a dust collector duct through a wall and hang strips of
heavy plastic in the doorway. Air will flow in through the strips
as the dust collector sucks it out.

Sawdust which normally covers the floors and work benches
in my shop, is now contained in one room. I still sweep the
shop, but less frequently and the air is much cleaner.

glue tray

1. Get a large, rectangular plastic food storage container with
a lid that closes tightly.

2. Screw through the bottom of the container into a beveled board
at one end so the glue will pool at the opposite end like a paint
tray. The glue is too thick to leak around the screws

3. Screw through the side of the container into a block inside for
the handles of your glue spreaders to sit on.

glue spreader

The best way to spread glue is with a painter's trim tool, either roller
or "Shur-line" style. I prefer a roller – 1 inch for edges and a 3 inch
for wide surfaces.

If the tray is at least half full with the lid closed, the spreader
won't dry out. If you won't be using the glue for a week or more,
add water to the container to keep the glue and the spreaders
from drying out. If you won't be using the glue for several
weeks, put the spreaders in a zip lock bag with some water and
pour the glue into a jar.

hidden assets - reclaimed lumber

Free wood is all around you. By finding and using it, you'll save money and reduce what goes to the landfill.

- In Minneapolis, where I live, people can put furniture out for the city to haul to the landfill. If it's solid wood, I take it.

- Tables are usually oak, maple or ash and some couches and stuffed chairs have solid poplar frames.

Use a metal detector to find hidden screws or nails in the wood.

- Most bookshelves made before 1980 were made of solid oak or 3/4 inch plywood and old cabinets were made of plywood, not particle board or composites.

other sources of free wood

- Let friends know you're looking for wood. I got some beautiful wood which had been sitting around a friend's garage for years and he was happy to get rid of them.

- There's a web site in Minneapolis that lists things people want to give away. A guy had a garage full of beautiful hardwoods and wanted to get rid of it all. I got a truck-load of oak, maple, walnut and a few exotic boards.

- Woodworking shops sometimes give their scraps away.

- If you're a wood-turner, you have a huge supply of free wood. Companies that remove trees have to haul the wood to a landfill where they pay a premium for disposal. They'd much rather give it to you because it saves them time and money. If you hear a chain saw in your neighborhood, ask the crew if you can have some of the wood. Usually they'll cut it to the length you want and even drop it off at your shop. Check out the types of trees you have in your area. You'll probably find some beautiful wood there.

- When a contractor finishes framing a building, there will be piles of half inch plywood waiting to be hauled to the dump. I've found full sheets with small defects like a corner cut off. I've gotten uncut 2x4 studs, sometimes with one or two nails. It costs a contractor more to pay someone to pull nails than get another board. It's a sad waste of resources but a great opportunity for those of us willing to put in a little work to save money, reduce what's being hauled to the landfill and save a few trees.

  - Home Depot (and probably other lumber yards) has a cart in the back of their stores near the radial arm saw that is often full of boards which have some defect – usually bowed or cracked – so they can't sell it at retail. I've also seen partial sheets of plywood on their carts.

    You also have materials in your shop you can reuse.

    - I keep scraps in a bucket which I use for small projects or to make pegs.

    - Scraps that are too small to use go into a bin which I use or share for kindling.

    - I put an email in our community list serve to let people know I have shavings from my planer and sawdust available. People use the sawdust in compost piles and the shavings as mulch in their gardens.

  - Fine sawdust sprinkled over fresh compost reduces odors.

  Note: Make sure to tell people if there's walnut shavings or sawdust in the mix because walnut will damage their plants.

How I Came to Love Woodworking

Chapter 3 - __the properties of a curved joint__ *starts on page 57.*

part 1

When I was a child, I never imagined that one day I'd be making my living as a woodworker. I never took a shop class in high school and I was twenty-three years old before I ever picked up a hammer.

I grew up in Albany Park, a mostly middle-class Jewish neighborhood of modest apartments on the north side of Chicago. People worked in shops and stores along Lawrence Avenue and in shadowy offices above them. They rode, packed and standing in commuter trains to work in skyscrapers and department stores downtown. They were teachers like my mother or salesmen like my father and none of them knew how to fix or build anything. The joke in my family was that Dad had to hire someone to change a light bulb. When our apartment was painted, my parents didn't buy paint, they called a painter. When they wanted a new door, they called a carpenter. That's what I knew about woodworking. When you need something done, call a carpenter.

We lived in a two-flat apartment building – two identical apartments stacked one over the other with a flat roof. My grandfather owned our building and lived downstairs. He knew how to fix things and had a workroom full of tools in a corner of our dank basement. He was an immigrant from Eastern Europe who didn't speak English. Since I didn't understand Yiddish, I never learned anything about tools or wood from him. Also, my main interest was sports. If it didn't have something to do with baseball or football, I didn't care about it. When grandpa died, my mother gave his tools to Goodwill because nobody in our family had any interest in them.

In high school, I was an all-conference linebacker, captain of the football team and a poor student. But, there was one class I never missed. I loved geometry. Somehow, everything about it seemed familiar to me. I could see shapes and relationships in my mind as clearly as you can see buildings on a street.

My geometry teacher commanded respect even though she never got angry. She was coldly serious about mathematics and nobody caused trouble in her class. One day, she was describing the intersection of two complex three dimensional shapes – a flat plane. It was long before computers, so there was no way to show the shapes in three dimensions without building a model and there wasn't enough time to do that for every lesson. So, she had to describe the shapes and their intersection. However, I could see that her description of the flat plane was wrong.

It wasn't a good idea to contradict her, but there was no question in my mind if I was right. I could see the points in the three dimensional shapes floating in space like two colliding galaxies of stars. I explained what I saw and held my breath.

"It doesn't matter if its wrong or right," she said. "That's not the point of the lesson.

I wished I hadn't said anything.

My grades were average but my scores on the college entrance exams were in the top one percent because even if I didn't know an answer, I knew enough to figure out what the writers of the test wanted. Despite my average grades, the test qualified me for a scholarship to the University of Illinois.

If I'd been a better student, if I had cared about school and worked harder, I might have become a lawyer or an executive in a corporation. But, I would have spent every day wishing I was working with my hands making something.

I went to college because my friends did and I couldn't think of anything else to do. I took the easiest classes I could find and when it was time to pick a major and a minor at the

end of my sophomore year, I chose writing and theater, not
because I wanted to be a writer or an actor, but because to get
an A, all you had to do was show up and look interested. I
could do that.

I got a few small roles and a good review for one of them
but memorizing lines was too hard for me. Something about
writing was attractive but I couldn't imagine sitting at a desk
day after day (which, however, is exactly what I did to write
this book). Being exposed to people with talent showed me
how things get done, but my writing professor changed the way
I thought.

Dr. Nuel Pharr Davis was six feet three inches tall, with a
clean-shaven head, a thin lanky frame, hunched shoulders and
a Texan's muddy drawl. I never met anyone like him before or
since. He had won a Pulitzer Prize for his book, Lawrence and
Openheimer, but in his mid-fifties, was an untenured professor
at this mostly disregarded liberal arts college in a university
known for agriculture and technology. His salvation was his
students. He lived to inspire us. We could write as little or as much
as we wanted, but we had to be thoughtful and creative, not only
in our work, but in our discussions. One day, it was my turn to
read one of my pieces. People were not impressed and said so.
Even though I didn't respond, Dr. Davis noticed it bothered me.
Writing, like all art, is an act of creation. If someone is critical, it
hurts in a very primal way.

"Mr. Lamm," he said so all could hear, "if someone
compliments your work, usually they are simply exhibiting the
social graces their mothers taught them. But when they criticize
your work, that means you've struck something inside them and
they can't resist making a comment even if it means ignoring good
manners to do so. Your work has forced them to think.
Congratulations."

Dr. Davis taught through stories. Some were personal. Most
had messages I struggled to understand. All made the point that
art must reveal truth, that you must pay attention, examine social
norms and not follow widely accepted points of view without
questioning them. He wanted us to think, to search for

extraordinary concepts like a diver digging in oysters looking for pearls. Few writers or artists sell anything, so money is rarely the reward for that search. The same is true for woodworkers. The reward for the work comes when you create something and especially when you do something you have never done before.

After graduation, friends moved home to begin careers. But, I didn't want to work in an office, so I moved back to Chicago and got a job driving a cab.

I did that for about seven months, earned enough money to buy a guitar and a car and moved back downstate.

(part 2 starts on page 117)

section two

the
techniques

chapter 3

the
properties
of a curved joint

Woodworking is applied geometry and is therefore governed by the laws of geometry.

A straight joint between two boards exists in a single plane – two dimensions along the X and Y axes in space (image 1). With proper techniques, a panel made with a straight joint will be as strong as the glue which holds it together. However, if the glue fails, the top of the joint will open as if it had hinges.

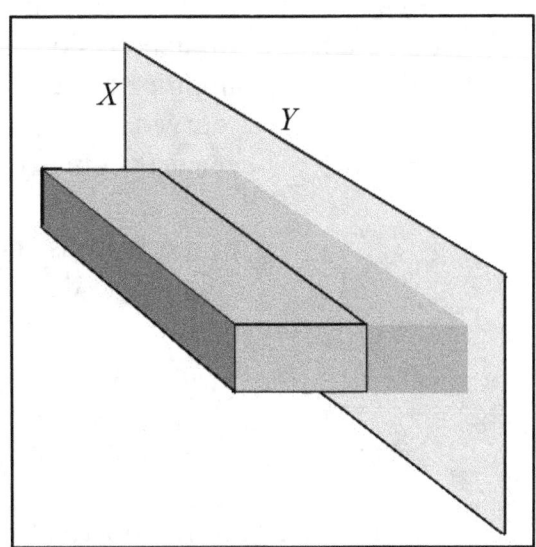

image 1 – the plane of a straight joint expanded

In a curved joint, two boards come together in three dimensions along the X, Y and Z axes (image 2). The intersection of the boards curves through space. The glue can't release because geometry won't allow the panel to hinge along a curved plane – the curved joint between the boards. For the joint to fail, the glue must have a complete failure and the boards must shear along its entire length.

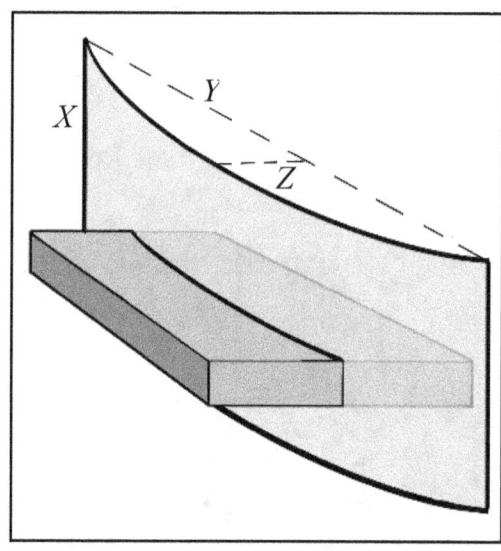

image 2 – curved joint expanded

In geometry, the X and Y axes are horizontal and the Z axis is vertical. However, in woodworking, glue joints are vertical so I drew the X axis vertical to reflect the vertical plane of the joint.

To see why a curved joint can't fail, draw a straight line on a piece of paper. This represents a standard straight joint between two boards. You can easily fold the paper along the line (image 3).

Draw a curved line. This represents a curved joint between two boards (image 4). You can't fold the paper along that line. The same is true in a curved joint. The joint can't hinge because geometry won't allow it.

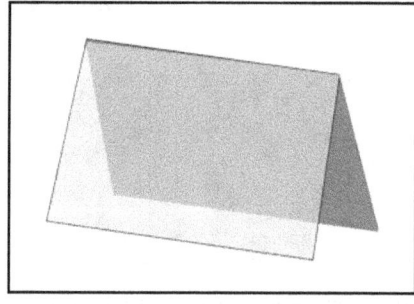

image 3 – sheet of paper folded along a straight line

A properly constructed curved joint can't fail. The wood may fail, but the joint can't.

A curved joint also makes a panel stronger in another way.

The strength of a board along its grain lines is far weaker than across them. A board with twisted grain lines is far more resistant to cracking or breaking than a board with straight grain lines because the curves of the grain lines are like a

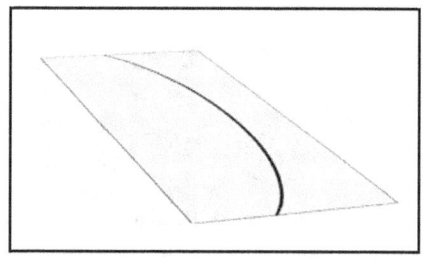

*image 4
paper with curved line*

curved joint – it functions in three dimensions. In the same way, boards joined along a diagonal with the direction of the lines of grain at an angle to each other will have more resistance than either board alone (image 6). The difference in the direction of grain between the two boards creates a situation similar to a curved line on a sheet of paper. The board cannot "fold" along two grain lines which run in different directions.

A curved joint adds even more strength by interweaving the grain lines that run at an angle to each other (image 7).

The most remarkable ability of curved joinery is in a flat butt joint. A standard flat butt joint without finger joints, plates, dowels or pins will fail because the glue doesn't penetrate the ends of the fibers as well as their sides. However, even a slight curve will give a butt joint enough stability to resist significant stress. I've made many curved butt joints and tested them with significant pressure but they don't break or flex.

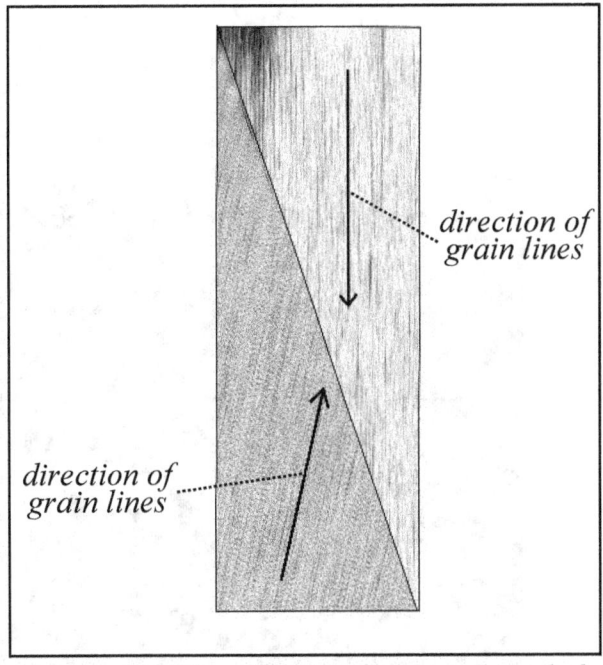

direction of grain lines

direction of grain lines

image 6 – 2 boards joined along an angled straight joint

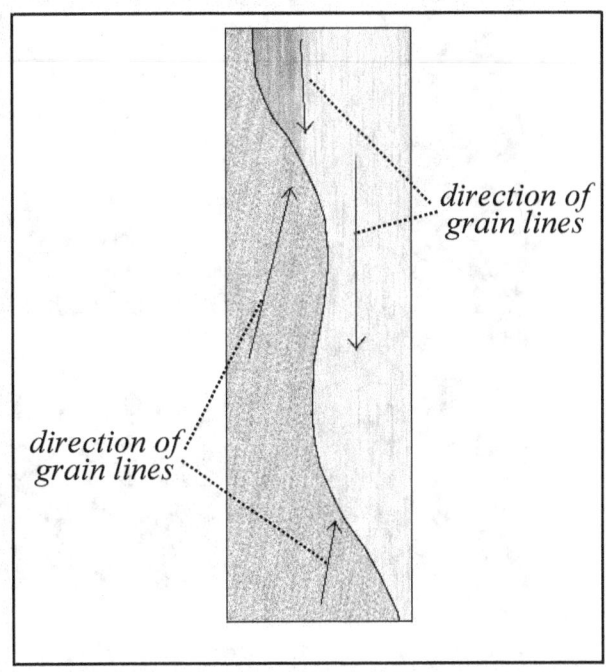

direction of grain lines

direction of grain lines

image 7 – boards joined in a curve

Panels I made years ago that include curved butt joints, are
    still in excellent condition.

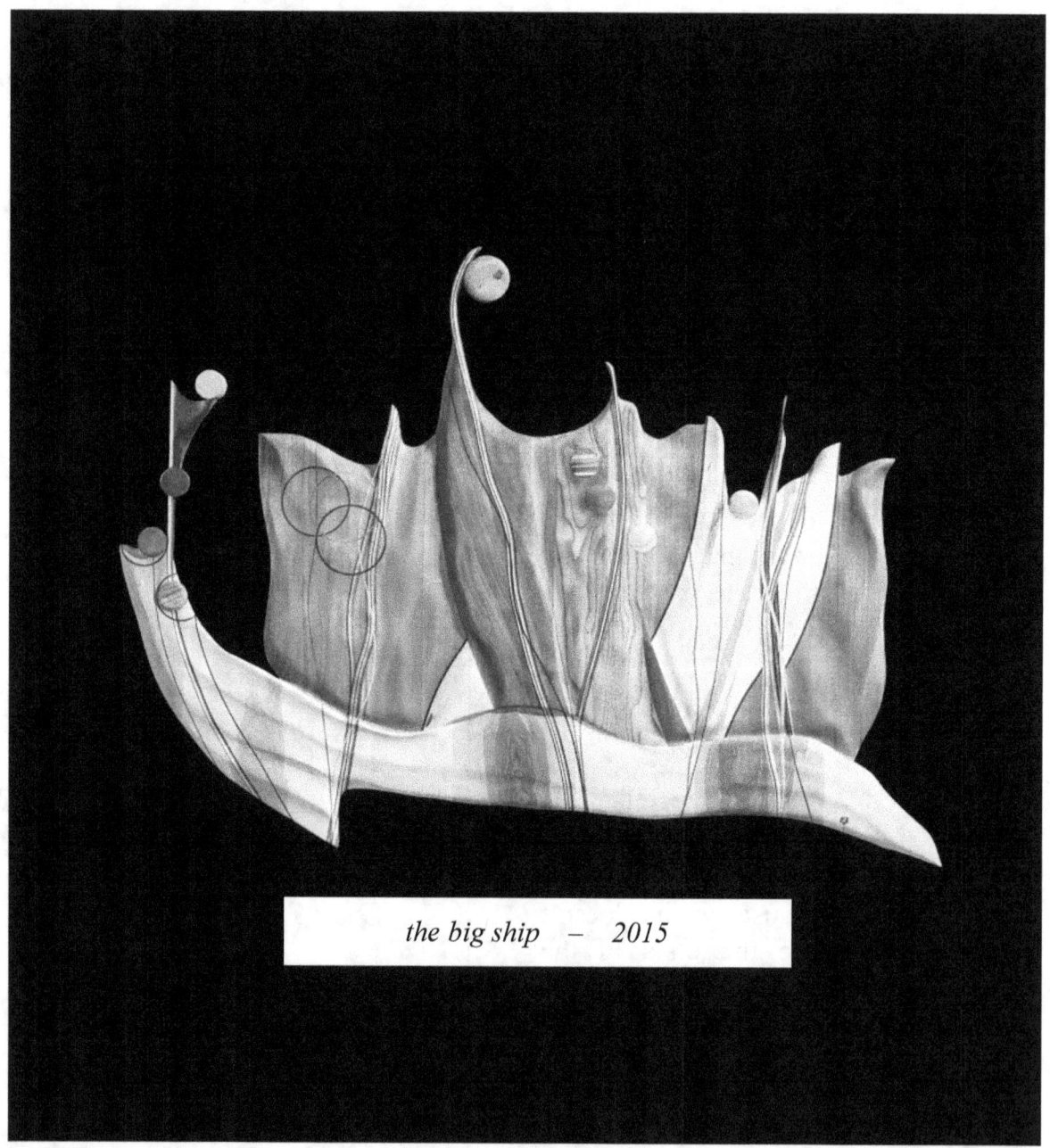

the big ship   —   2015

*This piece has a 5 foot long curved butt joint between the bottom and top sections.
The grain of all the boards in it run vertically.*

chapter 4

inserting strips
in curved cuts

The maple line in this walnut board is not an inlay. Inlays are thin narrow strips set into shallow grooves cut into the surface of a board. The technique used to make this board involves gluing solid wood strips between two halves of a board which was cut on a curve.

This technique is easier and simpler to do than an inlay yet the finished product is just as clean and precise and you can easily add strips to create complex designs.

While an inlay adds only aesthetics to a panel, every strip you add increases a panel's strength. Here's how that happens.

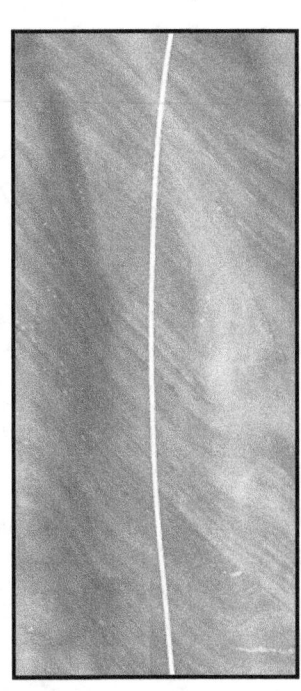

A board or a panel is weakest along the line of its grain but
it can be reinforced by inserting a strip as thin as 1/8 inch if
the strip is kept in a vertical position – directly in line with
the force exerted against it. Any tilt or twist in the strip will
significantly reduce its strength.

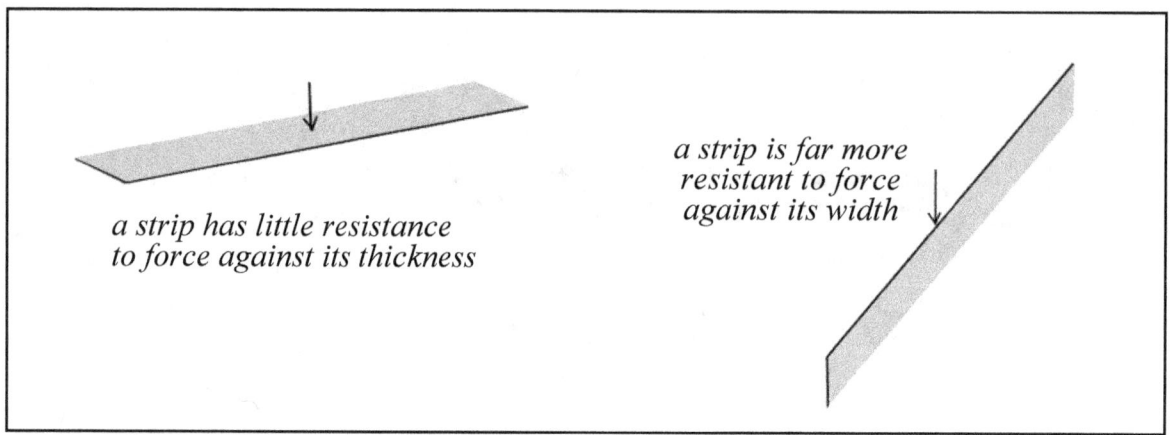

a strip has little resistance to force against its thickness

a strip is far more resistant to force against its width

Here's a test you can do to see how strong an eighth inch strip in a panel can be.

1. Cut an eighth inch strip from a board with straight grain.

2. Clamp two boards on one end of an eighth inch strip so they are flush with the bottom of the strip and are even with each other near the mid-point of the strip.

3. Clamp a second set of boards flush to the bottom of the strip leaving 1/2 inch of the strip exposed between the two sets of boards. This assembly will keep the strips in a vertical position like it would be in a board or panel.

4. Set two 2x2s on a work bench five inches apart.

5. Set the assembly on the two boards so that the exposed section of the strip is centered and square between them.

6. Set a 1x2 across the exposed section of the strip between the clamped boards.

7. Apply pressure to the 1x2 over the exposed strip.

8. Increase the pressure on the 1x2 until the strip breaks.

The amount of force required to break the strip is surprising. Since there's no gap in a board or panel along a strip, it will be even stronger than in this test.

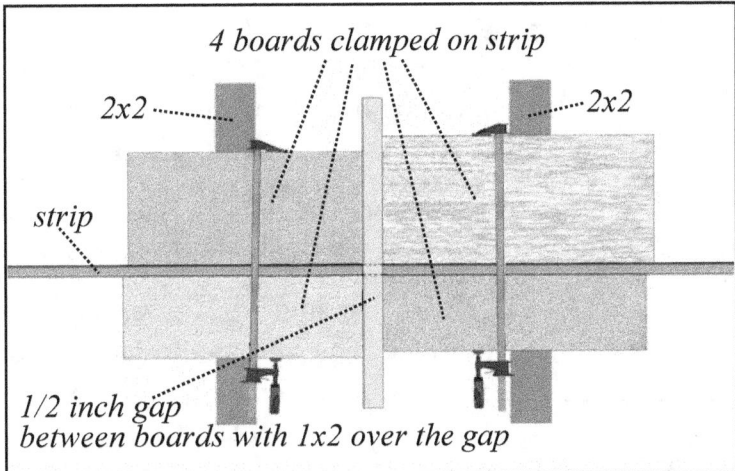

4 boards clamped on strip

2x2   *2x2*

strip

1/2 inch gap between boards with 1x2 over the gap

testing the tensile strength of a strip

When you cut a curve and glue a strip into it, the boards hold the strip in a vertical position as it crosses the lines of grain in them allowing maximum resistance to a vertical force as shown in the test. This reinforces the grain lines which it crosses making the board stronger than it was without the strip. Each strip that's added increases the board's strength.

how strips fixed a broken panel

One day, I glued up a large mahogany panel. When the glue was dry, I removed the clamps and leaned it against a wall. Later that day, I knocked it over and it broke along one of the grain lines. I glued it back together, carefully aligning the break. When the glue was dry, I cut a curve in the panel and glued a strip into it.

After the glue dried, I picked it up and pressed against the surface. It flexed, but didn't break – clearly stronger than it was before I added the strip. I inserted several more strips and the panel – which was once broken – had become as solid and stiff as a sheet of plywood.

inserting strips in curved cuts

1. Draw a line with a gentle arc from one end of the board to the other with a sharp, number 2 pencil or ball point pen.

2. The arc should be shallow without a sharp turn at any point so that the strip can easily follow the curve.

3. You can change the direction of your line but all the curves must be long and shallow. A gradual curve is easier to run through the band-saw and easier to align when assembling the joint.

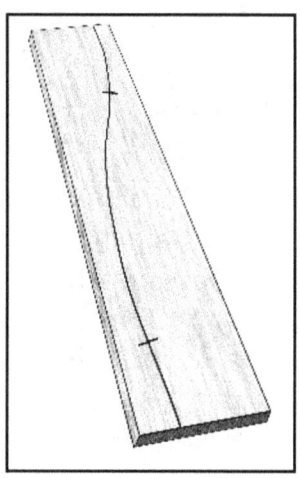

4. Draw hash marks across the line. You'll use these marks to align the joint when assembling the joint.

5. The hash marks should be perpendicular to point where it crosses the curve. A slanted line makes it more difficult to line up when it's separated by the strip. Hash marks should be dark and thick enough to be easily seen and there should be no question how the marks should lines up. It might be easier for you to make hash marks with a straight edge but it's not necessary.

curved line drawn with hash marks

With the line drawn, you're ready to cut the curve.

Some of the procedures in this chapter starting with __making the cut__, are also in the next chapter, __joining boards along a curve__. I did that so you can read either chapter and follow the instructions without having to flip to the other chapter.

cutting the curve

1. Before starting the cut, position the board so the first few inches of your line is in line with the blade.

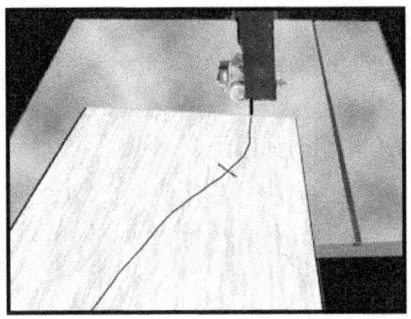

2. As you move the board through the blade, turn it so the next few inches of the line are aligned with the blade.

• If you move the board through the blade at an angle to the line, it will make deep saw marks on one side of the cut which may show when the piece is finished.

• Turning the board too quickly will make a sharp corner. The strip won't be able to make a sharp bend which will leave a gap.

Controlling forward and lateral movement is the art of making curved cuts. It's like baseball. Hitting the curve every time takes practice.

3. If you turn the board without moving it forward, the blade may twist and crease. A blade must be been in perfect condition to make a cut that is clean enough for any of these techniques. So, if you put a crimp in it, replace it.

4. Move the assembly at a moderate, constant and smooth rate through the blade.

5. Move the board laterally as you move it forward so the line of cut is always in line with the blade and move the board forward faster than you move it laterally. If your blade is sharp, the board should move easily. If the blade is dull, forcing the board through it will cause it to wander off the line.

6. With the cut complete, turn off the band-saw and wait for the blade to come to a complete stop before moving the two halves of the board onto the strong-backs of your work-station.

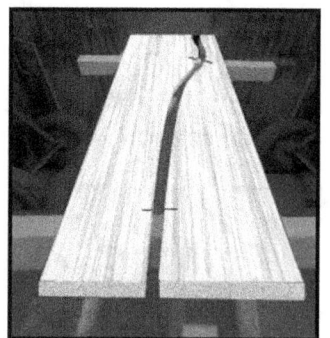

The next step is cutting strips. A standard insert for the blade of a table-saw allows thin strips to run down beside the blade. To solve that problem, make a low clearance insert plate.

Here's how to do that:

1. Check that your blade is square to the top of the saw table.

2. Drop the blade down so it's at least 1 inch below the surface of the table. Mark the position of the crank shaft handle on the body of the saw behind the handle with a piece of masking tape so you can return the handle to that position later.

3. Count the turns on the crank handle while raising the blade two inches above the surface of the table.

4. Drop the blade down the same number of turns you raised it and back to the position marked on the saw.

5. Clamp a stop board on the table of the saw two or three inches behind the space for the insert.

6. Set the blank phenolic (plastic) insert in place.

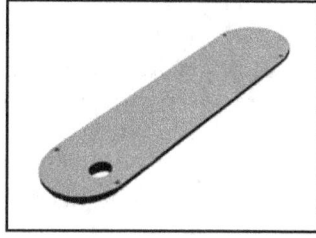

blank phenolic insert

7. Place a 12 inch square piece of 1/2 or 3/4 inch plywood over the insert and against the stop board. (See the drawings on next page.)

8. Hold the plywood in place with a long, solid stick.

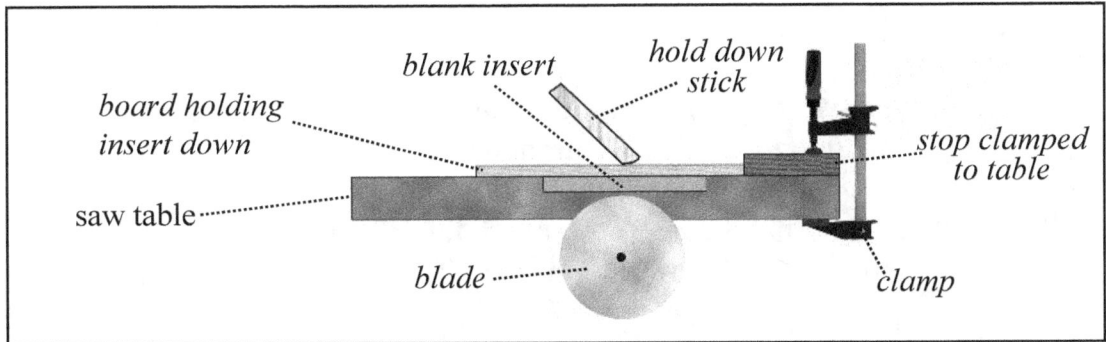

side view of table saw with stops in place

Never put your hand on the board that holds the insert down when the saw is on.

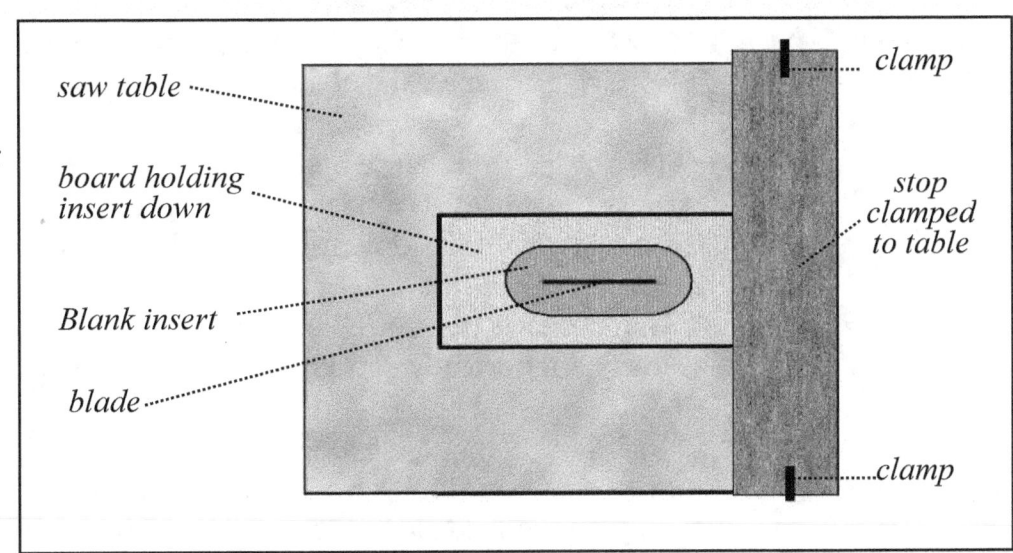

top view of table saw with stops in place

9. Turn the saw on and carefully raise the blade the same number of times you raised it for step 3.

10. Turn the saw off and remove the plywood square.

11. Raise the blade till it hits the front and back of the cut in the insert. The top of the blade should be approximately 2 inches above the saw table.

12. If you cut thicker materials, you can repeat this process and raise the blade higher.

13. This is your low clearance insert plate.

cutting strips

If you work slowly and carefully, you can get a smooth cut with an 80 tooth blade on your table-saw.

1. Use a hand square to ensure the blade is square to the table. If the blade isn't square, it will be difficult to make uniform strips.

1/16 to 1/8 inch strips work best, but, thickness is limited only by what will bend into a curved cut.

2. The fence must be parallel with the blade so the wood won't bind as it runs past the blade.

3. Make strips from hardwood. Fibers in a softwood strip can tear apart under even moderate stress. However, Douglas fir has enough integrity to withstand significant stress.

4. Use a fence extender (chapter 2) or a joiner to make one edge of the board perfectly straight, smooth and square to its surface.

5. Use a push stick or feather board to press the board against the fence as you run it through the blade. Side pressure should be only on the feed side of the blade so you don't bind the blade and scar the strips. The goal is to make strips with a uniform thickness and a reasonably smooth surface.

6. Always use a push stick to move the board through the blade.

7. Set the fence and cut the board.

8. Check the first strip. If the thickness is acceptable, continue cutting strips. Otherwise, adjust as necessary.

If you must sand a strip, use a hard rubber sanding block and go easy. Uniform thickness is more important than how smooth a strip is.

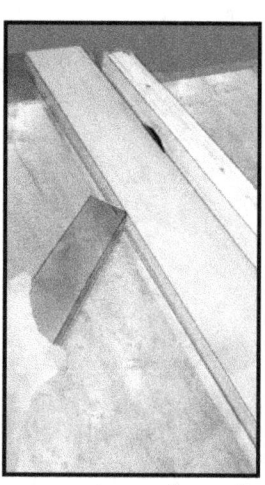

pressing a board against fence

gluing strips in a curve

1. You may find that your band-saw left feathers on the edge of the boards. Those feathers could get in the joint when you glue it up so remove them by running a wood file or hard rubber sanding block at an angle over the corner of the cut. It may take several passes.

2. If you must sand the surface of the edge, use minimum pressure and don't try to remove saw marks. Unless the saw marks are deep, if you cut the curve correctly, the marks won't show up in the finished panel.

3. Dry clamp the boards with a strip between them.

4. Align the hash-marks. If there's a slight but uniform gap in one area but the joint is tight at the ends, you should be able to close the gap when tightening the clamps.

• If the gaps are in more than one area or if you can't get the two boards to fit correctly, the hash marks may not be lined up. In that case, remove the clamps and adjust the boards till the hash marks line up.

If you can't make the joint work, set it aside. Sanding or re-sawing a joint won't fix it.

• If this doesn't correct the problem, move the boards one way and then the other. When you find the correct placement, make new hash marks.

• Don't use a warped board. It's difficult and often impossible to make a warped board work in curved joinery.

5. When you're satisfied with the fit of the joint, apply glue to both sides of the joint and both sides of the strip.

6. At the moment before clamping the boards together, the glue should look shiny like wet paint. If it looks dull, the wood has absorbed too much of the glue or the glue has started to set. In either case, apply another layer of glue to rejuvenate it. If the glue is fully dry and hard, you'll have to sand it off but that

will usually ruin the fit so it's best to set the boards aside and start over. To avoid this, whenever there's a delay in the assembly, refresh the glue by applying more. Too much glue may make a mess but if the glue dries before you clamp the joint, it will fail.

7. Set the strip between the boards and slide them against it to keep it vertical.

8. Space your clamps to apply uniform pressure. I set mine approximately twelve to sixteen inches apart with one at each end.

9. Add clamps where extra pressure is needed to draw a gap together. You can't hurt a joint with too many clamps but not using enough clamps might leave a gap.

Porous woods absorb glue quickly and need a second coat. Hard and dense woods need time for the glue to penetrate and a second coat to refresh the glue.

10. Pull the joint together but don't tighten the clamps.

11. Align the hash marks. You may have to tap one board with a mallet to move it.

12. Clamp the outside edges of the assembly to the strong-backs. When you put full pressure on a clamp, it pulls the edges of the assembly upward. Clamping the edges of the panel down to the strong-backs will keep the panel flat and allow you to safely apply whatever amount of pressure is necessary.

13. Tighten the clamps

14. Check the hash marks. If the alignment isn't correct, tap the end of one board until the marks line up. Sometimes, you'll have to give it a solid hit to get the boards to move. If necessary, use a scrap to protect the board when you hit it.

15. When you're satisfied the alignment is correct, tighten the clamps a little more but not fully tight.

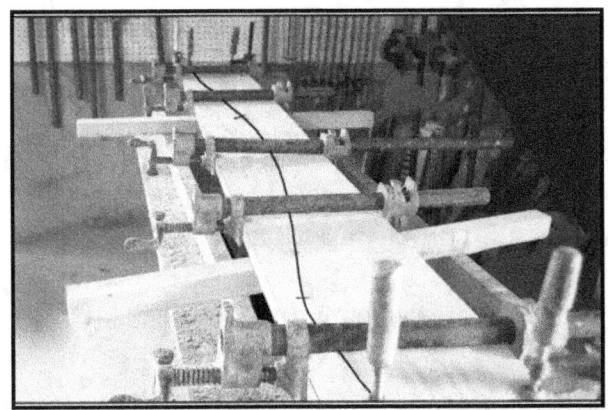

board clamped around strip

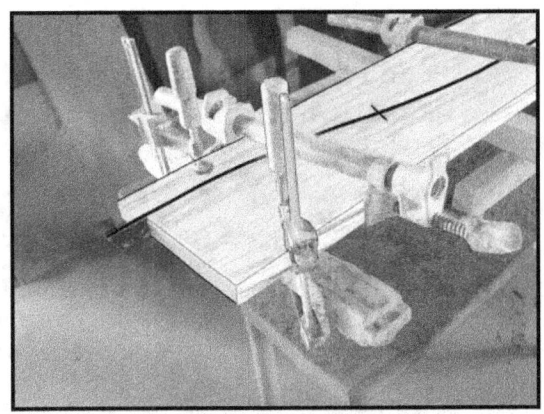

edges clamped to strong backs

16. Check the surface of the boards at the ends of the joint. They should be flush. If not, tap the higher side with a rubber mallet to drive it down flush to the other side or place a clamp over the joint to force them flush.

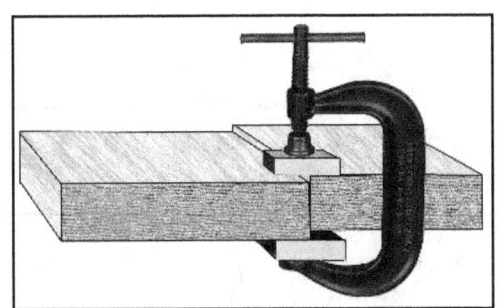

clamp w/ blocks to pull surface flush

17. If the middle of the joint isn't flush, tap the high side with a mallet to drive it down.

18. If that doesn't work, lay a 2x4 over the panel at that spot and clamp it to the strong-back which runs under that spot to sandwich the panel between them.

19. If that doesn't work, drive a wedge under that 2x4.

20. If that doesn't work, drive a wedge under the low side of the joint above the strong-back that runs below it.

21. With all adjustments made, tighten the clamps until there are no gaps in the joint or you see glue squeeze out uniformly along the joint. If you see a gap or don't see glue squeeze out uniformly, your joint may not be lined up correctly. Check the hash marks. If the dry run worked, and you have the joint lined up the same way, you can assume the joint will work now so apply full pressure.

22. If that doesn't work, loosen the clamps and check the glue.

23. From this point, you'll be doing trial and error until you find the correct alignment. Tap the end of one board to move it down the joint in the direction you think might work. Tighten the clamps and check the fit.

24. If necessary, repeat the process in the other direction.

25. When you're satisfied with the alignment, apply full pressure.

- Bar clamps can't put too much pressure on a joint but pipe clamps may. If glue is squeezing out everywhere along the joint, you have enough pressure.

26. If there is an area where glue is not squeezing out, you may need to increase the clamping pressure. If the joint is still out of alignment, loosen the clamps and repeat step 11.

27. With the clamps fully tight, the assembly is sturdy enough to move. You can't hurt a solidly clamped curved joint if it's clamped to strong-backs but be careful not to hurt your back or drop it on your foot.

With aliphatic glue, wait 1½ to 2 hours before removing the clamps and 3 to 4 hours before putting stress on the joint.

28. When you're confident the glue has set, put the assembly back on the table and take the clamps off in the following order.

- Release half the pressure on the primary clamps (those across the joint). Don't remove the clamps which hold the edges to the strong-backs until the primary clamps are removed or the edges will be pulled up and the panel may break.

- Release all pressure from the main clamps.

- Remove the clamps holding the assembly to the strong-backs.

You now have a board or panel with a solid wood strip glued into a curved cut.

overlaying strips

A board or panel with a strip can be used like any board or panel. It can be cut and joined to other boards or panels. It can be used in cabinets, tables or any woodworking project. You can also cut a curve in it to insert another strip.

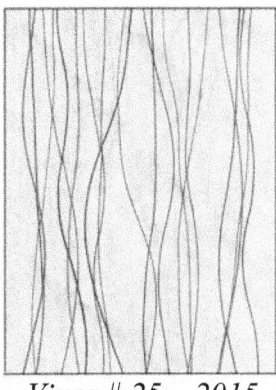

Vines # 25 – 2015

If you align the joints so there are no gaps, each strip will add strength to the panel and there is no limit to the number of strips you can insert. Follow the procedures listed in the previous section, **gluing strips in a curve** on page 69. The procedures are the same no matter how many strips you insert.

inserting multiple strips

There's no limit to the number of strips you can use in a curved cut. However, the thickness of the set of strips you insert will effect how the joint can be assembled.

When you cut a board along a curve and separate the two sides of the cut to insert a set of strips, you have created two identical arcs. Since the center of a circle or arc moves when the circle or arc moves, the centers of the two sides of the curved joint have also moved apart. It's critical to understand how that affects the assembly of a curved joint with multiple strips.

As you can see in image 1, when one of two equal circles is moved, the lines of the two circles overlap at two points. The part of each circle between these two points are arcs of the circle. Starting from the midpoint of the two arcs (A), as you move one way or the other, the distance between the arcs changes until they finally intersect at the ends of the arcs (B). In the same way, when you separate the two sides of a curved cut, the distance between the arcs changes as you move in either direction from the mid-point of the two arcs toward either end of the arcs (point A to point B).

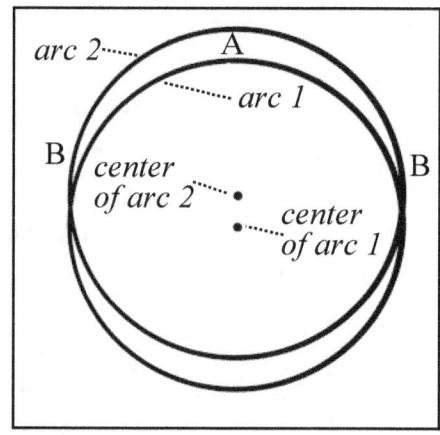

image 1 – two identical circles

In images 1 through 4, "A" represents the mid-point of the arc and "B" represents the end of the arc.

You can see how this affects short arcs, like those in curved joinery, by drawing a line up the center of a sheet of paper (image 2). Mark the line at 1 and 2 inches from the bottom of the sheet. Use a protractor to draw an arc with an eight inch radius from the 1 and 2 inch marks across the top of the sheet.

Set a ruler on the lower mark and measure the distance between the two arcs at A along the line. Move the ruler so it runs from the lower mark to the arcs at the left edge of the paper. Measure the distance between the two arcs at B. The measurement at B should be 1/8 inch less than at A. The differential between A and B is 1/8 inch.

As the space between the mid-points of the arcs increases, the differential between points A and B increases as well. In image 3, you can see that the wider space between arcs 2 and 3 creates a larger differential between A and B than between arcs 1 and

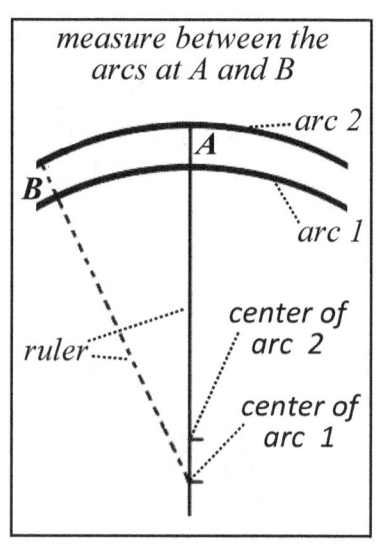

image 2 – identical arcs

2. In the same way, a thicker set of strips will create a greater differential between the center of a curved cut and the ends of it. This must be considered when drawing the line for a curved joint.

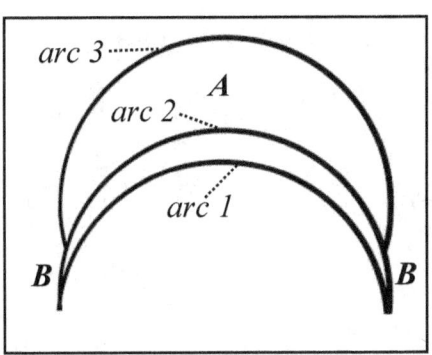

image 3

A second issue that must be considered when making a joint with multiple strips is the radius of the arc in the curved cut.

As you can see in image 4, when gentle arcs – arcs with a long radius – are separated, there is a very slight differential between A and B. The space between 2 and 3 is double that between arcs 1 and 2, yet the change in differential is minimal. So, even when the two sides of a curved cut are separated by a thick set of strips, a gentle arc will mitigate the effect of the separation.

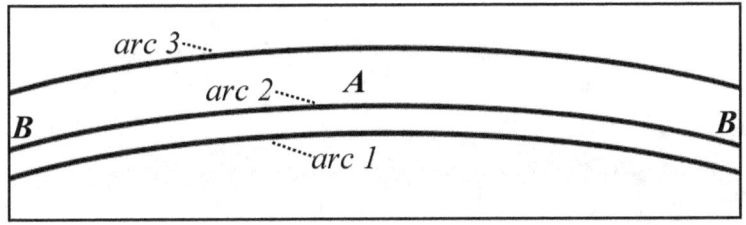

image 4 – arcs with identical long radii

If you're going to use a thick set of strips, cut a gentle arc. The wider the set of strips, the gentler the arc must be. If your arcs are too severe for the space between them, you'll have a gap in the middle of the arc and if it's too wide, you won't be able to draw it closed when you clamp the joint.

I've made panels with sixteen strips glued into a curved cut which separated the sides of the joint 2 inches.

procedures for inserting multiple strips

1. Cut the number and variety of strips you want to use.

2. Set the boards with the curved cuts on strong-backs on your work-station.

3. Make hash marks across the joint. (image 5)

4. This is a difficult process, so first, do a dry run.

5. Bundle the strips and lay them between the boards.

6. Set your clamps in place.

7. Draw the boards together, applying pressure uniformly on all clamps.

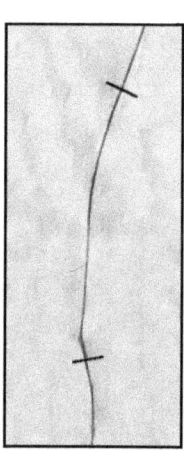

image 5
hash marks

8. Set small clamps on the edges of the board to hold them down to the strong-backs.

9. Because you'll be drawing the boards together several inches, you'll have to move the clamps which hold the edges of the boards to the strong-backs.

10. In some cases, you can find the correct position by squaring one set of hash marks across the strips.

Finding the right position may require realigning the joint several times.

11. A hash mark in the center of an arc will line up and put the joint in the correct position. Hash marks on the sides of the arc won't line up (image 6). However, if your curve has a reasonably uniform arc, you should be able to split the difference between the two hash marks to make a good joint.

12. When you've found the best position, erase or sand off the original marks and make new ones.

13. With a successful dry run, assemble the joint.

14. Set the boards with the curved cuts on strong-backs on your work-station.

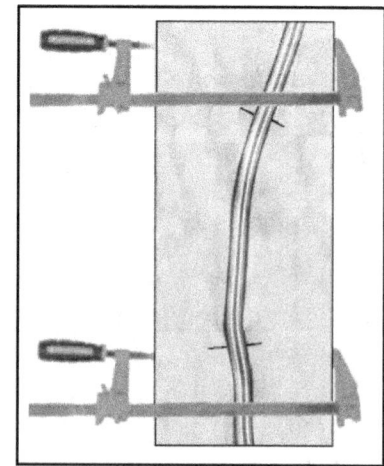

image 6
strips clamped

15. Arrange the strips on a table in the order they will appear in the joint.

16. Apply glue to one side of all the strips.

17. Set the glued strips against each other.

18. Don't apply glue to the strips which will face the edges of the boards.

19. Apply glue to the dry strips and set those together.

20. Repeat the process until all the strips are glued and set together.

21. Apply glue to the boards and the outsides of the strip set.

Making consistently successful curved joints with multiple strips requires patience, skill and practice.

22. Set the strips between the boards.

23. From here, the instructions are the same as those for doing a dry run starting with instruction 6 on the previous page.

24. There is so much glue involved with multiple strips that the assembly should be left to set up overnight.

25. When you're certain the glue is dry and set, remove the clamps in the following order: small clamps holding the edges to the strong-backs then the edge clamps.

The panel with multiple strips is done.

an anomaly

A curved joint with two or more arcs that go in opposite
directions usually won't work unless you know how to fix
the problem the condition creates.

Here's the nature of the problem:

In image 7, the two curved lines represent the sides of a kerf.
The curved lines have two arcs which run in opposite
directions from each other. Hash marks 1 and 2 run across the
kerf at the mid-point of each arc.

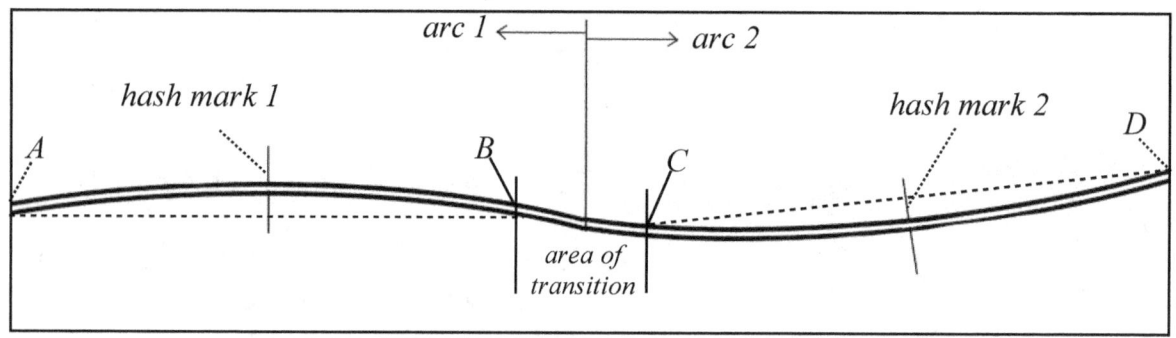

*image 7 – identical curves with arcs running in opposite
directions and hash marks at the center point of both arcs*

A, B, C and D are the end points of the two arcs. Dotted lines
connect the end points. The dotted lines are not parallel. They run
at an angle to each other and this condition creates a problem.

The two curving lines in image 8, represent the sides of the kerf
after they've been separated. The space between the two lines
represents a thick set of strips.

The separated hash marks are now called 1A and 1B, 2A and 2B.
Hash marks 1A and 1B line up across the joint as shown by the
dashed line. When hash marks at the midpoint of an arc line up
across a joint, the joint should be properly aligned. In this case,
arc 1 would line up correctly across the strips when the joint is
clamped together.

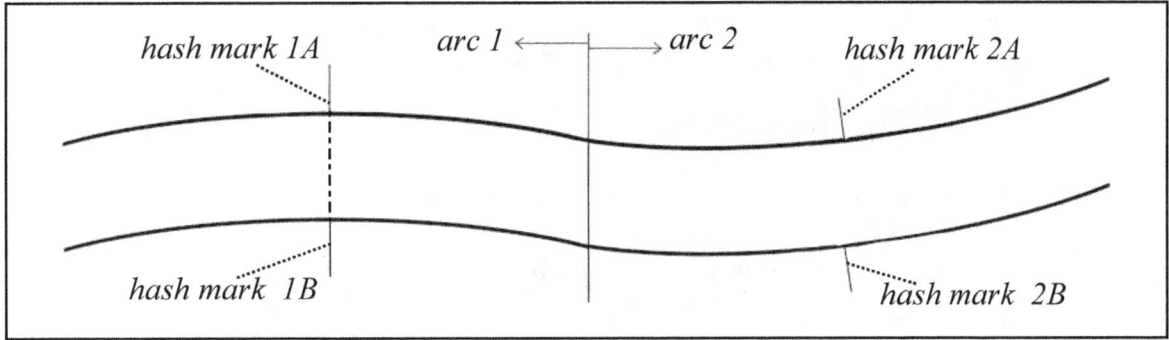

image 8 – identical curves with arcs running in opposite directions and hash marks at the center point of the arcs

However, because the two arcs aren't parallel, when the lines are separated, hash marks 2A and 2B are forced out of alignment. When hash marks don't line up, the joint can't be correctly aligned and will have gaps.

So, when you insert a thick set of strips in a curved cut with two or more arcs that run in opposite directions and aren't parallel to each other, there is no perfect alignment for the joint. The best you can do is find the best possible fit by moving the sides of the joint laterally. Often, the best possible fit leaves a gap or gaps somewhere in the joint and no adjustment or amount of pressure on the clamps can solve the problem.

However, there is a way to make the joint work.

1. Set the two sides of the joint together without strips and make hash marks.

2. Do a dry run with the strips inserted.

3. Clamp the joint tight and check the fit.

4. If there are gaps, loosen the clamps, move one of the boards laterally, tighten the clamps and check the fit again.

5. If there still are gaps, loosen the clamps, move the board in the opposite direction, tighten the clamps and check the fit again.

6. If you can't avoid gaps, find a position that produces the fewest and thinnest gaps. That will be the best possible fit.

7. Tighten the clamps.

8. Erase or sand off the original hash marks.

9. Make new hash marks for this position.

With diligence and proper execution, this operation can create a strong and durable joint.

10. Starting with instruction 14 on page 77, glue and clamp the joint to full pressure with the hash marks aligned and the edges clamped to strong-backs.

11. Make a set of thin strips in the desired color or colors. Cut or sand the strips to various thicknesses starting from almost paper thin.

12. Run a bead of glue over the gaps and press it into the gaps.

13. Apply glue to both sides of the shims.

14. Push or drive the shims into the gap. They must fit tight.

15. Fill the entire length of all gaps with shims.

16. Let the glue set up at least four hours before removing clamps.

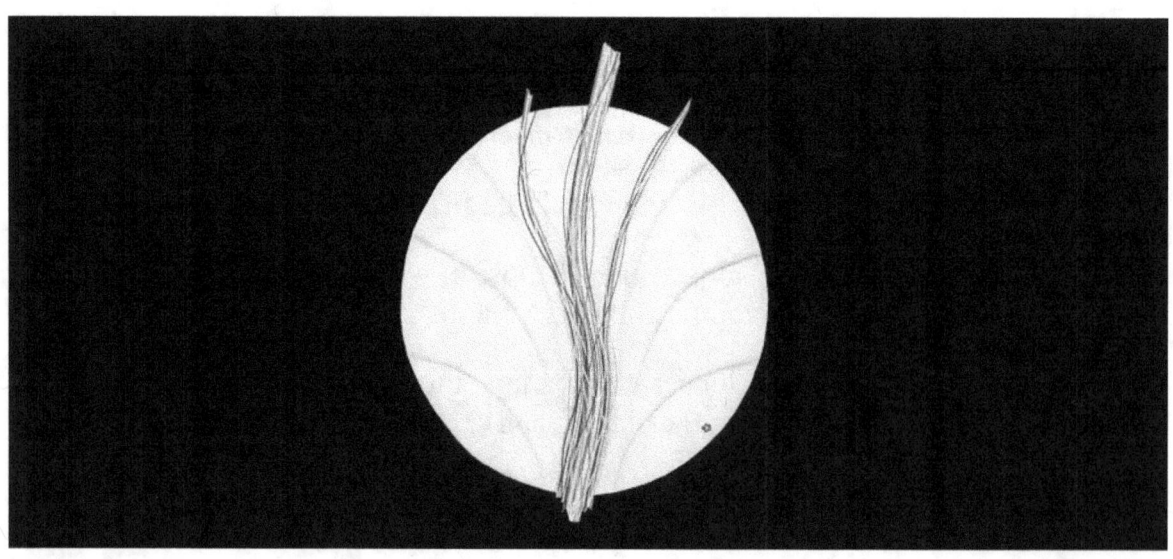

summary of chapter 4

inserting
strips
in curved cuts

your

notes

inserting strips in curved cuts

1. Draw a line with a gentle arc from one end of the board to the other with a sharp, number 2 pencil or ball point pen.

2. The arc should be shallow without a sharp turn at any point so that the strip can easily follow the curve.

3. You can change the direction of your line but all the curves must be long and shallow. A gradual curve is easier to run through the band saw and easier to align when assembling the joint.

4. Draw hash marks across the line. You'll use these marks to align the joint when assembling the joint.

5. The hash marks should be perpendicular to point where it crosses the curve. A slanted line makes it more difficult to line up when it's separated by the strip. Hash marks should be dark and thick enough to be easily seen and there should be no question how the marks should lines up. It might be easier for you to make hash marks with a straight edge but it's not necessary.

With the line drawn, you're ready to cut the curve.

cutting the curve

1. Before starting the cut, position the board so the first few inches of your line is in line with the blade.

2. As you move the board through the blade, turn it so the next few inches of the line are aligned with the blade.

• If you move the board through the blade at an angle to the line, it will make deep saw marks on one side of the cut which may show when the piece is finished.

• Turning the board too quickly will make a sharp corner. The strip won't be able to make a sharp bend which will leave a gap.

3. If you turn the board without moving it forward, the blade may twist and crease. A blade must be been in perfect condition to make a cut that is clean enough for any of these techniques. So, if you put a crimp in it, replace it.

4. Move the assembly at a moderate, constant and smooth rate through the blade.

5. Move the board laterally as you move it forward so the line of cut is always in line with the blade and move the board forward faster than you move it laterally. If your blade is sharp, the board should move easily. If the blade is dull, forcing the board through it will cause it to wander off the line.

6. With the cut complete, turn off the band saw and wait for the blade to come to a complete stop before moving the two halves of the board onto the strong-backs of your work-station.

The next step is cutting strips. A standard insert for the blade of a table saw allows thin strips to run down beside the blade. To solve that problem, make a low clearance insert plate.

Here's how to do that:

1. Check that your blade is square to the top of the saw table.

2. Drop the blade down so it's at least 1 inch below the surface of the table. Mark the position of the crank shaft handle on the body of the saw behind the handle with a piece of masking tape so you can return the handle to that position later.

3. Count the turns on the crank handle while raising the blade two inches above the surface of the table.

4. Drop the blade down the same number of turns you raised it and back to the position marked on the saw.

5. Clamp a stop board on the table of the saw two or three inches behind the space for the insert.

6. Set the blank phenolic (plastic) insert in place.

7. Place a 12 inch square piece of 1/2 or 3/4 inch plywood over the insert and against the stop board. (See the drawings on next page.)

8. Hold the plywood in place with a long, solid stick.

9. Turn the saw on and carefully raise the blade the same number of times you raised it for step 3.

10. Turn the saw off and remove the plywood square.

11. Raise the blade till it hits the front and back of the cut in the insert. The top of the blade should be approximately 2 inches above the saw table.

12. If you cut thicker materials, you can repeat this process and raise the blade higher.

13. This is your low clearance insert plate.

cutting strips

If you work slowly and carefully, you can get a smooth cut with an 80 tooth blade on your table saw.

1. Use a hand square to ensure the blade is square to the table. If the blade isn't square, it will be difficult to make uniform strips.

2. The fence must be parallel with the blade so the wood won't bind as it runs past the blade.

3. Make strips from hardwood. Fibers in a softwood strip can tear apart under even moderate stress. However, Douglas fir has enough integrity to withstand significant stress.

4. Use a fence extender (chapter 2) or a joiner to make one edge of the board perfectly straight, smooth and square to its surface.

5. Use a push stick or feather board to press the board against the fence as you run it through the blade. Side pressure should be only on the feed side of the blade so you don't bind the blade and scar the strips. The goal is to make strips with a uniform thickness and a reasonably smooth surface.

6. Always use a push stick to move the board through the blade.

7. Set the fence and cut the board.

8. Check the first strip. If the thickness is acceptable, continue cutting strips. Otherwise, adjust as necessary.

gluing strips in a curve

1. You may find that your band saw left feathers on the edge of the boards. Those feathers could get in the joint when you glue it up so remove them by running a wood

file or hard rubber sanding block at an angle over the corner of the cut. It may take several passes.

2. If you must sand the surface of the edge, use minimum pressure and don't try to remove saw marks. Unless the saw marks are deep, if you cut the curve correctly, the marks won't show up in the finished panel.

3. Dry clamp the boards with a strip between them.

4. Align the hash-marks. If there's a slight but uniform gap in one area but the joint is tight at the ends, you should be able to close the gap when tightening the clamps.

• If the gaps are in more than one area or if you can't get the two boards to fit correctly, the hash marks may not be lined up. In that case, remove the clamps and adjust the boards till the hash marks line up.

• If this doesn't correct the problem, move the boards one way and then the other. When you find the correct placement, make new hash marks.

• Don't use a warped board. It's difficult and often impossible to make a warped board work in curved joinery.

5. When you're satisfied with the fit of the joint, apply glue to both sides of the joint and both sides of the strip.

6. At the moment before clamping the boards together, the glue should look shiny like wet paint. If it looks dull, the wood has absorbed too much of the glue or the glue has started to set. In either case, apply another layer of glue to rejuvenate it. If the glue is fully dry and hard, you'll have to sand it off but that will usually ruin the fit so it's best to set the boards aside and start over. To avoid this, whenever there's a delay in the glue up, refresh the glue by applying more. Too much glue may make a mess but if the glue dries before you clamp the joint, it will fail.

7. Set the strip between the boards and slide them against it to keep it vertical.

8. Space your clamps to apply uniform pressure. I set mine approximately twelve to sixteen inches apart with one at each end.

9. Add clamps where extra pressure is needed to draw a gap together. You can't hurt a joint with too many clamps but not using enough clamps might leave a gap.

10. Pull the joint together but don't tighten the clamps.

11. Align the hash marks. You may have to tap one board with a mallet to move it.

12. Clamp the outside edges of the assembly to the strong-backs. When you put full pressure on a clamp, it pulls the edges of the assembly upward. Clamping the edges of the panel down to the strong-backs will keep the panel flat and allow you to safely apply whatever amount of pressure is necessary.

13. Tighten the clamps

14. Check the hash marks. If the alignment isn't correct, tap the end of one board until the marks line up. Sometimes, you'll have to give it a solid hit to get the boards to move. If necessary, use a scrap to protect the board when you hit it.

15. When you're satisfied the alignment is correct, tighten the clamps a little more but not fully tight.

16. Check the surface of the boards at the ends of the joint. They should be flush. If not, tap the higher side with a rubber mallet to drive it down flush to the other side or place a clamp over the joint to force them flush.

17. If the middle of the joint isn't flush, tap the high side with a mallet to drive it down.

18. If that doesn't work, lay a 2x4 over the panel at that spot and clamp it to the strong-back which runs under that spot to sandwich the panel between them.

19. If that doesn't work, drive a wedge under that 2x4.

20. If that doesn't work, drive a wedge under the low side of the joint above the strong-back that runs below it.

21. With all adjustments made, tighten the clamps until there are no gaps in the joint or you see glue squeeze out uniformly along the joint. If you see a gap or don't see glue squeeze out uniformly, your joint may not be lined up correctly. Check the hash marks. If the dry run worked, and you have the joint lined up the same way, you can assume the joint will work now so apply full pressure.

22. If that doesn't work, loosen the clamps and check the glue.

23. From this point, you'll be doing trial and error until you find the correct alignment. Tap the end of one board to move it down the joint in the direction you think might work. Tighten the clamps and check the fit.

24. If necessary, repeat the process in the other direction.

25. When you're satisfied with the alignment, apply full pressure.

• Bar clamps can't put too much pressure on a joint but pipe clamps may. If glue is squeezing out everywhere along the joint, you have enough pressure.

26. If there is an area where glue is not squeezing out, you may need to increase the clamping pressure. If the joint is still out of alignment, loosen the clamps and repeat step 11.

27. With the clamps fully tight, the assembly is sturdy enough to move. You can't hurt a solidly clamped curved joint if it's clamped to strong-backs but be careful not to hurt your back or drop it on your foot.

28. When you're confident the glue has set, put the assembly back on the table and take the clamps off in the following order.

•Release half the pressure on the primary clamps (those across the joint). Don't remove the clamps which hold the edges to the strong-backs until the primary clamps are removed or the edges will be pulled up and the panel may break.

•Release all pressure from the main clamps.

•Remove the clamps holding the assembly to the strong-backs.

You now have a board or panel with a solid wood strip glued into a curved cut.

overlaying strips

A board or panel with a strip can be used like any board or panel. It can be cut and joined to other boards or panels. It can be used in cabinets, tables or any woodworking project. You can also cut a curve in it to insert another strip.

If you align the joints so there are no gaps, each strip will add strength to the panel and there is no limit to the number of strips you can insert. Follow the procedures listed in the previous section, **gluing strips in a curve** on page 69. The procedures are the same no matter how many strips you insert.

procedures for inserting multiple strips

1. Cut the number and variety of strips you want to use.

2. Set the boards with the curved cuts on strong-backs on your work station.

3. Make hash marks across the joint. (image 5)

4. This is a difficult process so first, do a dry run.

5. Bundle the strips and lay them between the boards.

6. Set your clamps in place.

7. Draw the boards together, applying pressure uniformly on all clamps.

8. Set small clamps on the edges of the board to hold them down to the strong-backs.

9. Because you'll be drawing the boards together several inches, you'll have to move the clamps which hold the edges of the boards to the strong-backs.

10. In some cases, you can find the correct position by squaring one set of hash marks across the strips.

11. A hash mark in the center of an arc will line up and put the joint in the correct position. Hash marks on the sides of the arc won't line up (image 6). However, if your curve has a reasonably uniform arc, you should be able to split the difference between the two hash marks to make a good joint.

12. When you've found the best position, erase or sand off the original marks and make new ones.

13. With a successful dry run, assemble the joint.

14. Set the boards with the curved cuts on strong-backs on your work station.

15. Arrange the strips on a table in the order they will appear in the joint.

16. Apply glue to one side of all the strips.

17. Set the glued strips against each other.

18. Don't apply glue to the strips which will face the edges of the boards.

19. Apply glue to the dry strips and set those together.

20. Repeat the process until all the strips are glued and set together.

21. Apply glue to the boards and the outsides of the strip set.

22. Set the strips between the boards.

23. From here, the instructions are the same as those for doing a dry run starting with instruction 6 on the previous page.

24. There is so much glue involved with multiple strips that the assembly should be left to set up overnight.

25. When you're certain the glue is dry and set, remove the clamps in the following order: small clamps holding the edges to the strong-backs then the edge clamps.

The panel with multiple strips is done.

How to save a joint with gaps.

1. Set the two sides of the joint together without strips and make hash marks.

2. Do a dry run with the strips inserted.

3. Clamp the joint tight and check the fit.

4. If there are gaps, loosen the clamps, move one of the boards laterally, tighten the clamps and check the fit again.

5. If there still are gaps, loosen the clamps, move the board in the opposite direction, tighten the clamps and check the fit again.

6. If you can't avoid gaps, find a position that produces the fewest and thinnest gaps. That will be the best possible fit.

7. Tighten the clamps.

8. Erase or sand off the original hash marks.

9. Make new hash marks for this position.

10. Starting with instruction 14 on page 77, glue and clamp the joint to full pressure with the hash marks aligned and the edges clamped to strong-backs.

11. Make a set of thin strips in the desired color or colors. Cut or sand the strips to various thicknesses starting from almost paper thin.

12. Run a bead of glue over the gaps and press it into the gaps.

13. Apply glue to both sides of the shims.

14. Push or drive the shims into the gap. They must fit tight.

15. Fill the entire length of all gaps with shims.

16. Let the glue set up at least four hours before removing clamps.

chapter 5

joining boards along a curve

I have a warm spot in my heart for this technique because it was the first one I developed in 1996. I remember the day I tried it for the first time. I wasn't sure it could work and I wasn't sure what to do with it if it did. Now, it's my favorite technique because the options it offers are unlimited.

Over the years, I've improved the procedures for the technique and now I can make a curved joint as fast and as accurately as a standard straight joint. You'll do just as well if you carefully read and practice the procedures in this chapter.

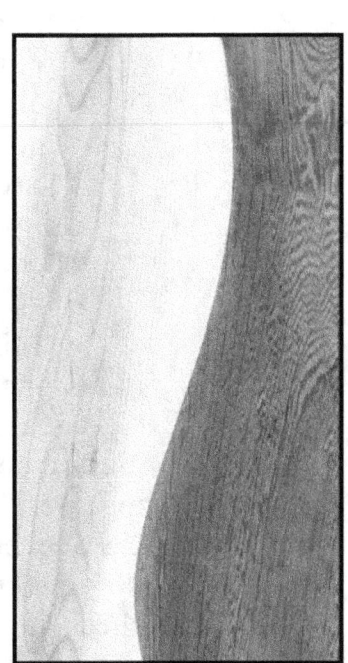

Douglas fir and wenge joined along a curve

selecting lumber

Color is my first and often my only consideration. I don't care much about using highly figured wood because the panels I make have a lot of detail and highly figured wood can make it too busy. It's amazing how many colors of wood you can find. I have books that have photos of wood from around the world but the pictures are always of straight grained boards. Pictures can't give an accurate portrayal of wood and one picture can't show the variety of features every species provides. Imagine seeing a photo of a walnut board and not knowing walnut can have complex multi toned highlights or seeing birch without the convoluted green and brown patterns like storms in the wood.

The best introduction you can get to the wide variety of wood available to you is at a hardwood lumber-yard. Walk around the racks to see what they have and what the various types of wood look like in person. Every city has a commercial hardwood lumber yard that stocks domestic woods like maple, oak, cherry and walnut as well as common exotic woods like padauk, purpleheart and wenge. If you ask around or check the web sites of hardwood suppliers, you should be able to find a yard that stocks a variety of hardwoods. If that isn't available, some lumber yards will ship boards to you. However, weight and size makes shipping expensive and you can't see the boards before you buy them.

In Minneapolis, where I live, Youngblood Lumber has a reasonable selection and I buy most of my wood there. However, years ago, when I lived in Olympia, Washington, I'd go up to Seattle and spend hours walking around Crosscut Hardwoods' huge warehouse. It was like a Toy-R-Us of lumber – racks and racks of every type and color of wood imaginable. If you live in the Northwest or are passing through Seattle, take an afternoon and check it out. I love Minneapolis but I miss Crosscut Hardwoods. If you're lucky, there's a place like that somewhere near you. It would be worth your time finding it.

Here are some of the colors I use that are available in my area.

red – bloodwood

rust – African mahogany, sapele, jatoba

purple – purpleheart (although it may darken toward brown)

light green – treated, one inch exterior decking. It has a green tint, doesn't change with time and – except for variations in the grain – is uniform throughout. The preservatives used now in wood don't have arsenic and are deemed safe for human contact. However, you should work in a well ventilated space and wear a dust mask when sanding or cutting treated wood so you don't inhale the preservative.

black and blackish brown – wenge

white – hard maple

brown – walnut

off-white to beige – birch and soft maple

tan – oak

yellow/orange – Douglas fir

procedures

1. Cut the boards to the length and width you want to use. The only limit on the size is your work space, your tools and your skills. (Until you're comfortable with the procedures, use boards that are no more than 3 feet long.) For the purpose of this lesson, let's call the two boards AB and CD. Board AB will become boards A & B. Board CD will become boards C & D.

2. Lay one board over the other with the wider one on the bottom. To start out, keep the edges parallel. When you're comfortable with the process, you can set the boards as much as 45 degrees off parallel. However, the farther the boards are from parallel, the more difficult the assembly will be.

3. Drill a pilot hole through the top board as far to the end as possible so you can cut it off when trimming the finished panel. Pick a spot that will be out of the line of your cut.

If a screw breaks off, use a vice grip to turn it out. If the stem won't turn, drill small holes as close as possible around it. That will loosen it, so you can turn it out with a vice grips.

• The drill bit you use to make the pilot hole should be slightly thicker than the screw you use so the screw will go through it easily but not have any play when pushing the board through the band-saw.

4. For 3/4 inch boards, use 1-1/4 inch screws. For 1 inch boards, use 1-5/8 inch screws. I use sheet rock screws because they are case hardened and have a solid grip on the wood.

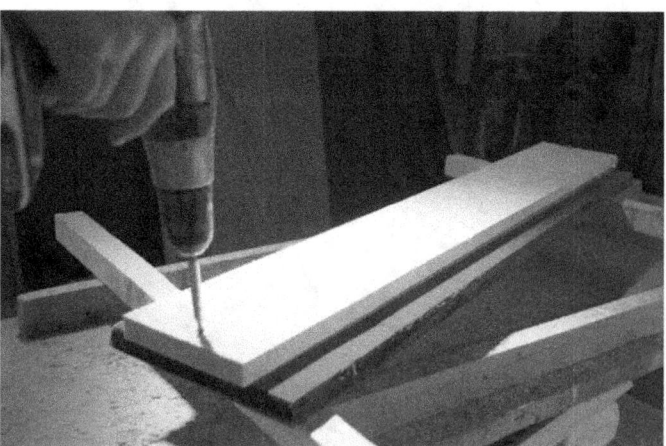

screwing the boards together before cutting them on a band-saw.

5. Drive the screw head till the boards are held firmly together but not tight.

6. Check the boards halfway between the screws. They must lay flat against each other. A gap will allow the assembly to vibrate during the cut which could ruin the fit of the joint.

• If one of the boards is warped, set it aside. It's difficult, and in some cases impossible, to make a successful curved joint with a warped board.

7. If one of the boards bows up on its surface, set it so the bow is down – like a valley rather than a hill. You want the gaps to be at the ends rather than in the middle of the boards.

8. With the gaps at the ends, screw one end of the boards together, draw the other end down with a clamp and screw it together.

• Thin gaps in the middle of the boards shouldn't be a problem.

• Be careful when you screw the boards together. If the bottom board is a dense hardwood, the screw could break off when you remove it. To prevent this, you have two choices. You can drill a small pilot hole in the bottom board or – a quicker method – you can coat the threads of the screw with bees wax before using it. Bees wax is the best lubricant for screws – better, by far, than oil, soap or WD40 – and it doesn't penetrate or stain the wood. You can get bees wax from a wax ring, which is used for setting a toilet and is sold in the plumbing department.

9. Test the assembly by gently trying to pull it apart. The screws don't have to withstand a lot of stress but they must hold the boards together while you're working on them.

10. Draw a line on the top board for the curve you'll cut.

• Although some styles allow it, for the purpose of this lesson, don't run your line off the side.

- Keep the line away from the screws. I've ruined a few band-saw blades by nicking a screw.

  - You can change the direction of your line as often as you like but make the curves long and shallow. A gradual curve is easier to run through the band-saw and is easier to work with during assembly.

Some of the procedures in the following sections starting with **making the cut**, *are also in the previous chapter,* **inserting strips in curved cuts**. *I did that so you can read either chapter and follow the instructions without having to flip to the other chapter.*

---

making the cut

1. Before starting the cut, position the board so the first few inches of your line is in line with the blade.

2. As you move the board through the blade, turn it so the next few inches of the line are aligned with the blade.

   - If you move the board through the blade at an angle to the line, it will make deep saw marks on one side of the cut which may show when the piece is finished.

3. If you turn the board without moving it forward, the blade may twist and crease which will make an irregular cut from that point on. A bent or creased blade should be replaced.

4. Move the assembly at a moderate, constant and smooth rate through the blade.

5. Move the board laterally as you move it forward so the line of cut is always in line with the blade. In any case, always

move the board forward faster than you move it laterally. If your blade is sharp, the board should move easily. Forcing it can cause the blade to wander off the line.

6. With the cut complete, turn off the band-saw and wait for the blade to come to a complete stop before moving the two halves of the board, then set them on the strong-backs of your assembly table.

assembling the panel

Boards AB and CD are now boards A, B, C and D.

Do as little sanding as possible. If you take off more material from one area than another, you'll have a gap in the joint.

1. Set all four boards on your strong-backs and arrange them so the cuts match.

2. Remove boards B and D leaving boards A and C.

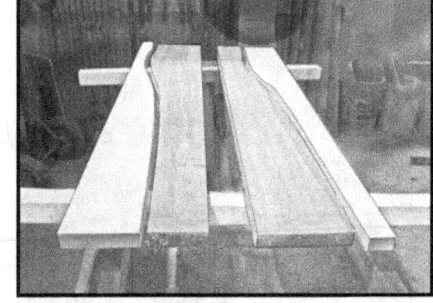

3. You may find that your band-saw left feathers on the edges of the boards. Those feathers could get in the joint when you glue it up so remove them by running a wood file or a sanding block over the corner of the cut at an angle. It may take several passes. Make sure you don't sand the surface of the edge.

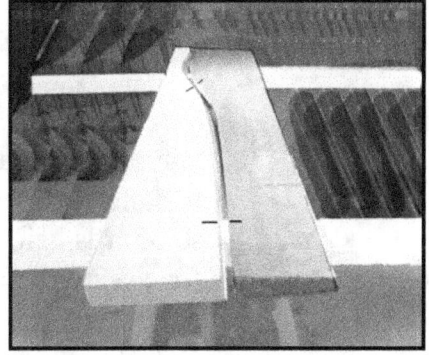

4. If you must sand the surface of the edge, don't try to remove the saw marks. If you've cut the curve correctly, the marks won't show in the finished panel but if you sand too much you could create a gap.

100

5. Dry align the boards with a strip between them. Align the
hash marks. If there is a slight but uniform gap in one area
of the joint, it should close when you pull the joint tight
with clamps.

- If the gaps are in more than one area or if you can't get the
two boards to fit correctly, the hash marks may not be lined
up. In that case, remove the clamps and adjust the boards so
the hash marks line up.

- If this doesn't correct the problem, a poor cut may be the
cause. If so, set the boards aside and start over. Trying to fix
a bad fit with a sander or by re-sawing the joint won't work.
You'll spend a lot less time getting it right by starting over. If
you glue the board back together, it should be useable again.

- Don't use a warped board. It's extremely difficult and often
impossible to make a warped board work in curved joinery.

6. When the hash marks have lined up correctly and you are
satisfied with the dry run, apply glue to both sides of the joint
and to both sides of the strip.

Porous woods absorb glue so quickly you may have to apply a second coat. Hard and dense woods need to sit for a minute or two and need a second coat to refresh the glue.

- Before setting the boards together, check the glue. It should look shiny like wet paint. If it looks dull, the wood has absorbed too much of the glue or the glue has dried. In either case, apply another layer of glue. It will mix with the previous layer and create a good bond. If the glue has hardened, you'll have to sand it off but that may cause other problems so it's best to set the boards aside and start over. To avoid this, if there is a delay in the assembly, keep the glue fresh by applying more. You can't hurt anything by applying too much glue but not enough can cause a failure.

7. Arrange your clamps where you want to apply pressure. I
set my clamps approximately twelve to sixteen inches apart
with one at each end. Add clamps in places where extra

pressure is needed to draw a gap together. You can't hurt a joint with too many clamps but too few might leave a gap.

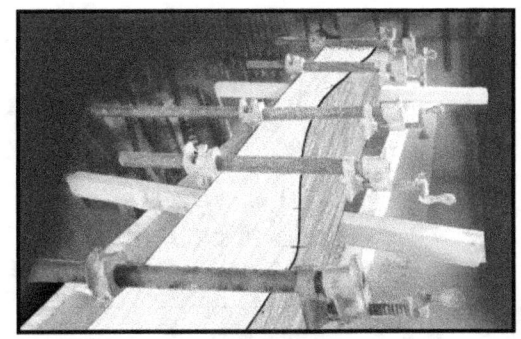

setting clamps

8. Clamp the boards together with minimum pressure and align the hash marks.

9. Pull the joint together with moderate pressure. Don't tighten the clamps.

10. Clamp the outside edges of the assembly down to the strong-backs. With full pressure, a clamp can pull the edges of the panel assembly upward. Clamping the edges to the strong-backs will keep the panel flat and allow you to safely apply whatever amount of pressure is necessary.

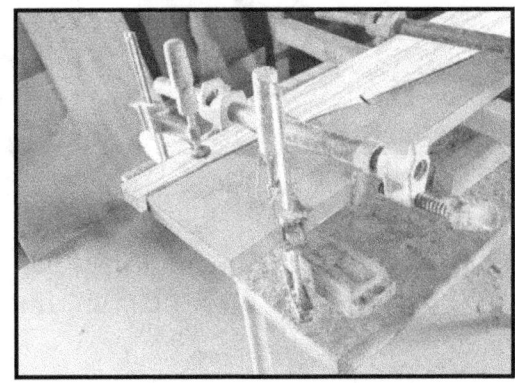

edges clamped to strong back

11. Again, check to make sure the hash marks on the boards are lined up, then tighten the clamps. Don't put full pressure on them yet.

• If the alignment isn't perfect, tap the end of one board until the marks line up. Sometimes, you'll have to hit it hard to get the boards where you want them. Use a scrap to protect the end grain when you hit it.

• If the gaps are in more than one area or if you can't get the two boards to fit correctly, you may not have the hash marks lined up correctly. In that case, remove the clamps and adjust the boards so the hash marks line up.

• If this does not correct the problem, your cut may have left the edges irregular. If so, set the boards aside and start over. Trying

to fix a bad fit with a sander or by re-sawing the joint won't
work. You'll spend a lot of time on it and probably still won't
be happy with the fit so accept that you'll have to start over.

12. When you are satisfied the alignment is correct, tighten
the clamps a little more but not fully tight.

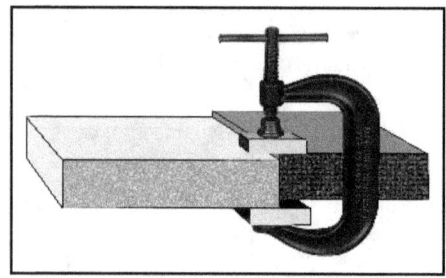

clamp with blocks

13. Check the surface of the boards at the
ends of the joint. They should be flush. If
not, tap the higher side with a rubber mallet
to drive it down flush to the other side or use
a clamp over the joint to force them flush.

14. If the surfaces in the middle of the joint aren't
flush, tap the high side with a hammer or mallet
to drive it down to flush. If that doesn't work, lay
a 2x4 over the panel at that spot and clamp it to the strong-back
which runs under that spot to sandwich the panel between them.

• That should force the boards to flush. If not, drive a wedge
between the 2x4 which runs over the panel and the high side of
the panel at the joint. If that doesn't work, drive a wedge under
the low side of the joint and the strong-back below it.

• If the joint isn't flush in several places, and won't move when
you tap it, you'll have to use several sets of strong-backs and
wedges.

15. With all adjustments made, tighten the clamps until there are
no gaps in the joint or you see glue squeeze out uniformly along
the joint. If you see a gap or don't see glue squeeze out uniformly,
your joint may not be lined up correctly. Check the hash marks.
If they line up and the dry run worked, you know that the gaps
will disappear when you apply full pressure.

• If you're not sure of the condition, loosen the clamps but don't
take all the pressure off the joint.

- Tap the end of one of the boards to move it down the joint in the direction you think might work. Tighten the clamps.

  - If you still suspect a gap, repeat the process but move the board in the other direction.

    - You may have to work the fit until you find the correct alignment. Glue between boards set against each other will remain fresh much longer than if it's fully exposed so you should have time to do this.

      - I've moved boards several times before getting it right. Getting a curved joint to line up is an art so keep working at it and your rate of success will improve.

        - When you're satisfied with the alignment, reapply full pressure.

        - Bar clamps can't put too much pressure on a joint but pipe clamps may. The harder the wood, the more pressure is allowed. If you have glue squeezing out everywhere along the joint, you have enough pressure.

With aliphatic glue, wait 1½ to 2 hours before removing the clamps and 3 to 4 hours before putting stress on the joint.

- If there's place with a gap in the joint, you may need to increase pressure on the clamps. It's possible that with all your checking and double checking the joint is still out of alignment. Check it again. If it's off, loosen the clamps, check the glue and begin the clamping process again.

  - At this point, the panel assembly is sturdy enough to move. You can't hurt a solidly clamped curved joint if it's clamped to strong-backs but be careful not to hurt your back or drop it on your foot.

16. When you're confident the joint has set, put the assembly back on the table and take the clamps off in a specific order. First, remove pressure from the edge clamps. After all the edge

clamps have been released, remove the small clamps holding the edges of the assembly to the strong-backs. If you release the small clamps holding the edges of the assembly to the strong-backs first, the panel may bow up with the pressure of the edge clamps and put stress on the joint.

You now have a panel with two species of wood joined along a curve.

overlapping curved joints

At this point, the new panel is stronger than the boards you started with. You can treat the panel the same way you would handle any board or panel. You can make mitered, dovetail or rabbet joints. You can use it for cabinet sides or table tops. You can insert strips into curved cuts through the panel or you can join the new panel to other boards along a curved joint. And you can add as many strips or curved joints as you like. If you do it correctly, you'll actually be making the panel stronger with each one.

In chapter 10, I describe how to make cabinets and furniture with these panels.

procedures for overlapping curved joints

1. Set a board on your panel so it intersects both of the first two boards. It should be set at no more than 45 degrees to either board.

2. Screw it to the panel in the same way you did making the first curved joint. If there's bridging over a short distance, that won't cause a problem. If you're concerned the boards will chatter while you cut them, set shims between the boards where necessary.

3. Once the new panel and the board are fastened together, follow the same procedures you used for creating the first

curved joint. If all your curved joints are constructed correctly, they will be stable no matter how many times you cut through them as long as the grain of one board is not more than 45 degrees off the direction of the grain of any board it's joined to.

The overlapping joints create a web of curved joints and grain lines which give a panel extraordinary strength.

You can enhance the appearance of the panel by inserting black (wenge) strips in all the curved cuts when you assemble the joints. As you can see on the cover, this produces an outline for the segments.

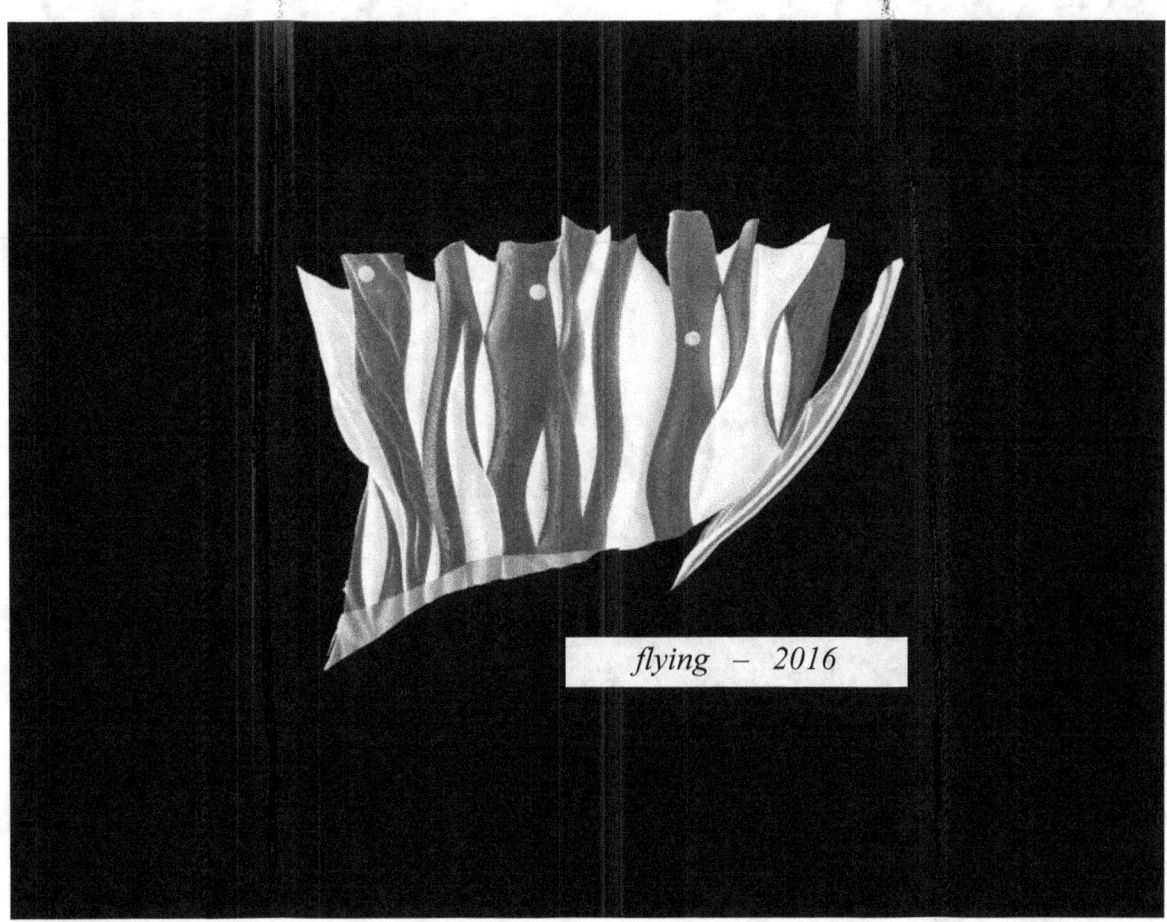

flying – 2016

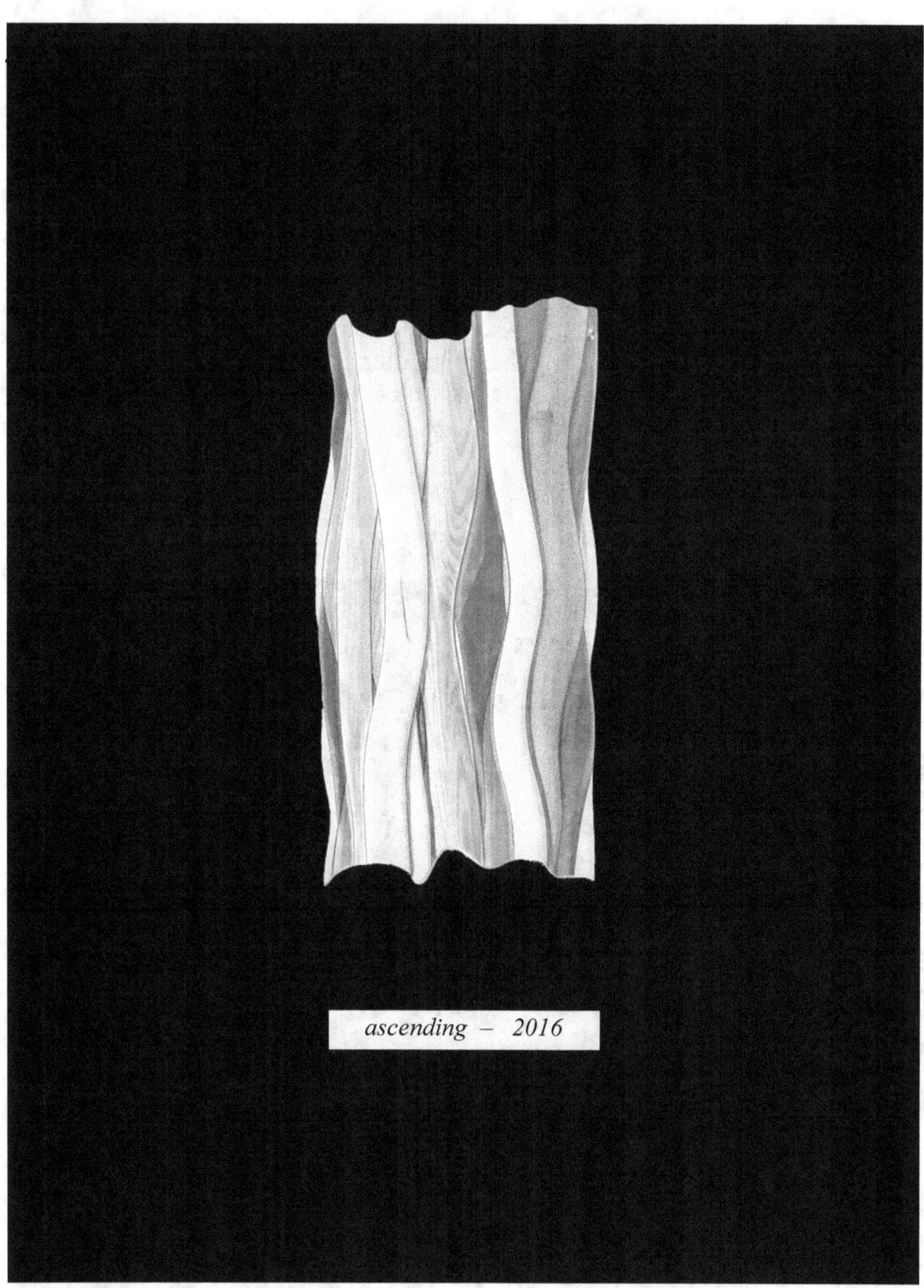

ascending – 2016

summary of chapter 5

joining boards along a curve

your

notes

procedures

1. Cut the boards to the length and width you want to use. The only limit on the size is your work space, your tools and your skills. (Until you're comfortable with the procedures, use boards that are no more than 3 feet long.) For the purpose of this lesson, let's call the two boards AB and CD. Board AB will become boards A & B. Board CD will become boards C & D.

2. Lay one board over the other with the wider one on the bottom. To start out, keep the edges parallel. When you're comfortable with the process, you can set the boards as much as 45 degrees off parallel. However, the farther the boards are from parallel, the more difficult the assembly will be.

3. Drill a pilot hole through the top board as far to the end as possible so you can cut it off when trimming the finished panel. Pick a spot that will be out of the line of your cut.

• The drill bit you use to make the pilot hole should be slightly thicker than the screw you use so the screw will go through it easily but not have any play when pushing the board through the band-saw.

4. For 3/4 inch boards, use 1-1/4 inch screws. For 1 inch boards, use 1-5/8 inch screws. I use sheet rock screws

because they are case hardened and have a solid grip on the wood.

5. Drive the screw head till the boards are held firmly together but not tight.

6. Check the boards halfway between the screws. They must lay flat against each other. A gap will allow the assembly to vibrate during the cut which could ruin the fit of the joint.

• If one of the boards is warped, set it aside. It's difficult, and in some cases impossible, to make a successful curved joint with a warped board.

7. If one of the boards bows up on its surface, set it so the bow is down – like a valley rather than a hill. You want the gaps to be at the ends rather than in the middle of the boards.

8. With the gaps at the ends, screw one end of the boards together, draw the other end down with a clamp and screw it together.

• Thin gaps in the middle of the boards shouldn't be a problem.

• Be careful when you screw the boards together. If the bottom board is a dense hardwood, the screw could break off when you remove it. To prevent this, you have two choices. You can drill a small pilot hole in the bottom board or – a quicker method – you can coat the threads of the screw with bees wax before using it. Bees wax is the best lubricant for screws – better, by far, than oil, soap or WD40 – and it doesn't penetrate or stain the wood. You can get bees wax from a wax ring, which is used for setting a toilet and is sold in the plumbing department.

9. Test the assembly by gently trying to pull it apart. The screws don't have to withstand a lot of stress but they must hold the boards together while you're working on them.

10. Draw a line on the top board for the curve you'll cut.

• Although some styles allow it, for the purpose of this lesson, don't run your line off the side.

• Keep the line away from the screws. I've ruined a few band-saw blades by nicking a screw.

• You can change the direction of your line as often as you like but make the curves long and shallow. A gradual curve is easier to run through the band-saw and is easier to work with during assembly.

making the cut

1. Before starting the cut, position the board so the first few inches of your line is in line with the blade.

2. As you move the board through the blade, turn it so the next few inches of the line are aligned with the blade.

• If you move the board through the blade at an angle to the line, it will make deep saw marks on one side of the cut which may show when the piece is finished.

• Turning the board too quickly will make a sharp corner. The strip won't be able to make a sharp bend which will leave a gap.

3. If you turn the board without moving it forward, the blade may twist and crease which will make an irregular cut from that point on. A bent or creased blade should be replaced.

4. Move the assembly at a moderate, constant and smooth rate through the blade.

5. Move the board laterally as you move it forward so the line of cut is always in line with the blade. In any case, always move the board forward faster than you move it laterally. If your blade is sharp, the board should move easily. Forcing it can cause the blade to wander off the line.

6. With the cut complete, turn off the band-saw and wait for the blade to come to a complete stop before moving the

two halves of the board, then set them on the strong-backs of your assembly table.

assembling the panel

Boards AB and CD are now boards A, B, C and D.

1. Set all four boards on your strong-backs and arrange them so the cuts match.

2. Remove boards B and D leaving boards A and C.

3. You may find that your band-saw left feathers on the edges of the boards. Those feathers could get in the joint when you glue it up so remove them by running a wood file or a sanding block over the corner of the cut at an angle. It may take several passes. Make sure you don't sand the surface of the edge.

4. If you must sand the surface of the edge, do it carefully and don't try to remove any saw marks. If you've cut the curve correctly, the marks won't show up in the finished panel but if you sand too much you could create a gap.

5. Dry align the boards with a strip between them. Align the hash marks. If there is a slight but uniform gap in one area of the joint, it should close when you pull the joint tight with clamps.

• If the gaps are in more than one area or if you can't get the two boards to fit correctly, the hash marks may not be lined up. In that case, remove the clamps and adjust the boards so the hash marks line up.

• If this doesn't correct the problem, a poor cut may be the cause. If so, set the boards aside and start over. Trying to fix a bad fit with a sander or by re-sawing the joint won't work. You'll spend a lot less time getting it right by starting over. If you glue the board back together, it should be useable again.

• Don't use a warped board. It's extremely difficult and often impossible to make a warped board work in curved joinery.

6. When the hash marks have lined up correctly and you are satisfied with the dry run, apply glue to both sides of the joint and to both sides of the strip.

• Before setting the boards together, check the glue. It should look shiny like wet paint. If it looks dull, the wood has absorbed too much of the glue or the glue has dried. In either case, apply another layer of glue. It will mix with the previous layer and create a good bond. If the glue has hardened, you'll have to sand it off but that may cause other problems so it's best to set the boards aside and start over. To avoid this, if there is a delay in the assembly, keep the glue fresh by applying more. You can't hurt anything by applying too much glue but not enough can cause a failure.

7. Arrange your clamps where you want to apply pressure. I set my clamps approximately twelve to sixteen inches apart with one at each end. Add clamps in places where extra pressure is needed to draw a gap together. You can't hurt a joint with too many clamps but too few might leave a gap.

8. Clamp the boards together with minimum pressure and align the hash marks.

9. Pull the joint together with moderate pressure. Don't tighten the clamps.

10. Clamp the outside edges of the assembly down to the strong-backs. With full pressure, a clamp can pull the edges of the panel assembly upward. Clamping the edges to the strong-backs will keep the panel flat and allow you to safely apply whatever amount of pressure is necessary.

11. Again, check to make sure the hash marks on the boards are lined up, then tighten the clamps. Don't put full pressure on them yet.

• If the alignment isn't perfect, tap the end of one board until the marks line up. Sometimes, you'll have to hit it hard to get the boards where you want them. Use a scrap to protect the end grain when you hit it.

• If the gaps are in more than one area or if you can't get the two boards to fit correctly, you may not have the hash marks lined up correctly. In that case, remove the clamps and adjust the boards so the hash marks line up.

• If this does not correct the problem, your cut may have left the edges irregular. If so, set the boards aside and start over. Trying to fix a bad fit with a sander or by re-sawing the joint won't work. You'll spend a lot of time on it and probably still won't be happy with the fit so accept that you'll have to start over.

12. When you are satisfied the alignment is correct, tighten the clamps a little more but not fully tight.

13. Check the surface of the boards at the ends of the joint. They should be flush. If not, tap the higher side with a rubber mallet to drive it down flush to the other side or use a clamp over the joint to force them flush.

14. If the surfaces in the middle of the joint aren't flush, tap the high side with a hammer or mallet to drive it down to flush. If that doesn't work, lay a 2x4 over the panel at that spot and clamp it to the strong-back which runs under that spot to sandwich the panel between them.

• That should force the boards to flush. If not, drive a wedge between the 2x4 which runs over the panel and the high side of the panel at the joint. If that doesn't work, drive a wedge under the low side of the joint and the strong-back below it.

• If the joint isn't flush in several places, and won't move when you tap it, you'll have to use several sets of strong-backs and wedges.

15. With all adjustments made, tighten the clamps until there are no gaps in the joint or you see glue squeeze out uniformly along the joint. If you see a gap or don't see glue squeeze out uniformly, your joint may not be lined up correctly. Check the hash marks. If they line up and the dry run worked, you know that the gaps will disappear when you apply full pressure.

- If you're not sure of the condition, loosen the clamps but don't take all the pressure off the joint.

- Tap the end of one of the boards to move it down the joint in the direction you think might work. Tighten the clamps.

- If you still suspect a gap, repeat the process but move the board in the other direction.

- You may have to work the fit until you find the correct alignment. Glue between boards set against each other will remain fresh much longer than if it's fully exposed so you should have time to do this.

- I've moved boards several times before getting it right. Getting a curved joint to line up is an art so keep working at it and your rate of success will improve.

- When you're satisfied with the alignment, reapply full pressure.

- Bar clamps can't put too much pressure on a joint but pipe clamps may. The harder the wood, the more pressure is allowed. If you have glue squeezing out everywhere along the joint, you have enough pressure.

- If there's place with a gap in the joint, you may need to increase pressure on the clamps. It's possible that with all your checking and double checking the joint is still out of alignment. Check it again. If it's off, loosen the clamps, check the glue and begin the clamping process again.

- At this point, the panel assembly is sturdy enough to move. You can't hurt a solidly clamped curved joint if it's clamped to strong-backs but be careful not to hurt your back or drop it on your foot.

16. When you're confident the joint has set, put the assembly back on the table and take the clamps off in a specific order. First, remove pressure from the edge clamps. After all the edge clamps have been released, remove the small clamps holding the edges of the assembly to the strong-backs. If you release the small clamps holding the edges of the assembly to the strong-backs first, the panel may bow up with the pressure of the edge clamps and put stress on the joint.

You now have a panel with two species of wood joined along a curve.

overlapping curved joints

At this point, the new panel is stronger than the boards you started with. You can treat the panel the same way you would handle any board or panel. You can make mitered, dovetail or rabbet joints. You can use it for cabinet sides or table tops. You can insert strips into curved cuts through the panel or you can join the new panel to other boards along a curved joint. And you can add as many strips or curved joints as you like. If you do it correctly, you'll actually be making the panel stronger with each one.

procedures for overlapping curved joints

1. Sand or plane the surface of the panel to remove extremely high spots.

2. Select a board you want to add to the panel.

3. Set the board on your panel so that it intersects the first two boards. It should be set at no more than 45 degrees to either board.

4. Screw the board to the panel in the same way you did making the first assembly. If you were not able to get the surface at the joints flush during the last assembly, there may be some voids between the panel and the board you are adding to it. If the bridging is over a short distance, that won't cause a problem. If you are concerned the boards will chatter as you run them through the band-saw, set shims under the board at the area of bridging to firm it up.

5. Once the new panel and the board are fastened together, follow the same procedures you used for creating the first curved joint. If all your curved joints are constructed correctly, they will be stable no matter how many times you cut through them as long as the grain of one board is not more than 45 degrees off the direction of the grain of any board it's joined to.

You can enhance the appearance of the panel by inserting black (wenge) strips in all the curved cuts when you assemble the joints. As you can see on the cover, this produces an outline for the segments.

How I Came to Love Woodworking

Chapter 6,
patterns of pegs
starts on
page 121

part 2

In the summer of 1972, I moved back downstate and lived in a rundown old house on two acres at the edge of Urbana, Illinois. The owner of the house, Mrs. Harrison, was the sweet, evangelical widow of a man who, although blind, built the house with his son using six panel garage doors they got at a junk yard. It was a tenement the day it was finished and perfect for me. A friend called it the House of Doors and the name stuck.

One day, I poked around a shed hidden in the overgrown weeds out back and found a hammer with a cracked handle, a coffee can full of bent nails and several old boards. I straightened the nails, scraped mud off the boards and turned the shed into a chicken coop. Unfortunately for the chickens, I wasn't much of a carpenter, so when the raccoons came around, I couldn't keep them out. I sent the survivors to a farm south of town. My days as a farmer were over but my life as a woodworker was about to begin.

Early the next year, I got a job working for a cabinet maker, even though I knew nothing about woodworking. I hauled materials, sanded panels and caught boards as he fed them through the table saw. It was menial work but I loved it.

Since I could see shapes in my mind, I quickly understood what he was doing and paid close attention. However, I could also recognize what he was doing wrong and, as I did with my geometry teacher, I told him about it. He fired me the next day.

I felt bad about it but I didn't want to stop working with wood. A few weeks later, I bought a table saw, some tools and set up a shop of my own.

That summer, I fell in love with woodworking. My first
commission was a set of bookshelves with casters and hinges.
An interior designer saw them and asked me to design and
build a terrarium end table for the lobby of a bank – an
inverted pyramid with a hinged glass top and glass sides with
oak frames. She evidently didn't realize how little experience
I had and I didn't realize how difficult the project would be
for me. I spent hours figuring out every joint and did every
operation in the slowest and most difficult way. I fixed so
many mistakes I could have made the whole thing twice.
Somehow, it turned out well. After that, I was always busy,
in part, because of a steady stream of work, but more because
it took so long for me to do the work.

In 1974, some friends and I moved to a hundred and
sixty-five acre farm eight miles east of Waynesboro, Tennessee
and I built a shop in a barn. In the summer of '76, I made a
traditional cedar chest which the Waynesboro chief of police
bought. I expected that to give a good boost to my business.

About that time, a friend gave me a magazine designed for
dedicated woodworkers that had just started publication. It was
Fine Woodworking by Taunton Press. An article highlighted a
woman who made furniture by gluing plywood into massive slabs
which she carved into thick chairs with an auto body grinder. I
loved the flowing shapes and the unorthodox method. About that
time, the county sheriff came to see me. He saw the cedar chest I
made and wanted one. "You make it the way you want," he said.
I did.

It had pull out trays and a lid with chain restraints just like
any cedar chest. But, the sides and top of the box flowed onto
each other like a perfect loaf of bread. I loved it. When the sheriff
came for it, he stopped hard at the door.

"I thought you'd make it like the other one," he said.

It was disappointing for both of us. Clearly, rural Tennessee
was not going to be a good market for my work.

The other guys on our farm had been building decks and
sheds for people in town – small jobs that didn't require much

experience or skill. Somehow, one of the guys convinced a lawyer that they could build his four thousand square foot house. I needed work so I joined them. But, it was a complex project. It had dormers, flat valleys and forty foot long rafters, a long stairway and a cathedral ceiling with a ridge that dog-legged. Experienced carpenters would have had a hard time building it. We were way over our heads. One of the guys had a book on construction which we kept on a bench beside the blue prints. We were students without a teacher, paid to go to class.

Although we were making more money than any of us had ever made, we were charging the lawyer half what he would have paid a contractor. Unfortunately, we took more than twice as long to build the house. But, the lawyer was patient and kind and when it was finally finished, he was happy with it and we were happy to be done.

In the Spring of 1977, I moved to Olympia, Washington where I got a job framing houses – simple ramblers which the contractor wanted built as fast and as cheaply as possible. Quality was not a consideration. Once I learned how to work fast, there was little more to learn from him. I heard somewhere that you could take a test and if you passed it you'd become a journeyman in the carpenter's union. I decided to give that a shot.

The union business agent was very nice. He took me to a room next to his office, gave me the exam and said I had an hour to finish it. The geometry was easy and I knew the answers to most of the questions about framing. The questions on concrete and interior finish were another matter. I didn't know much about those. However, I knew enough that I could figure out the answers even if I didn't know them. I passed the test and got a union card, but that didn't get me a job.

Jobs were controlled by the business agent. If a company needed a carpenter, they'd call the union office and the business agent would go to the list of members who had at least five hundred hours in the past year. If all of those members were working, he'd go to the list of those with two hundred or more hours. After that, he go to members with less than two hundred

hours but more than zero. If all of them were working, he'd
call someone with no hours. That would be me. My chances
of being called were probably zero. If I was going to get a
job, I had to get it myself. I drove around for days and finally
found someone who'd hire me.

"Go get a dispatch," he said.

"What?" I said.

"I can't hire you without a dispatch from the union."

I didn't know that rule when I started this whole process
and I wasn't optimistic about my chances of getting one but
I went to the office anyway.

Above the Brotherhood Tavern on Capital Way, the office
of Carpenters Local Union 1148 probably looked the same as
it did in the 1950's, with walnut stained oak paneling, wide
cove molding and Douglas fir flooring. On the other side of a
thick, dark, wood counter, the business agent – the same guy
who had given me the test – talked to an older man who looked
like he'd been out in the weather most of the last thirty years.

"Can I help you?" the agent said.

"I need a dispatch," I said.

He looked at me as if I'd said something stupid or rude. "You
got a job yourself?" he said.

"Yeah."

He shook his head. "That's not how it's done. But as of today
Jack's the business agent. I'm just filling him in on a few things.
It's your call, Jack."

The older man seemed uncomfortable with that. Clearly, he
would have been more comfortable making decisions on a job
site than in an office. I kept my mouth shut and didn't flinch while
he stared at me.

"I suppose it's okay," he said.

(part 3 starts on page 233)

chapter 6

patterns
of pegs

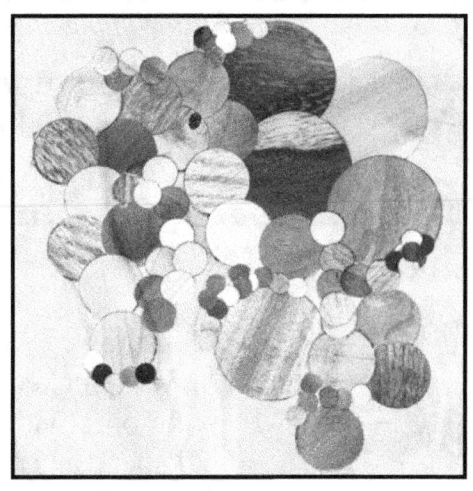

Pegs – also called dowels – have been used in various civilizations around the world for thousands of years. Egyptians used them in furniture long before the pyramids were built. Fourteen hundred years ago, Japanese artisans used them to construct a temple. Leif Eriksson sailed from Norway to Newfoundland a thousand years ago on ships constructed of planks fastened together, in part, with pegs. For centuries, buildings have been constructed with heavy beams joined to massive posts with mortise and tenon joints that were held together with pegs.

It's common practice to insert a peg over a countersunk screw in furniture, a cosmetic fix that, one day in 1997, gave me an idea that became the technique I describe in this chapter – making designs with pegs. Over the years, my designs have evolved to the point they can cover several square feet in some pieces. It's a time consuming process and you may never make more than a small design but it will be a useful and interesting technique to have in your portfolio.

To create interest, a pegging design must have a significant variety of sizes and colors. Lumber and hardware stores have a limited selection of dowel rods, so you'll have to make them yourself.

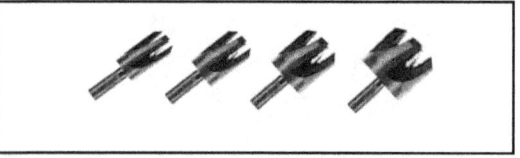

1/8, 1/4, 3/8 and 1/2 inch plug cutters

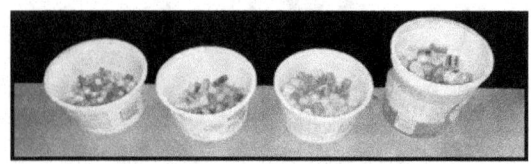

1/8, 1/4, 3/8 and 1/2 inch pegs

A standard set of plug cutters runs from 1/8 inch to 1/2 inch but you can find sets up to one inch. There are two types of plug cutters. One leaves the end square to the sides of the peg and the other leaves it with a slight dome. Both work fine but the one with a dome is a little easier to start into a hole.

Cutting pegs from both edge and end grain will double your variety because each has a unique appearance and you should save scraps from any board with an unusual color or highlight. I save every scrap that could make a peg in buckets. I have a bucket for every color of wood and one for prized scraps – the ones with very unusual features. Once every six months or so, I spend an entire day making pegs of every size for every color I have. I have one container for each size with tightly fitting lids so if it gets knocked over I don't have to pick two hundred little pegs out of the sawdust.

Sometimes when cutting pegs, one will break off inside the cutter and has to come out before you can cut the next one. To remove it, set the tip of a small flat screw driver against the peg as high up the side of the cutter as possible. Tap the screwdriver with a hammer but not hard so you don't bend the shaft of the

cutter or damage the drill press chuck. Rotate the cutter and
tap another spot. You may have to do this a few times.

Pegs cut in edge grain will break off inside the cutter if the
board has a crack. Soft woods are more prone to breaking in
the plug cutter than hard woods and the chance of a peg
breaking off increases as pegs get smaller. Working slowly
helps keep a peg in tact. 1/8 inch pegs should be cut in end
grain because they rarely survive being cut in edge grain.

making pegs in edge grain

1. Use a board which is at least 3/4 inch thick so the plug will
remain in the board when you draw the plug cutter out. If the
plug cutter goes all the way through the board, you'll have to drive
the plug out of the cutter which adds a lot of time to the operation.

2. Rip the boards so they are no more than three inches wide. This
allows you to safely run them through a band-saw to separate the
pegs from the board.

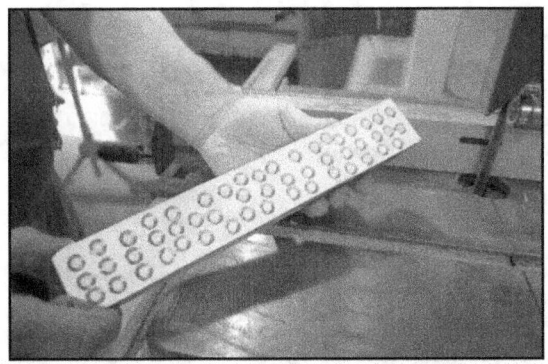

*Leave space around each peg so the
cutter won't nick the last one you cut.*

3. Use a clamp or a jig with a stop board
on the drill press table to prevent the board
from spinning when cutting pegs.

4. The cutter has no center point to hold
the board steady so it can kick the board
out. Pull the cutter down to the board
slowly till it barely hits the surface
and ease it down till it is fully seated
in the surface of the board.

5. Increase pressure, but not too
much or you might burn or
darken the wood.

6. Repeat the process until you have filled the entire board. Throw all those boards into a bucket to take to the band-saw.

cutting pegs in end grain

1. Cut a board into blocks with both ends square to the sides. The length of the block should be less than its narrowest width so it will be stable against the force of the plug cutter.

2. Glue and screw two short boards onto a piece of plywood creating a ninety degree crotch for the block to sit in.

3. Clamp the block firmly in the crotch. The board must be secure and stable when drilling it for pegs.

4. Keep your fingers clear of the cutter. If the top and bottom of the block are square, all the tips of the plug cutter will make contact with the block at the same time. If not, the cutter will kick out the block with surprising force.

If you drill near the edge of a block, it may split and fly apart.

removing pegs from the board

With all the edge and end grain pegs cut in the blocks and boards, the next step is removing them. A table saw or chop saw are not safe to use for this.

1. If you don't have a band-saw, pry the pegs out of edge grain using a thin screwdriver or an awl. You can't pry pegs out of end grain so if you don't have a band-saw, use a hand saw to remove them.

2. A larger plug cutter will make a longer peg than a smaller one. Measure the depth of the plug cutter and set the fence on your band-saw to slightly less than that.

3. Cut a piece of plywood large enough to cover the table of the band-saw up to the fence. This will help keep loose pegs from getting caught on the uneven surface between the insert and the table.

4. Run the plywood through the blade along the fence and stop when it reaches the back edge of the table. This will leave a strip behind the blade next to the fence.

5. Clamp the plywood to the table in a spot away from the line of the cut. Place a large bin behind the band-saw to catch everything that falls off the back of the table.

6. The side of the board showing the pegs must face the fence. In other words, you won't be able to see the pegs when you cut the board.

7. Press the board against the fence with a fixed feather board or a push stick in your right hand.

8. Use a second push stick to move the board through the band-saw blade. Hold this push stick in a way to keep your fingers out of the line of cut and away from the blade.

9. When the board is fully past the blade, use your push stick to move it fully past the blade. The pegs will be in the slice that is against the fence and should be loose.

10. If the pegs are still attached to the board, the fence was set too far from the blade. In that case, remove the plywood from the table, move the fence slightly toward the blade and run a clean edge of plywood as described in 3, 4 and 5 above.

11. If the pegs are loose, you have two halves of the board. One half has holes where

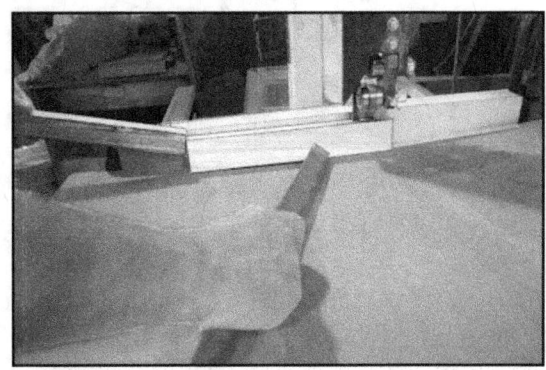

The push stick in your left hand will be cut, so have more sticks available.

the pegs were cut and the other is a thinner, solid piece. That piece should have no more than a very slight groove left from the plug cutter. If the groove is deep, the fence was set too far from the blade and you're wasting valuable peg length. In that case, remove the plywood from the table, move the fence slightly away from the blade and run a clean edge of the plywood as described in 3, 4 and 5 above.

12. To make end grain pegs, you'll be cutting relatively short blocks rather than boards which can be difficult to control. Blocks should be at least 3 inches wide on one side so you can hold them securely down on the table of the band-saw. Use a push stick which holds the block down as it pushes it through the blade and a second stick to hold it against the fence.

• To make this push stick, draw a square corner at approximately 35 degrees at the end of a 12 to 16 inch board that tapers from 3 inches to 1 inch. Cut the square corner with a band-saw or hand saw.

13. When all the boards and blocks have been cut, the bin will have sawdust, small chunks of wood and your pegs. Remove the pegs and put them into plastic food containers with secure lids. Be sure the lids are secure. It's not fun picking hundreds of pegs off the floor.

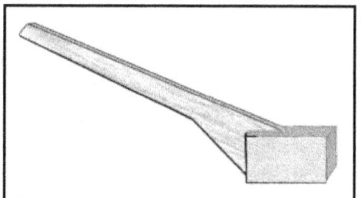

This type of push stick holds a block down as it pushes it forward

14. Measure the depth of the next plug cutter, set the fence and repeat the procedures listed above.

cutting pegs with a hole saw

You can make pegs that are larger than plug cutters make with a hole saw.

1. Your hole saw will be cutting all the way through the board, so set a piece of plywood on the drill press table to prevent the blade from hitting the metal table.

2. Use a hole saw with a pilot bit to make a jig in 3/4 inch plywood .

3. The blade must cut smoothly and evenly so the jig will be exactly the diameter of the hole saw.

4. Remove the disk from inside the hole saw.

5. To cut a peg, loosen the set screw in the side of the arbor and remove the pilot bit from the hole saw arbor. Using a hole saw without a pilot bit allows you to make a peg without a hole at its center. However, without a pilot bit, the saw will vibrate, wander and could kick the board out.

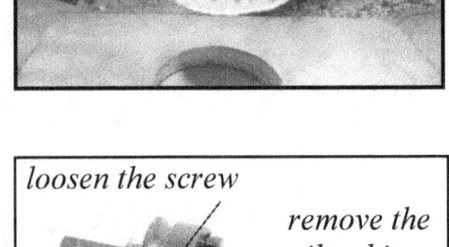

loosen the screw

remove the pilot bit

hole saw arbor

6. Clamp the jig and the board to the drill press table. Even with the jig, there will be some vibration. You can reduce vibration by drilling slowly.

7. Ease the hole saw down to the board until it barely touches. If one side hits first, remove the board or block and sand the area where the saw hit first.

8. Repeat that process until the bit hits the board evenly. Go slowly until the saw makes a fine spray of dust, then continue until the entire circumference of the hole saw is approximately one-eighth inch below the surface of the board. Continue the cut with steady and moderate force. A delicate touch yields the best results.

9. If your jig doesn't fit tight on the hole saw there may be some vibration while you drill. If so, loosen the clamp enough that you can put light pressure against the side of the hole saw as it contacts the board. The jig will steady the hole saw enough to allow it to bite into the wood.

If a hole saw wobbles, it will leave an uneven cut and a rough edge

10. Cut all the way through the board so that the peg is left inside the hole saw.

11. Remove the peg by putting a thin screw driver or thick nail set through the slots in the top of the hole saw. Lightly tap down against the peg with a hammer till it drops out. Don't use too much force or you could bend or damage the arbor.

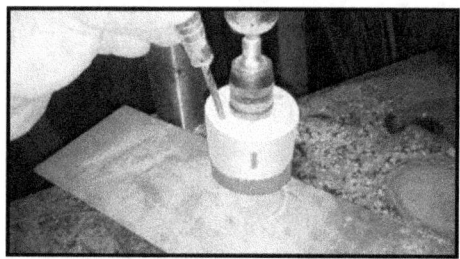 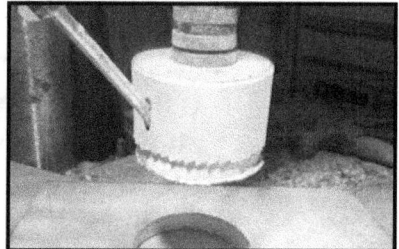

12. You could also put an awl or small screwdriver through a slot in the side of the hole saw to push the peg down. Turn the hole saw and push down through various sides of the peg until it drops out.

drilling and setting pegs

Each plug cutter and the peg it makes has a corresponding Forstner style drill bit.

• Use a drill press. You can't hold a hand drill steady enough to make a precise fit for the pegs.

Don't drill all the way through the board. Without wood below the peg, you'll push it through the bottom when you drill for the next peg. Set a stop so you don't drill too deeply. I stop when the top of the cylindrical cutter is flush with the top of the board.

- If you drill through the board, set the peg and wait for the glue to set up which will hold the peg when you drill the next hole. However, this will add time to the operation.

- Pour a small puddle of glue onto a food container lid. Dip the tip of a peg into the glue and drive it into the hole with a hammer.

- Don't put glue in the hole because it will prevent the peg from reaching the bottom of the hole and leave a void when the glue dries.

- If you're working near the edge of a board, putting glue in the hole can cause a hydraulic effect which can create enough lateral pressure to crack or split the board.

creating patterns with pegs

1. After driving a peg, use a chisel to cut it off. Start high on the peg to see which way the grain goes. Continue cutting from the low side of the grain.

2. Position the board so the drill bit will take off some of the first peg leaving a crescent.

3. Pull the bit down into the wood slowly so it doesn't wander or chip the last peg then raise the bit slowly and carefully.

4. Repeat the process to add pegs.

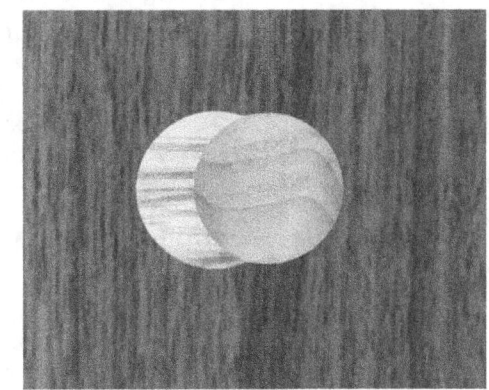

second peg drilled into the first

drilling holes for large pegs

Forstner bits run up to four inches in diameter. Those bits are not an exact match for the pegs you make with a hole saw but they're close enough that the gap they leave can easily be mitigated as I'll explain later.

The area to be drilled must be flat and level with the drill press table or the teeth of the bit will catch the wood before the point in the bit touches and throw the board out with surprising force. Sand or scrape the area so the point of the bit will hit first or clamp the board to the drill press table.

If you drill for a plug that's larger than the bits you have, use a hole saw to create the hole. Here's how to do that:

1. Set the depth gauge on the drill press so the hole saw will cut approximately half way through the board.

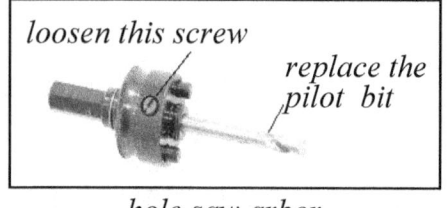

loosen this screw

replace the pilot bit

hole saw arbor

2. Replace the pilot bit in the hole saw arbor.

3. Bring the pilot bit down to the table and adjust the table so the bit lines up with the hole.

4. Clamp the board to the table.

5. Ease the hole saw down until it barely touches it. Continue slowly until you see a fine spray of dust.

6. Continue gently until the entire circumference of the hole saw is below the surface of the board.

7. Continue the cut with steady and moderate force.

• If the blade wobbles, use a jig to steady it. You may have to gently press one side of the jig against the hole saw as you draw it down into the board. Once the saw is fully seated in the bole, you won't need the jig.

8. When you have reached the correct depth of cut, set the board aside and replace the hole saw with a Forstner bit of any size.

9. Unlock the drill press depth gauge.

10. Set the stop to allow the bit to go down approximately half the thickness of the board.

11. Put the board back on the table.

12. Pull the drill bit down so the edge of it cuts into the inside edge of the kerf made by the hole saw till you hit the stop.

13. Raise the bit and check the hole. You shouldn't see any more than a trace of the hole saw kerf.

14. Reset the depth gauge if necessary.

15. With the depth correct, continue drilling with the Forstner bit until all or most of the area inside the hole is removed. Be careful not to drill outside the hole saw kerf.

16. Take the board to a workstation.

17. Use a chisel or scraper to remove anything the drill left.

18. Sand or scrape the bottom of the hole to get it as flush as possible. It must be flat but doesn't have to be smooth

setting large pegs

1. The holes made by a large Forstner style bit or by a hole saw won't match the size of a peg made with a hole saw. The peg will be slightly smaller than the hole and won't be stable in the hole until the glue sets.

2. Pour a small puddle of glue into the bottom of the hole.

3. Set the large peg into the hole and twist it till you feel some resistance. This will create enough bonding to hold the peg in place while the glue sets up.

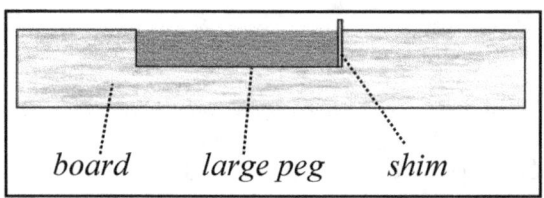

board   large peg   shim

When you drill for the next peg, you'll cut through the shim but the drill bit will hold the last peg in place.

4. Drive a shim on one side of the peg to push it against the opposite side of the hole.

5. Tap the peg to make sure it sits on the bottom of the hole.

6. Drill for the next peg and set it.

7. Shim the peg so it presses against the first peg.

• If you must put shims in an area which won't be drilled out, use a wood which matches either the peg or the surrounding wood so when you fill in the gap with a matching putty, the shim will disappear. (For information on making matching putty, go to chapter 12, **filling voids** on page 223.)

8. Repeat the process to add as many pegs as you like.

———————————

If you drill too far and go though the bottom of a board, there will be nothing to hold the peg in place. Here's how to save the situation:

1. Screw a piece of 1/4 inch plywood to the back of the board over the hole.

2. Turn the board over, put glue on the plywood, set the peg and twist it till there is some resistance.

3. Clamp the peg to the plywood or secure it with screws through the back of the plywood.

4. Let this sit till the glue sets.

Another method which can save the situation:

1. Put wax paper on a flat surface.

2. Set the board on the wax paper.

3. Put the peg in the hole.

4. Wedge the peg firmly in place with shims glued around it on three or more sides.

5. Let this sit till the glue sets.

6. Drill a hole centered on the line or gap between the peg and the board. The hole should be drilled half way through the thickness of the board and peg.

One or more pegs should be at least half the size of the first peg to work as a gusset between the peg and the board.

7. Set a second peg and shim it into position.

8. Continue drilling and setting pegs around the first peg to create a design.

No matter how you fix the problem, drilling through the bottom of a board will add a lot of time to a project.

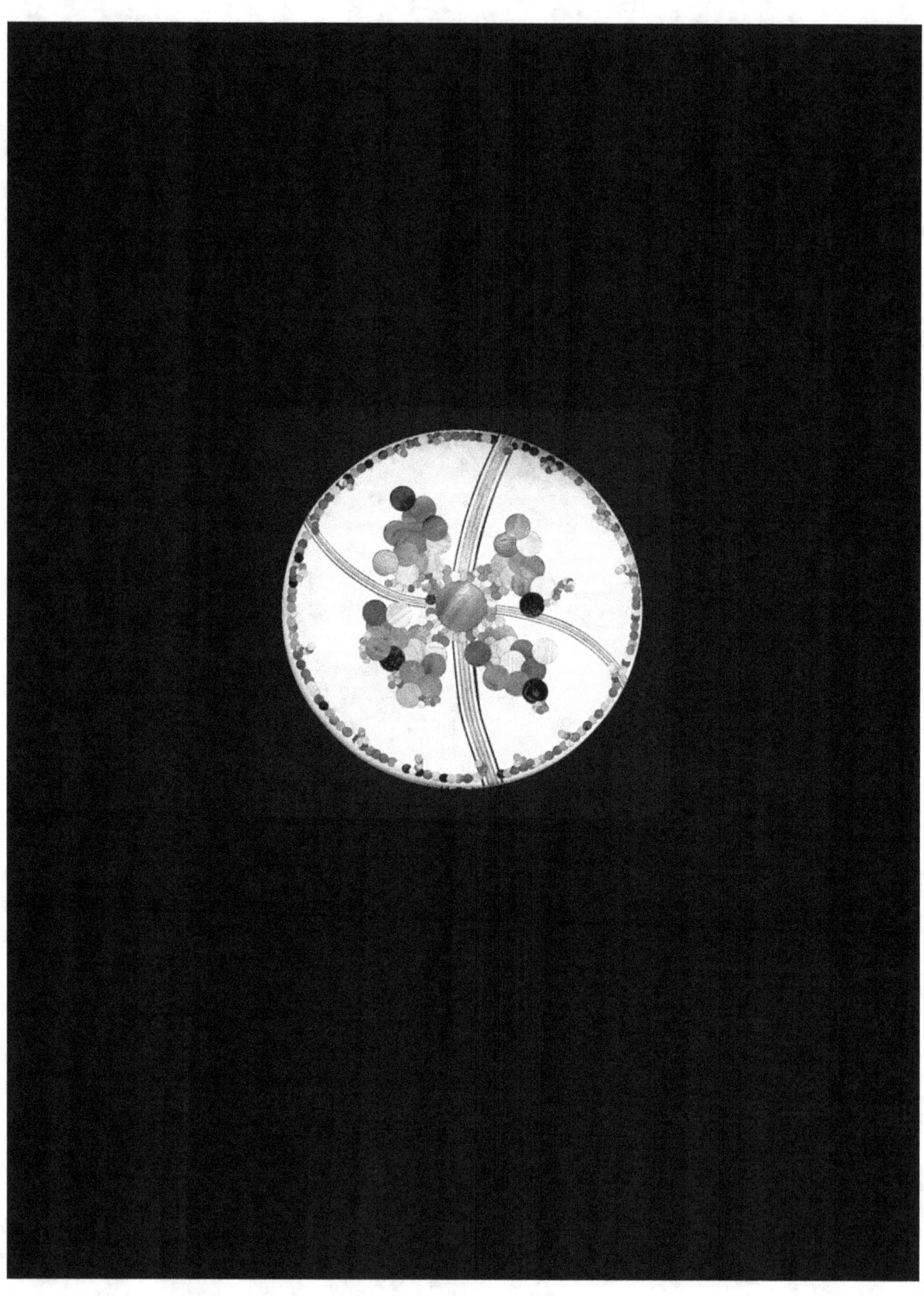

summary of chapter 6

pegging

designs

making pegs in edge grain

1. Use a board which is at least 3/4 inch thick so the plug will remain in the board when you draw the plug cutter out. If the plug cutter goes all the way through the board, you'll have to drive the plug out of the cutter which adds a lot of time to the operation.

2. Rip the boards so they are no more than three inches wide. This allows you to safely run them through a band-saw to separate the pegs from the board.

3. Use a clamp or a jig with a stop board on the drill press table to prevent the board from spinning when cutting pegs.

4. The cutter has no center point to hold the board steady so it can kick the board out. Pull the cutter down to the board slowly till it barely hits the surface and ease it down till it is fully seated in the surface of the board.

5. Increase pressure but not too much. Too much pressure can burn and darken the wood.

6. Repeat the process until you have filled the entire board. Throw all those boards into a bucket to take to the band-saw.

cutting pegs in end grain

1. Cut a board into blocks with both ends square to the sides. The length of the block should be less than its narrowest width so it will be stable against the force of the plug cutter.

2. Glue and screw two short boards onto a piece of plywood creating a ninety degree crotch for the block to sit in.

3. Clamp the block firmly in the crotch.

4. Keep your fingers clear of the cutter. If the top and bottom of the block are square, all the tips of the plug cutter will make contact with the block at the same time. If not, the cutter will kick out the block with surprising force.

removing pegs from the board

With all the edge and end grain pegs cut in the blocks and boards, the next step is removing them. A table saw or chop saw are not safe to use for this.

1. If you don't have a band-saw, pry the pegs out of edge grain using a thin screwdriver or an awl. You can't pry pegs out of end grain so if you don't have a band-saw, use a hand saw to remove them.

2. A larger plug cutter will make a longer peg than a smaller one. Measure the depth of the plug cutter and set the fence on your band-saw to slightly less than that.

3. Cut a piece of plywood large enough to cover the table of the band-saw up to the fence. This will help keep loose pegs from getting caught on the uneven surface between the insert and the table.

4. Run the plywood through the blade along the fence and stop when it reaches the back edge of the table. This will leave a strip behind the blade next to the fence.

5. Clamp the plywood to the table in a spot away from the line of the cut. Place a large bin behind the band-saw to catch everything that falls off the back of the table.

6. The side of the board showing the pegs must face the fence. In other words, you won't be able to see the pegs when you cut the board.

7. Press the board against the fence with a feather board or push stick.

8. Use a second push stick to move the board through the band-saw blade. Hold this push stick in a way to keep your fingers out of the line of cut and away from the blade.

9. When the board is fully past the blade, use your push stick to move it fully past the blade. The pegs will be in the slice that is against the fence and should be loose.

10. If the pegs are still attached to the board, the fence was set too far from the blade. In that case, remove the plywood from the table, move the fence slightly toward the blade and run a clean edge of plywood as described in 3, 4 and 5 above.

11. If the pegs are loose, you have two halves of the board. One half has holes where the pegs were cut and the other is a thinner, solid piece. That piece should have no more than a very slight groove left from the plug cutter. If the groove is deep, the fence was set too far from the blade and you're wasting valuable peg length. In that case, remove the plywood from the table, move the fence slightly away from the blade and run a clean edge of the plywood as described in 3, 4 and 5 above.

12. To make end grain pegs, you'll be cutting relatively short blocks rather than boards which can be difficult to control. Blocks should be at least 3 inches wide on one side so you can hold them securely down on the table of the band-saw. Use a push stick which holds the block down as

it pushes it through the blade and a second stick to hold it against the fence.

• To make this push stick, draw a square corner at approximately 35 degrees at the end of a 12 to 16 inch board that tapers from 3 inches to 1 inch. Cut the square corner with a band-saw or hand saw.

13. When all the boards and blocks have been cut, the bin will have sawdust, small chunks of wood and your pegs. Remove the pegs and put them into plastic food containers with secure lids. Be sure the lids are secure. It's not fun picking hundreds of pegs off the floor.

14. Measure the depth of the next plug cutter, set the fence and repeat the procedures listed above.

cutting pegs with a hole saw

You can make pegs that are larger than plug cutters make with a hole saw.

1. Your hole saw will be cutting all the way through the board, so set a piece of plywood on the drill press table to prevent the blade from hitting the metal table.

2. Use a hole saw with a pilot bit to make a jig in 3/4 inch plywood .

3. The blade must cut smoothly and evenly so the jig will be exactly the diameter of the hole saw.

4. Remove the disk from inside the hole saw.

5. To cut a peg, loosen the set screw in the side of the arbor and remove the pilot bit from the hole saw arbor. Using a hole saw without a pilot bit allows you to make a peg without a hole at its center. However, without a pilot bit, the saw will vibrate, wander and could kick the board out.

6. Clamp the jig and the board to the drill press table. Even with the jig, there will be some vibration. You can reduce vibration by drilling slowly.

7. Ease the hole saw down to the board until it barely touches. If one side hits first, remove the board or block and sand the area where the saw hit first.

8. Repeat that process until the bit hits the board evenly. Go slowly until the saw makes a fine spray of dust, then continue until the entire circumference of the hole saw is approximately one-eighth inch below the surface of the board. Continue the cut with steady and moderate force. A delicate touch yields the best results.

9. If your jig doesn't fit tight on the hole saw there may be some vibration while you drill. If so, loosen the clamp enough that you can put light pressure against the side of the hole saw as it contacts the board. The jig will steady the hole saw enough to allow it to bite into the wood.

10. Cut all the way through the board so that the peg is left inside the hole saw.

11. Remove the peg by putting a thin screw driver or thick nail set through the slots in the top of the hole saw. Lightly tap down against the peg with a hammer till it drops out. Don't use too much force or you could bend or damage the arbor.

12. You could also put an awl or small screwdriver through a slot in the side of the hole saw to push the peg down. Turn the hole saw and push down through various sides of the peg until it drops out.

drilling and setting pegs

Each plug cutter and the peg it makes has a corresponding Forstner style drill bit.

• Use a drill press. You can't hold a hand drill steady enough to make a precise fit for the pegs.

Don't drill all the way through the board. Without wood below the peg, you'll push it through the bottom when you drill for the next peg. Set a stop so you don't drill too deeply. I stop when the top of the cylindrical cutter is flush with the top of the board.

• If you drill through the board, set the peg and wait for the glue to set up which will hold the peg when you drill the next hole. However, this will add time to the operation.

• Pour a small puddle of glue onto a food container lid. Dip the tip of a peg into the glue and drive it into the hole with a hammer.

• Don't put glue in the hole because it will prevent the peg reaching the bottom of the hole and leave a void when the glue dries.

• If you're working near the edge of a board, putting glue in the hole can cause a hydraulic effect which can create enough lateral pressure to crack or split the board.

creating patterns with pegs

1. After driving the first peg, sand it or cut it off with a chisel.

2. Position the board so the drill bit will take off some of the first peg leaving a crescent.

3. Pull the bit down into the wood slowly so it doesn't wander or chip the last peg then raise the bit slowly and carefully.

4. Repeat the process to add pegs.

drilling holes for large pegs

Forstner bits run up to four inches in diameter. Those bits are not an exact match for the pegs you make with a hole saw but they're close enough that the gap they leave can easily be mitigated as I'll explain later.

The area to be drilled must be flat and level with the drill press table or the teeth of the bit will catch the wood before the point in the bit touches and throw the board out with surprising force. Sand or scrape the area so the point of the bit will hit first or clamp the board to the drill press table.

If you drill for a plug that's larger than the bits you have, use a hole saw to create the hole. Here's how to do that:

1. Set the depth gauge on the drill press so the hole saw will cut approximately half way through the board.

2. Replace the pilot bit in the hole saw arbor.

3. Bring the pilot bit down to the table and adjust the table so the bit lines up with the hole.

4. Clamp the board to the table.

5. Ease the hole saw down until it barely touches it. Continue slowly until you see a fine spray of dust.

6. Continue gently until the entire circumference of the hole saw is below the surface of the board.

7. Continue the cut with steady and moderate force.

• If the blade wobbles, use a jig to steady it. You may have to gently press one side of the jig against the hole saw as you draw it down into the board. Once the saw is fully seated in the bole, you won't need the jig.

8. When you have reached the correct depth of cut, set the board aside and replace the hole saw with a Forstner bit of any size.

9. Unlock the drill press depth gauge.

10. Set the stop to allow the bit to go down approximately half the thickness of the board.

11. Put the board back on the table.

12. Pull the drill bit down so the edge of it cuts into the inside edge of the kerf made by the hole saw till you hit the stop.

13. Raise the bit and check the hole. You shouldn't see any more than a trace of the hole saw kerf.

14. Reset the depth gauge if necessary.

15. With the depth correct, continue drilling with the Forstner bit until all or most of the area inside the hole is removed. Be careful not to drill outside the hole saw kerf.

16. Take the board to a workstation.

17. Use a chisel or scraper to remove anything the drill left.

18. Sand or scrape the bottom of the hole to get it as flush as possible. It must be flat but doesn't have to be smooth

setting large pegs

1. The holes made by a large Forstner style bit or by a hole saw won't match the size of a peg made with a hole saw. The peg will be slightly smaller than the hole and won't be stable in the hole until the glue sets.

2. Pour a small puddle of glue into the bottom of the hole.

3. Set the large peg into the hole and twist it till you feel some resistance. This will create enough bonding to hold the peg in place while the glue sets up.

4. Drive a shim on one side of the peg to push it against the opposite side of the hole.

5. Tap the peg to make sure it sits on the bottom of the hole.

6. Drill for the next peg and set it.

7. Shim the peg so it presses against the first peg.

• If you must put shims in an area which won't be drilled out, use a wood which matches either the peg or the surrounding wood so when you fill in the gap with a matching putty, the shim will disappear. (For information on making matching putty, go to chapter 11, **filling voids** on page 223.)

8. Repeat the process to add as many pegs as you like.

———————————

If you drill too far and go though the bottom of a board, there will be nothing to hold the peg in place. Here's how to save the situation:

1. Screw a piece of 1/4 inch plywood to the back of the board over the hole.

2. Turn the board over, put glue on the plywood, set the peg and twist it till there is some resistance.

3. Clamp the peg to the plywood or secure it with screws through the back of the plywood.

4. Let this sit till the glue sets.

Another method to save the situation:

1. Put wax paper on a flat surface.

2. Set the board on the wax paper.

3. Put the peg in the hole.

4. Wedge the peg firmly in place with shims glued around it on three or more sides.

5. Let this sit till the glue sets.

6. Drill a hole centered on the line or gap between the peg and the board. The hole should be drilled half way through the thickness of the board and peg.

7. Set a second peg and shim it into position.

8. Continue drilling and setting pegs around the first peg to create a design.

As you can imagine, either method will add a lot of time to a project so it's best not to drill through the bottom of a board.

chapter 7

creating

circles

of wood

In chapter 6, I described how setting a large peg in a board leaves a gap around it. You could cover the gap with a series of small pegs or you could use a technique I developed for this situation.

The circle you see in the board at right is made of solid wood strips inserted in a circular kerf. This technique will fill the gap around a large peg, but it can also be used as a stand alone element.

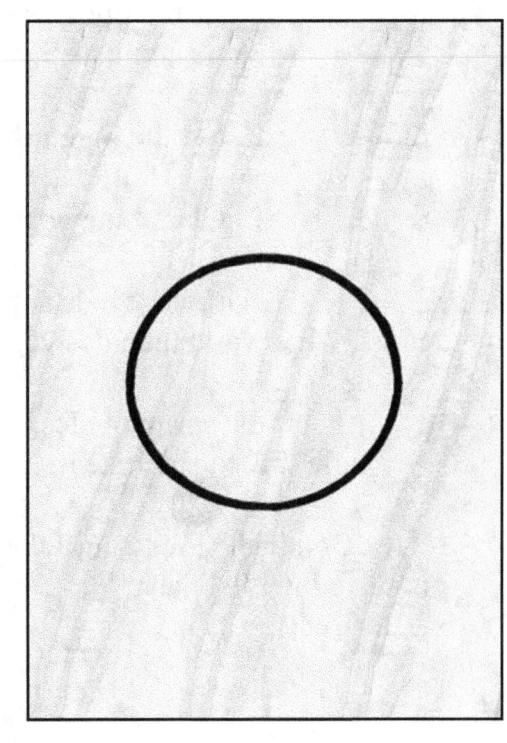

how to create circles of wood

1. Cover the drill press table with a piece of plywood to keep the hole saw from hitting the table.

2. Make a simple jig for large pegs.

3. Replace the pilot bit in the hole saw arbor.

4. Drill through a piece of 3/4 inch plywood with the hole saw you'll be using to make the peg.

5. Remove the disk from inside the hole saw.

6. Remove the pilot bit.

7. Lock the hole saw in the drill press chuck.

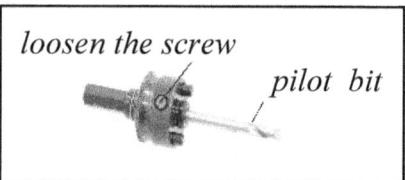

hole saw arbor

8. Set the stop on the drill press gauge to a depth of approximately half the thickness of the board or mark the side of the hole saw. You could also mark the side of the hole saw at the correct depth.

9. Set the jig on the board.

10. Clamp the board to the drill press table.

11. Draw the hole saw down through the jig until it barely touches the wood then use very slight pressure to start the cut.

12. If the saw wobbles, gently press the jig against the side of the hole saw to stabilize it.

13. Continue slowly until the entire circumference of the blade is seated in the board.

14. Increase pressure and continue drilling until you hit the correct depth.

If you will be inserting a peg in the hole:

15. Drill out and remove the material inside the kerf as described on page 130.

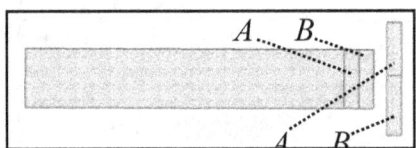

*large peg centered
for this technique
with temporary shims*

16. Pour glue in the hole and press the peg into it.

17. Turn the peg till you feel some resistance.

18. Center the peg in the hole with four shims.

19. Clamp the peg to the bottom of the hole.

With the peg centered and secure
or if you leave the hole saw kerf as is, proceed to the next step.

making wood inserts

A standard insert plate for the blade of a table-saw leaves too much space around the blade to safely cut strips. Use a low clearance insert. If you don't have one, follow the instructions on page 66.

1. Make sure the blade is square to the table.

2. Use a board that is 2 to 3 feet long and no less than six inches wide.

3. Plane or sand the top, bottom and edges of the board. Check to make sure the edges are square to the top and bottom.

• The top and bottom of a board become the edges of a strip. When the inserts are set in the kerf, the edges face each other which is why the top and bottom of the board must be smooth and clean.

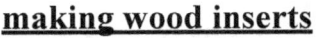

*how inserts cut from a board
are set together in the kerf*

4. The fence must be exactly parallel to the blade.

5. As you cut, the leading edge must always be firmly against the fence.

6. Use a push stick to move the board through the blade and a second stick or feather board to press the board against the fence.

7. Keep the board moving. If you stop, the blade may scar the strip.

8. Cut a strip and test it in the kerf.

An eighty tooth blade will leave a strip smooth enough to join.

9. If it's too tight, adjust the fence to make the next strip slightly thinner.

10. The strip should be snug but you should be able to push it to the bottom of the groove by hand or with the gentle tap of a hammer.

11. Cut more strips than you'll need so there's no chance you'll run out.

12. Set the fence on your band-saw to approximately half the width of the strip.

13. Run a piece of plywood through the blade and stop when it meets the end of the table. The plywood will keep strips from sliding under the fence.

14. Clamp the plywood to the table of the band-saw.

15. Use a push stick to move strips through the blade and another to hold them against the fence.

16. Remove the plywood and the fence.

17. Attach a one foot long 1x2 to the miter gauge of your band-saw.

18. Set a piece of masking tape on the table of the saw approximately 3/4 inch to the left of the blade.

19. Set the strips against the 1x2 lined up to the masking tape.

20. Run the strips slowly through the blade. Use a push stick to move the pieces away from the blade. These are your inserts.

21. Clean the kerf of sawdust and debris.

22. Pour glue into the kerf until half of it is nearly full. Don't fill the entire kerf.

From here on, the gap around a peg will be called the kerf.

23. Push the first insert down to the bottom of the kerf by hand or gently with a hammer.

24. Move it to square with the surface of the board by pushing it with the tip of a small screwdriver in the kerf.

25. Drive the next insert into the kerf and gently push it against the first insert with the screwdriver. Be careful not to push the first insert off square.

26. Continue setting inserts around the circle.

27. If the inserts get out of square to the board and you can't move them, cut or sand one edge of an insert at an angle to make a wedge shape and press it against the last insert to get back to square.

28. The glue must be high enough in the kerf to coat the walls of the kerf around the insert. As you drive the inserts, the glue will be pushed along in the kerf.

29. When there is only enough space for one last insert, trim the edge of this last insert until it fits tight in the space.

- Because the edges of the inserts are square, there will be very slight spaces between the inserts. These spaces disappear unless a different color of sawdust gets into them.

  - Don't cut or sand the inserts or anywhere around the circle until the glue is totally dry to avoid driving sawdust of another color into spaces between the strips.

    30. When the glue is dry, cut or sand the inserts until they are flush with the surface.

    31. Blow as much sawdust as possible out of the circle with an air compressor.

    32. Press a suitable filler into the circle and let it dry before sanding it.

    The circle is complete.

making a segmented circle

1. Select two boards of different colors.

1. Determine the correct thickness of the strips.

2. Set the fence of your band-saw at slightly less than half the width of the strips.

3. Run a piece of 1/2" plywood which is approximately the size of the table through the blade. Stop when it meets the end of the table. This will prevent strips from sliding under the fence.

4. Cut strips using push sticks.

5. Rip remaining strips to make them all the same width.

6. Attach a 1 foot long 1x2 to the miter gauge of your band-saw.

7. Set a piece of masking tape on the table of the saw approximately 3/4 inch to the left of the blade.

8. Set the strips against the miter gauge and to the masking tape.

9. Carefully cut the strips. Use a push stick to move the pieces away from the blade. These are your inserts.

10. The kerf should be clean.

11. Set an insert about 1/4 inch into the groove without glue.

12. Set insert of second color in groove beside the first.

13. Continue setting inserts in that manner until you are left with one insert of the correct color. That insert must be at least as wide as the last space.

14. The last insert must not match the first one.

15. Adjust width of inserts to produce the correct interval widths.

16. When inserts are correct, remove them and set them aside.

17. Pour glue into the one half of the kerf. The glue should be just below the top of the kerf so the entire surface of the kerf has glue on it.

18. Push the first insert to the bottom of the kerf by hand or gently with a hammer.

19. Use a thin screwdriver to push it sideways until it is square with the surface of the board.

20. Select an insert of the second color and press or drive it against the first insert with the screwdriver. Too much pressure against the second insert could push the first insert off square.

21. Continue setting inserts around the circle alternating between the two colors.

22. As you drive the inserts, the glue will be pushed along the kerf. The glue should always be high enough to coat the walls of the kerf around the insert.

23. The kerf must be at least partially filled with glue during the entire operation.

24. The inserts must be square to the surface of the board. If the inserts get off square, the angle will make them wider at the surface and ruin the spacing. When the top of inserts are level with the board, that indicates they are square to it.

If you made adjustments before starting, you shouldn't be far off.

25. When you have approximately one quarter of the circle left to fill, test to see that the remaining inserts will finish out the circle with the correct intervals.

26. When all the inserts have been installed, don't sand or cut them because that may put the wrong color of sawdust into the spaces between the inserts.

making a spoked circle

Follow the instructions in the section, **making wood inserts** on page 147, then follow these:

1. Cut a strip approximately 1/16 inch thick and at least 2 feet long.

2. With a 1 foot long 2x4 on your miter gauge, cut the strip into short pieces. These are spacers.

3. The kerf should be clean and clear of all sawdust.

4. Pour glue into the kerf until half of it is nearly full.

5. Push the first insert down to the bottom of the kerf by hand or gently with a hammer.

6. Use a thin screwdriver to push it sideways until it is square with the surface of the board by setting the tip of the screwdriver into the kerf and against the insert. If the top of an insert is level with the board, the strip should be square to it.

7. Place one of the spacers beside the first insert.

Inserts must be square to the surface to keep the intervals equal.

8. Push a second insert down to the bottom of the kerf and against the spacer.

9. Put a spacer beside the second insert.

10. Push a third insert down to the bottom of the kerf and just barely against the 1/16 spacer.

11. Continue setting spacers and inserts around the circle.

12. As you drive the inserts, the glue will be pushed along the kerf. The glue should always be high enough to coat the walls of the kerf around the insert.

13. The last insert should be approximately the same width as all others. When you have approximately one quarter of the circle left to fill, test to see if the remaining inserts will finish out the circle correctly. If not, make adjustments to the remaining inserts to make them work out right.

You won't be able to remove the spacers. You'll sand them out later.

14. When all the inserts have been installed, sand them flush while also sanding the surface of the board. This will push sawdust from the board into the spaces between the inserts making spokes.

adding circles to your design

When the glue is dry, you can overlay circles by using the same methods described in this chapter. There is no limit to the number of overlapping circles you can add.

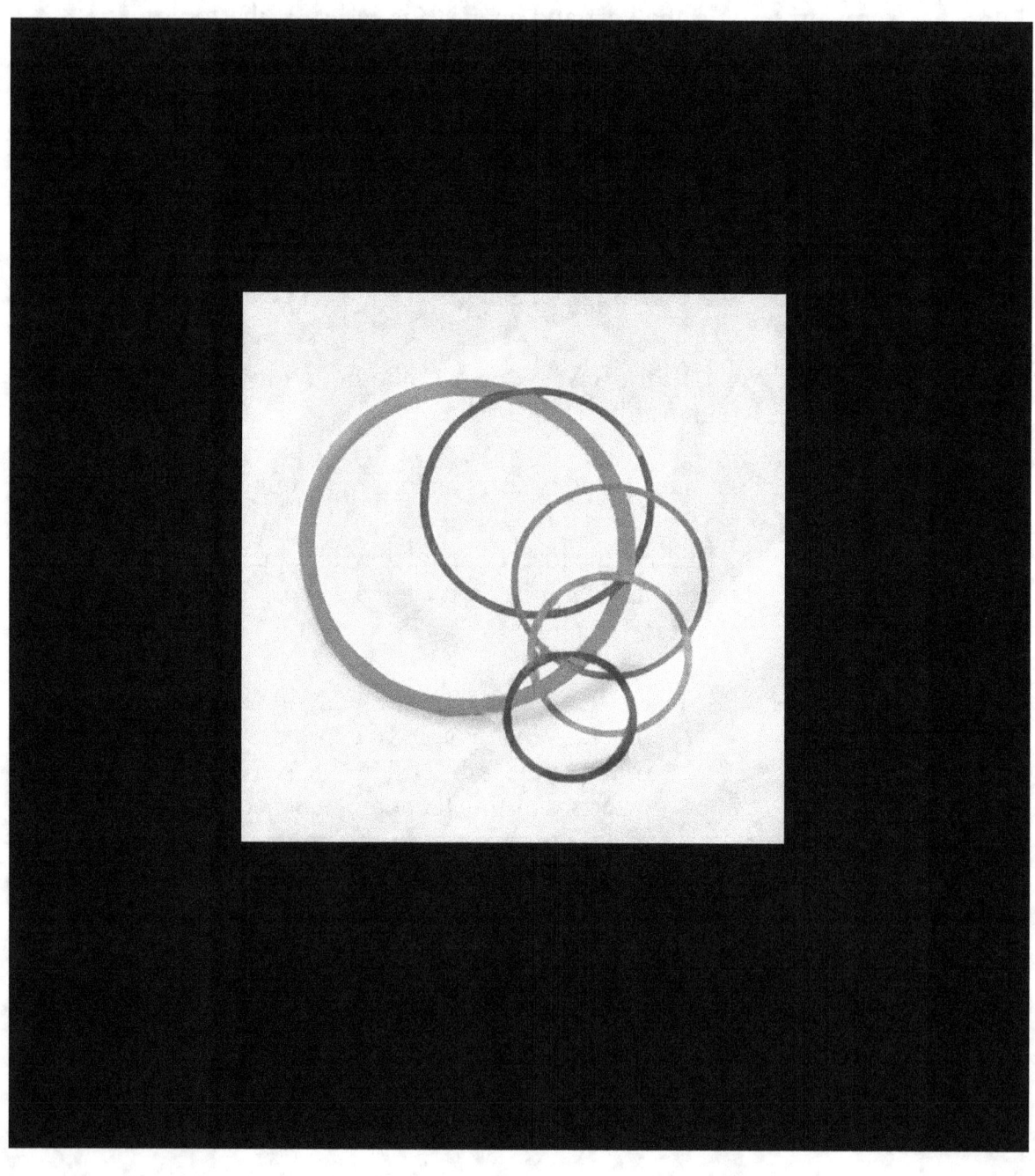

summary of chapter 7

creating circles of wood

how to create circles of wood

1. Cover the drill press table with a piece of plywood to keep the hole saw from hitting the table.

2. Make a simple jig for large pegs.

3. Replace the pilot bit in the hole saw arbor.

4. Drill through a piece of 3/4 inch plywood with the hole saw you'll be using to make the peg.

5. Remove the disk from inside the hole saw.

6. Remove the pilot bit.

7. Lock the hole saw in the drill press chuck.

8. Set the stop on the drill press gauge to a depth of approximately half the thickness of the board or mark the side of the hole saw. You could also mark the side of the hole saw at the correct depth.

9. Set the jig on the board.

10. Clamp the board to the drill press table.

11. Draw the hole saw down through the jig until it barely touches the wood then use very slight pressure to start the cut.

12. If the saw wobbles, gently press the jig against the side of the hole saw to stabilize it.

13. Continue slowly until the entire circumference of the blade is seated in the board.

14. Increase pressure and continue drilling until you hit the correct depth.

If you will be inserting a peg in the hole:

15. Drill out and remove the material inside the kerf as described on page 130.

16. Pour glue in the hole and press the peg into it.

17. Turn the peg till you feel some resistance.

18. Center the peg in the hole with four shims.

19. Clamp the peg to the bottom of the hole.

With the peg centered and secure

or if you leave the hole saw kerf as is, proceed to the next step.

making wood inserts

A standard insert plate for the blade of a table-saw leaves too much space around the blade to safely cut strips. Use a low clearance insert. If you don't have one, follow the instructions on page 66.

1. Make sure the blade is square to the table.

2. Use a board that is 2 to 3 feet long and no less than six inches wide.

3. Plane or sand one edge of the board. Check to make sure it is square to the surface of the board.

4. Plane or sand the top and bottom surfaces of the board.

5. The fence must be exactly parallel to the blade.

6. As you cut, the leading edge must always be firmly against the fence.

7. Use a push stick to move the board through the blade and a second stick or feather board to press the board against the fence.

8. Keep the board moving. If you stop, the blade may scar the strip.

9. Cut a strip and test it in the kerf.

10. If it's too tight, adjust the fence to make the next strip slightly thinner.

11. The strip should be snug but you should be able to push it to the bottom of the groove by hand or with the gentle tap of a hammer.

12. Cut more strips than you'll need so there's no chance you'll run out.

13. Set the fence on your band-saw to approximately half the width of the strip.

14. Run a piece of plywood through the blade and stop when it meets the end of the table. The plywood will keep strips from sliding under the fence.

15. Clamp the plywood to the table of the band-saw.

16. Use a push stick to move strips through the blade and another to hold them against the fence.

17. Remove the plywood and the fence.

18. Attach a one foot long 1x2 to the miter gauge of your band-saw.

19. Set a piece of masking tape on the table of the saw approximately 3/4 inch to the left of the blade.

20. Set the strips against the 1x2 lined up to the masking tape.

21. Run the strips slowly through the blade. Use a push stick to move the pieces away from the blade. These are your inserts.

22. Clean the kerf of sawdust and debris.

23. Pour glue into the kerf until half of it is nearly full. Don't fill the entire kerf.

24. Push the first insert down to the bottom of the kerf by hand or gently with a hammer.

25. Move it to square with the surface of the board by pushing it with the tip of a small screwdriver in the kerf.

26. Drive the next insert into the kerf and gently push it against the first insert with the screwdriver. Be careful not to push the first insert off square.

27. Continue setting inserts around the circle.

28. If the inserts get out of square to the board and you can't move them, cut or sand one edge of an insert at an angle to make a wedge shape and press it against the last insert to get back to square.

29. The glue must be high enough in the kerf to coat the walls of the kerf around the insert. As you drive the inserts, the glue will be pushed along in the kerf.

30. When there is only enough space for one last insert, trim the edge of this last insert until it fits tight in the space.

• Because the edges of the inserts are square, there will be very slight spaces between the inserts. These spaces disappear unless a different color of sawdust gets into them.

• Don't cut or sand the inserts or anywhere around the circle until the glue is totally dry to avoid driving sawdust of another color into spaces between the strips.

31. When the glue is dry, cut or sand the inserts until they are flush with the surface.

32. Blow as much sawdust as possible out of the circle with an air compressor.

33. Press in suitable filler into the circle and let dry before sanding.

The circle is complete.

making a segmented circle

1. Select two boards of different colors.

1. Determine the correct thickness of the strips.

2. Set the fence of your band-saw at slightly less than half the width of the strips.

3. Run a piece of 1/2" plywood which is approximately the size of the table through the blade. Stop when it meets the end of the table. This will prevent strips from sliding under the fence.

4. Cut strips using push sticks.

5. Rip remaining strips to make them all the same width.

6. Attach a 1 foot long 1x2 to the miter gauge of your band-saw.

7. Set a piece of masking tape on the table of the saw approximately 3/4 inch to the left of the blade.

8. Set the strips against the miter gauge and to the masking tape.

9. Carefully cut the strips. Use a push stick to move the pieces away from the blade. These are your inserts.

10. The kerf should be clean.

11. Set an insert about 1/4 inch into the groove without glue.

12. Set insert of second color in groove beside the first.

13. Continue setting inserts in that manner until you are left with one insert of the correct color. That insert must be at least as wide as the last space.

14. The last insert must not match the first one.

15. Adjust width of inserts to produce the correct interval widths.

16. When inserts are correct, remove them and set them aside.

17. Pour glue into the one half of the kerf. The glue should be just below the top of the kerf so the entire surface of the kerf has glue on it.

18. Push the first insert to the bottom of the kerf by hand or gently with a hammer.

19. Use a thin screwdriver to push it sideways until it is square with the surface of the board.

20. Select an insert of the second color and press or drive it against the first insert with the screwdriver. Too much pressure against the second insert could push the first insert off square.

21. Continue setting inserts around the circle alternating between the two colors.

22. As you drive the inserts, the glue will be pushed along the kerf. The glue should always be high enough to coat the walls of the kerf around the insert.

23. The kerf must be at least partially filled with glue during the entire operation.

24. The inserts must be square to the surface of the board. If the inserts get off square, the angle will make them wider

at the surface and ruin the spacing. When the top of inserts are level with the board, that indicates they are square to it.

25. When you have approximately one quarter of the circle left to fill, test to see that the remaining inserts will finish out the circle with the correct intervals.

26. When all the inserts have been installed, don't sand or cut them because that may put the wrong color of sawdust into the spaces between the inserts.

making a spoked circle

Follow the instructions in the section, **making wood inserts** on page 147, then follow these:

1. Cut a strip approximately 1/16 inch thick and at least 2 feet long.

2. With a 1 foot long 2x4 on your miter gauge, cut the strip into short pieces. These are spacers.

3. The kerf should be clean and clear of all sawdust.

4. Pour glue into the kerf until half of it is nearly full.

5. Push the first insert down to the bottom of the kerf by hand or gently with a hammer.

6. Use a thin screwdriver to push it sideways until it is square with the surface of the board by setting the tip of the screwdriver into the kerf and against the insert. If the top of an insert is level with the board, the strip should be square to it.

7. Place one of the spacers beside the first insert.

8. Push a second insert down to the bottom of the kerf and against the spacer.

9. Put a spacer beside the second insert.

10. Push a third insert down to the bottom of the kerf and just barely against the 1/16 spacer.

11. Continue setting spacers and inserts around the circle.

12. As you drive the inserts, the glue will be pushed along the kerf. The glue should always be high enough to coat the walls of the kerf around the insert.

13. The last insert should be approximately the same width as all others. When you have approximately one quarter of the circle left to fill, test to see if the remaining inserts will finish out the circle correctly. If not, make adjustments to the remaining inserts to make them work out right.

14. When all the inserts have been installed, sand them flush while also sanding the surface of the board. This will push sawdust from the board into the spaces between the inserts making spokes.

adding circles to your design

When the glue is dry, you can overlay circles by using the same methods described above. There is no limit to the number of overlapping circles you can add.

chapter 8

fans

creating a fan with straight joints

You'll find instructions on how to make and use a jig for cutting tapers in boards or panels in chapter 2, on page 33. You'll use that jig for this technique.

1. Select two or more boards which will look good side by side.

2. Join both edges of each board.

3. Using the jig (image 1), cut a taper on both boards. The angle should be less than 22½ degrees so the combined angle of intersecting grain lines is not more than 45 degrees. This will give you four segments. (image 2)

4. Set one segment from each of the two boards against each other. (image 2)

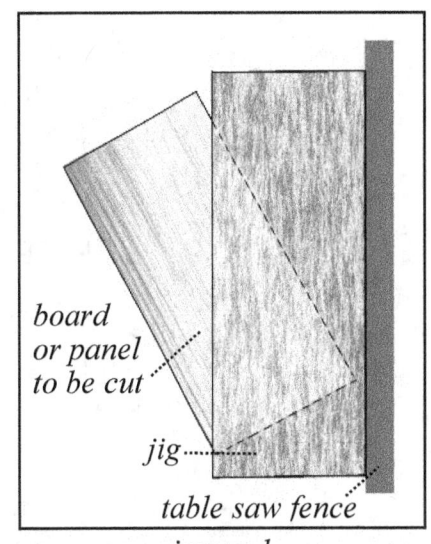

board or panel to be cut

jig

table saw fence

image 1

5. Cut 2 pieces of 3/4 inch plywood at the same angle as each tapered board. (image 3)

6. Place one of the plywood sections on each side of the two boards so you have parallel edges for your clamps. (image 3)

7. Set a board against the top and bottom of the assembly. (image 3)

8. Clamp the edges of the assembly down to strong-backs. (See image at the top of page 71.)

9. Set at least two clamps horizontally – one across the grain, and one vertically – in line with the grain. (image 3)

10. Apply firm pressure to the vertical clamp.

11. Increase pressure on the horizontal and vertical clamps incrementally at the same time.

12. When the glue has set, repeat these steps to make an identical tapered section.

13. Set the two sections with the points facing in the same direction. (image 4)

14. Cut 2 pieces of 3/4 inch plywood at the same angle as each of the two sections. (image 4)

15. Place one of the plywood sections on each side of the assembly so you have parallel edges for your clamps. (image 4)

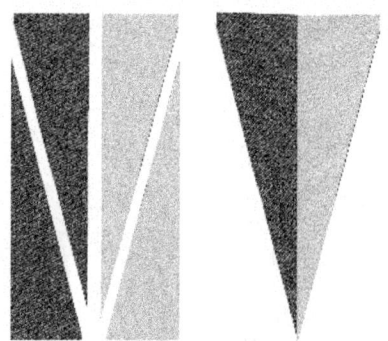

image 2

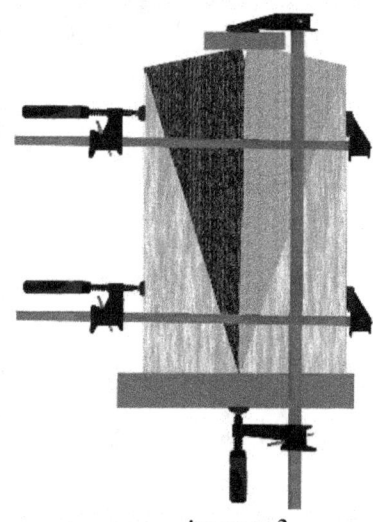

image 3

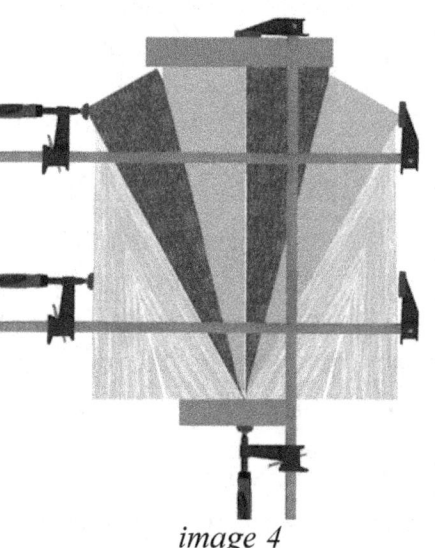

image 4

16. Set a board against the top and bottom of the assembly and clamp them together firmly. (image 4)

17. Clamp the edges of the plywood down to the strong-backs.

18. Set two or more clamps horizontally on the assembly. (image 4) You can set both clamps on the plywood or flatten the corners and set one of the clamps on them.

19. Increase pressure on the horizontal and vertical clamps incrementally at the same time.

20. When the glue has set, you can add more tapered boards using these procedures to make a fan with as many segments as you like.

21. At some point in adding segments, you'll need to place a clamp across the top of the fan. To do this, cut a small notch in the top of two segments on opposite sides of the joint you're gluing. The sides of the notches must be roughly parallel for the clamps to work. (image 5)

22. As you can see in image 5, when the edges of the assembly are near 90 degrees to each other, tapered plywood blocks won't work. Apply clamps as shown. You may want to add more clamps diagonally across the piece.

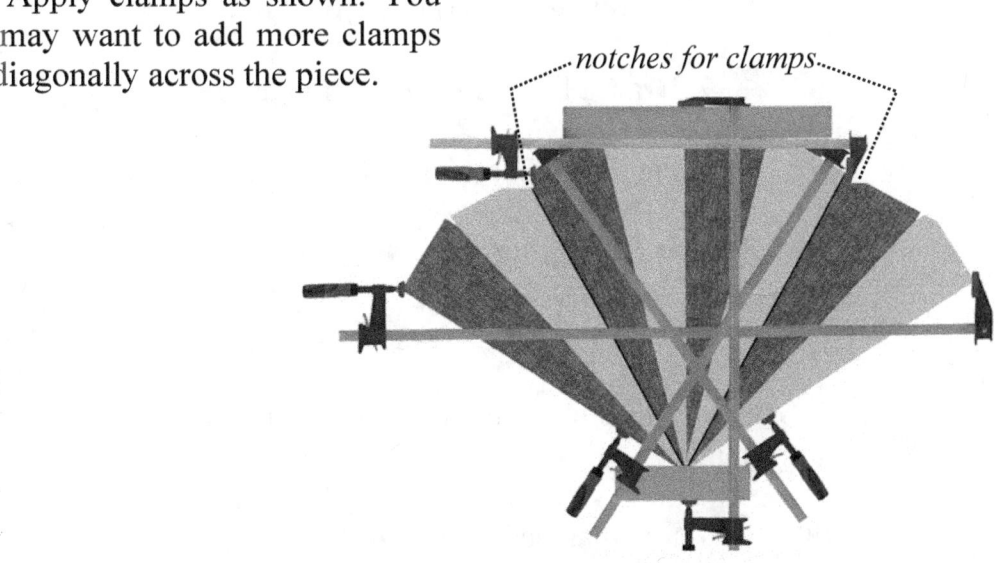

notches for clamps

image 5

making a fan with curved joints

1. Select two or more boards which will look good side by side.

2. Join both edges of the each board.

3. Set one board over the other in the shape of an "X". (image 6) Clamp them together to hold the boards in position till they are screwed together.

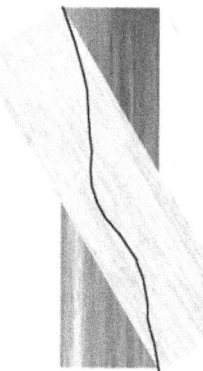

image 6

4. With a bit that's slightly larger than the screws, drill holes through the top board approximately one inch to the side of the crotches of the "X" and near the ends of the board. This will keep the screws out of the line of cut.

5. Drill pilot holes in the bottom board with a bit that's slightly smaller than the screws.

6. Screw the two boards together.

7. Draw a line for the cut. (image 6)

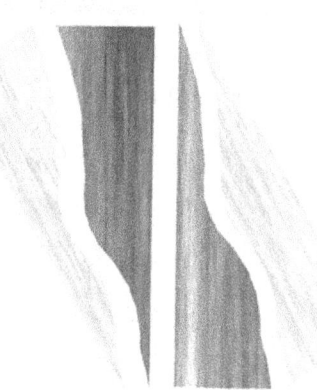

image 7

8. Cut the line on your band-saw using the techniques described in chapter 5, **joining boards along a curve**, starting on page 96. This will give you four sections. (image 7)

9. Set the opposite segments beside each other. (image 7)

10. With the boards matched, make hash marks in two or three places along the joint. (image 8)

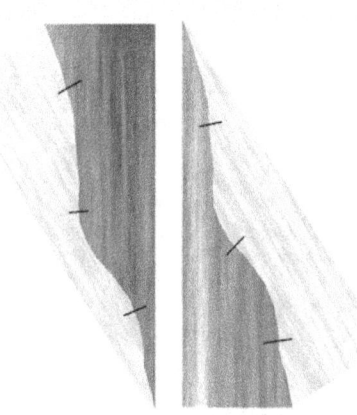

image 8

Note: The images for clamping the sections together are identical to the images on pages 164 and 165 in the section, __creating a fan with straight joints__.

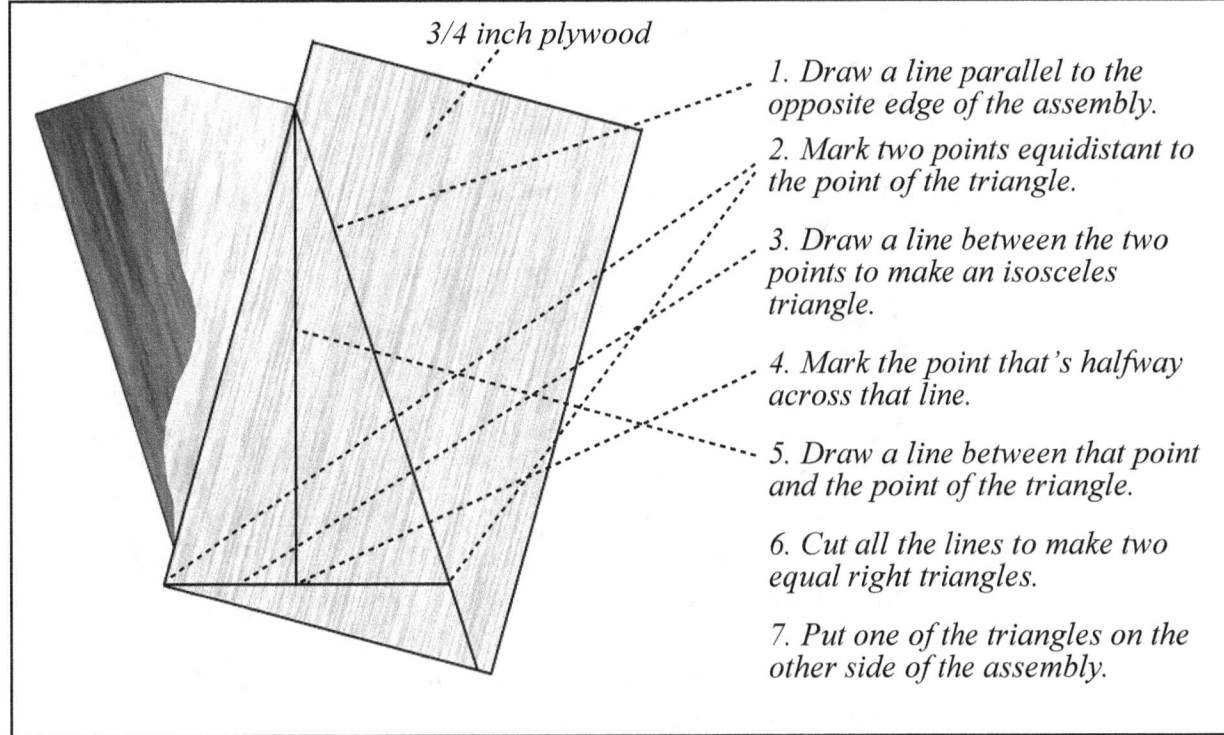

3/4 inch plywood

1. Draw a line parallel to the opposite edge of the assembly.

2. Mark two points equidistant to the point of the triangle.

3. Draw a line between the two points to make an isosceles triangle.

4. Mark the point that's halfway across that line.

5. Draw a line between that point and the point of the triangle.

6. Cut all the lines to make two equal right triangles.

7. Put one of the triangles on the other side of the assembly.

image 9 – clamping boards for curved joinery segments

11. Set one pair of segments beside a piece of 3/4 inch plywood. (image 9)

12. Draw a line parallel to the far edge of the assembly.

13. Mark two points equidistant to the point of the triangle.

14. Draw a line between the two points to make an isosceles triangle.

15. Mark the point that's halfway across that line.

16. Draw a line between that point and the point of the triangle.

17. Cut all the lines to make two equal right triangles.

18. Put one of the triangles on the other side of the assembly.

19. The edges of the assembly are now parallel so the clamps won't slip when you apply pressure. (image 3)

20. Set a board against the top and bottom of the assembly.

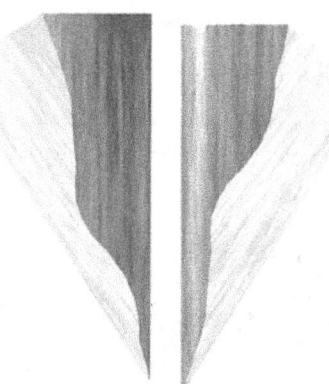

image 10

21. Clamp the edges of the assembly down to strong-backs.

22. Set 2 clamps horizontally and one vertically. (image 3)

23. Increase pressure on all clamps incrementally at the same time.

24. When the glue has set, repeat the steps listed above for the third and fourth boards.

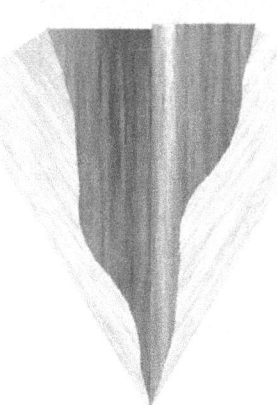

image 11

25. When the clamps are off, flip one of the two segments over so the points face the same way. (image 10)

26. Set the two segments together to make the center of the fan. (image 11)

27. Draw and cut a line that roughly bisects the acute angle of one of the plywood right triangles.

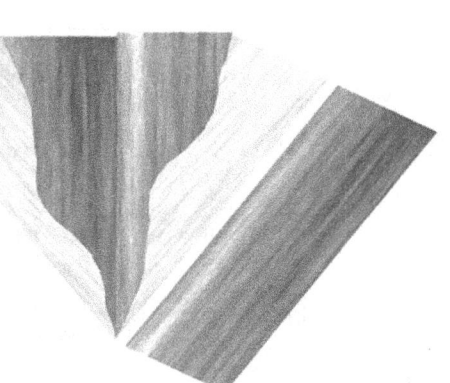

28. Glue the parts together using the configuration shown in image 4.

image 12

29. At this point, to increase the size of the fan, add single boards to the existing assembly. (image 12)

30. Set the board under the assembly with a board under one end of the assembly to keep it level.

31. Set the board where you want it to be cut.

32. Screw the two parts together with the screws out of any possible cut.

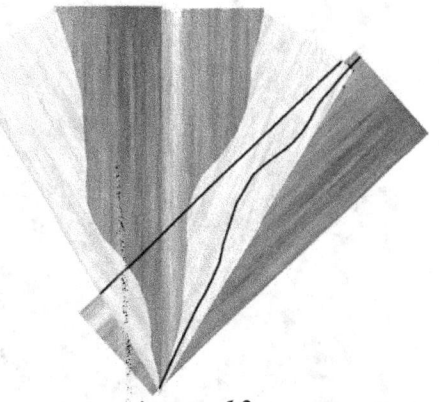

image 13
line showing edge of main panel and line to be cut

33. To avoid cutting through the edge of the board, draw a line showing the edge of the board on top of the assembly. (image 13)

34. Draw a curved line. (image 13)

35. Cut the curved line (image 14) using the techniques described in chapter 5, page 96.

36. Set the parts together and add hash marks. (image 15)

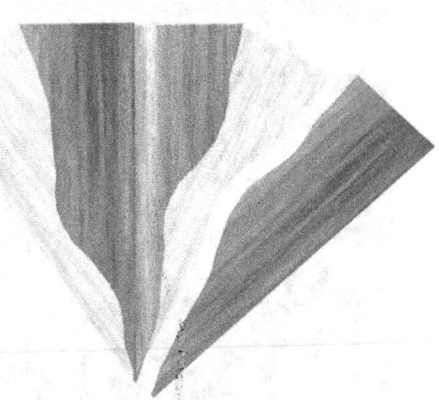

image 14 — after the cut

37. Glue and clamp the sections together. (similar to image 5)

38. You can add more boards but at some point you'll have to place a clamp across the top of the assembly. (image 5)

39. To do that, cut a small notch in the top of two segments on opposite sides of the joint. The sides of the notch facing each other must be parallel to work with the clamp. (image 5)

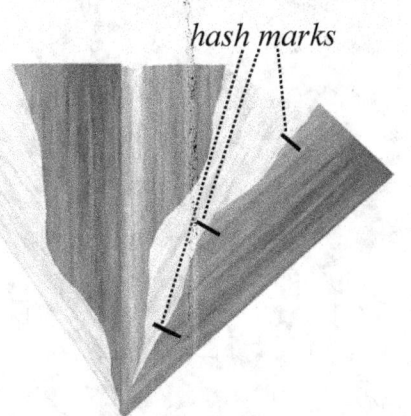

hash marks

image 15

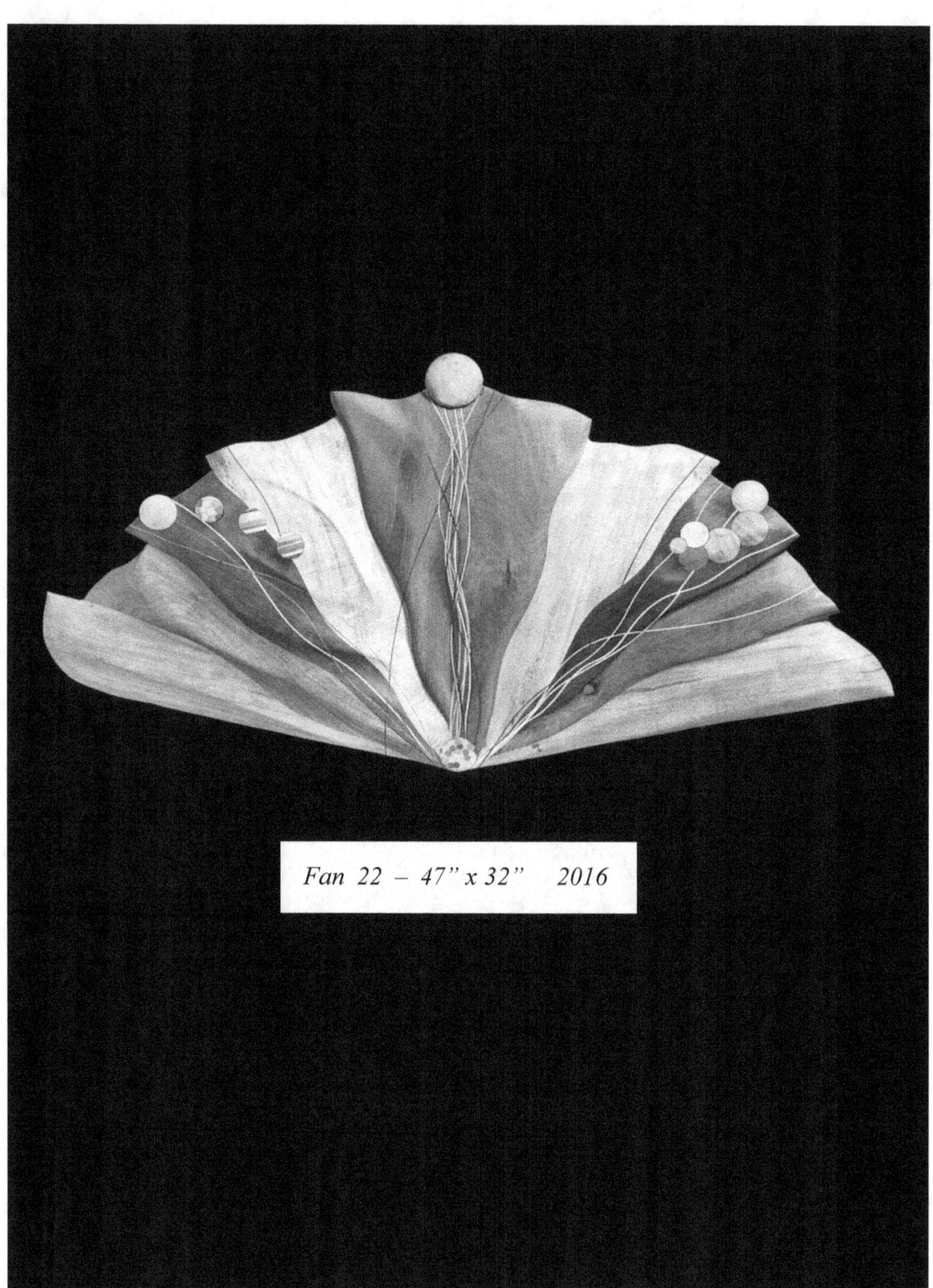

Fan 22 – 47" x 32"   2016

summary of chapter 8

fans

You'll find instructions on how to make and use a jig for cutting tapers in boards or panels in chapter 2, on page 33. You'll use that jig for this technique.

1. Select two or more boards which will look good side by side.

2. Join both edges of each board.

3. Using the jig (image 1), cut a taper on both boards. The angle should be less than 22½ degrees so the combined angle of intersecting grain lines is not more than 45 degrees. This will give you four segments. (image 2)

4. Set one segment from each of the two boards against each other. (image 2)

5. Cut 2 pieces of 3/4 inch plywood at the same angle as each tapered board. (image 3)

6. Place one of the plywood sections on each side of the two boards so you have parallel edges for your clamps. (image 3)

7. Set a board against the top and bottom of the assembly. (image 3)

8. Clamp the edges of the assembly down to strong-backs. (See image at the top of page 71.)

9. Set at least two clamps horizontally – one across the grain, and one vertically – in line with the grain. (image 3)

10. Apply firm pressure to the vertical clamp.

11. Increase pressure on the horizontal and vertical clamps incrementally at the same time.

12. When the glue has set, repeat these steps to make an identical tapered section.

13. Set the two sections with the points facing in the same direction. (image 4)

14. Cut 2 pieces of 3/4 inch plywood at the same angle as each of the two sections. (image 4)

15. Place one of the plywood sections on each side of the assembly so you have parallel edges for your clamps. (Image 4)

16. Set a board against the top and bottom of the assembly and clamp them together firmly. (image 4)

17. Clamp the edges of the plywood down to the strong-backs.

18. Set two or more clamps horizontally on the assembly. (image 4) You can set both clamps on the plywood or flatten the corners and set one of the clamps on them.

19. Increase pressure on the horizontal and vertical clamps incrementally at the same time.

20. When the glue has set, you can add more tapered boards using these procedures to make a fan with as many segments as you like.

21. At some point in adding segments, you'll need to place a clamp across the top of the fan. To do this, cut a small notch in the top of two segments on opposite sides of the joint you're gluing. The sides of the notches must be roughly parallel for the clamps to work. (image 5)

22. As you can see in image 5, when the edges of the assembly are near 90 degrees to each other, tapered

plywood blocks won't work. Apply clamps as shown. You may want to add more clamps diagonally across the piece.

making a fan with curved joints

1. Select two or more boards which will look good side by side.

2. Join both edges of the each board.

3. Set one board over the other in the shape of an "X". (image 6) Clamp them together to hold the boards in position till they are screwed together.

4. With a bit that's slightly larger than the screws, drill holes through the top board approximately one inch to the side of the crotches of the "X" and near the ends of the board. This will keep the screws out of the line of cut.

5. Drill pilot holes in the bottom board with a bit that's slightly smaller than the screws.

6. Screw the two boards together.

7. Draw a line for the cut. (image 6)

8. Cut the line on your band-saw using the techniques described in chapter 5, **joining boards along a curve**, starting on page 96. This will give you four sections. (image 7)

9. Set the opposite segments beside each other. (image 7)

10. With the boards matched, make hash marks in two or three places along the joint. (image 8)

11. Set one pair of segments beside a piece of 3/4 inch plywood. (image 9)

12. Draw a line parallel to the far edge of the assembly.

13. Mark two points equidistant to the point of the triangle.

14. Draw a line between the two points to make an isosceles triangle.

15. Mark the point that's halfway across that line.

16. Draw a line between that point and the point of the triangle.

17. Cut all the lines to make two equal right triangles.

18. Put one of the triangles on the other side of the assembly.

19. The edges of the assembly are now parallel so the clamps won't slip when you apply pressure. (image 3)

20. Set a board against the top and bottom of the assembly.

21. Clamp the edges of the assembly down to strong-backs.

22. Set 2 clamps horizontally and one vertically. (image 3)

23. Increase pressure on all clamps incrementally at the same time.

24. When the glue has set, repeat the steps listed above for the third and fourth boards.

25. When the clamps are off, flip one of the two segments over so the points face the same way. (Image 10)

26. Set the two segments together to make the center of the fan. (image 11)

27. Draw and cut a line that roughly bisects the acute angle of one of the plywood right triangles.

28. Glue the parts together using the configuration shown in image 4.

29. At this point, to increase the size of the fan, add single boards to the existing assembly. (Image 11)

30. Set the board under the assembly with a board under one end of the assembly to keep it level.

31. Set the board where you want it to be cut.

32. Screw the two parts together with the screws out of any possible cut.

33. To avoid cutting through the edge of the board, draw a line showing the edge of the board on the assembly. (image 13)

34. Draw a curved line. (image 13)

35. Cut the curved line (image 14) using the techniques described in chapter 5, page 96.

36. Set the parts together and add hash marks. (image 15)

37. Glue and clamp the sections together. (similar to image 5)

38. You can add more boards but at some point you'll have to place a clamp across the top of the assembly. (image 5)

39. To do that, cut a small notch in the top of two segments on opposite sides of the joint. The sides of the notch facing each other must be parallel to work with the clamp. (image 5)

chapter 9

preparing

your panel

for use

If you've built a panel using the techniques in this book, it could be warped but it's certainly rough and uneven. Before you can use it in a project, you'll have to prepare it.

This chapter will show you how to remove the warp from a panel and flatten both sides while giving it a uniform thickness.

The side of a panel that will be seen most is side A. Work on side B first so if you have any problems, you'll recognize them before working on side A.

1. Move the panel to a work-station which is sturdy enough to handle the lateral force of planing the surface. Secure the panel with bench stops or clamps.

2. Set a straight edge on the panel diagonally in both directions. If the panel is flat, the straight edge will touch both corners and the center of the panel in both directions.

If the panel is warped:

3. Set a large hand plane or electric hand planer to take a medium cut.

4. Plane diagonally from one high corner to the other.

5. Continue making diagonal cuts in that direction.

6. Check the diagonal from the low corners until the straight edge is approximately 1/4 inch above the two low corners.

7. Proceed to the next set of instructions.

If the panel isn't warped or you've leveled it:

8. Plane diagonally in one direction from corner to corner. (image 1)

9. Move to one side of the diagonal cut to plane in the same direction.

10. Move to the side of that cut and continue planing.

11. Continue until you've gone to the corner.

12. Repeat this on the other side of the diagonal.

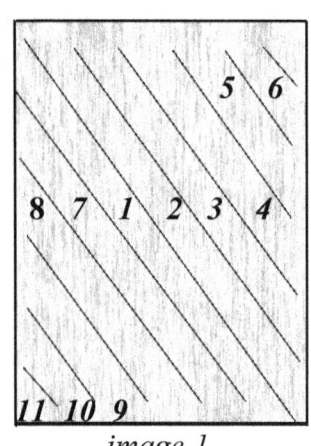

image 1
1ˢᵗ order of planing

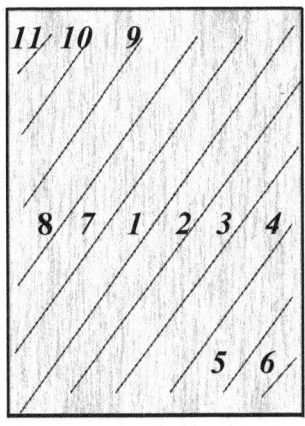

image 2
2ⁿᵈ order of planing

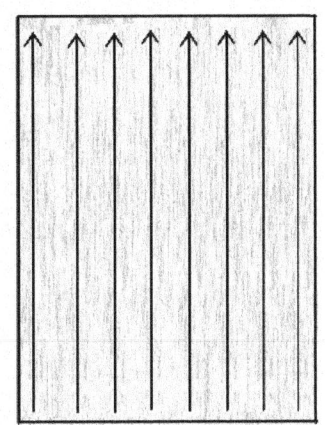

image 3 – planing in
line with grain

13. When you've made one pass over the entire panel in one direction, turn and make a pass diagonally from the other two corners. (image 2) You'll be planing across the first set of cuts.

14. After you've gone over the entire panel diagonally in both directions, check the surface diagonally in both directions with a straight edge. At this point, the panel should be reasonably flat with small depressions which you'll clean up later.

15. Set your plane or planer to make a smaller cut.

16. Plane in line with the grain line starting at one edge.

17. Continue making passes till you have reached the other edge. (image 3)

18. As you work along the grain, you'll be taking out grooves left by planing diagonally. You may have to go over the panel several more times to clean up the surface.

19. Look for spots where the plane or planer has torn out or chipped the surface. Tear out or chipping indicates you've gone against the grain. If so, reverse direction and go over the panel again.

20. If you can't avoid tear out in either direction, the grain is reversing. Make sure your blade is sharp, set it to take a very slight cut and go over the entire panel diagonally.

21. If that doesn't work, use a panel scraper or a power sander.

22. At this point, the panel should be flat and reasonably smooth.

23. Look for any slight tear out and mark it with a pencil.

24. What's left to do on this side will be done with sanding.

Now, it's time to start on side A.

25. Turn the panel over and secure it on your work-station.

26. If you haven't taken much off the surface of side B, the thickness of the panel should be reasonably uniform.

27. If side B was warped, side A will be warped as well. In that case, follow 3 through 21 starting on page 178.

28. If you suspect the panel varies in thickness, a panel caliper can help you determine where and how much it varies.

truing a panel with a caliper

1. Set the ends of the panel on sawhorses so the caliper can reach below it.

2. Work in a 6 to 8 inch grid to create a clear picture of the surface.

3. Place one end of the caliper on the panel.

Complete instructions for making a panel caliper are in chapter 2 on page 34.

4. Keep the jaw on the panel by holding the caliper slightly to the side of its center.

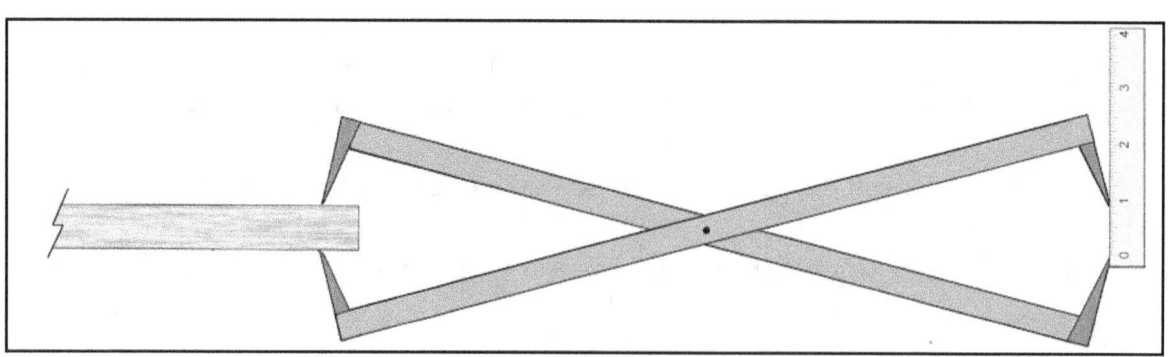

5. Don't press the jaw too hard on the panel or you may get an incorrect measurement.

6. Set a small ruler against the open jaw to read the thickness of the panel.

7. Write that measurement at the corresponding spot on the panel.

8. When you've checked the entire panel, find the thinnest and thickest spots and circle them. There may be more than one. These are control points.

9. Look for a set of high spots that run consecutively in a line or curve making a ridge. There may be more than one set.

10. Draw a thick line around the set or sets of high spots.

11. Look for a set of low spots that run consecutively in a line or curve making a valley. Again, there may be more than one set.

12. Draw a thick line around the set or sets of low spots.

13. Move the panel to a work-station that is sturdy enough to withstand the lateral force created when you plane the surface and secure it with bench stops or clamps.

14. Plane along the ridge of high spots.

15. As you work, your plane will begin to hit other high spots and flattened areas will expand.

16. As you continue planing, you should be hitting all the spots with matching measurements at the same time.

At some point, all the measurements will be planed off and the entire panel will be flattened although there may be traces of the lowest spots on the surface. You'll remove those later.

summary of chapter 9

preparing your panel for use

The side of a panel that will be seen more than the other is the A side. Work on the B side first so if you have any problems, you'll recognize them before working on the A side.

1. Move the panel to a work-station which is sturdy enough to handle the lateral force of planing the surface. Secure the panel with bench stops or clamps.

2. Set a straight edge on the panel diagonally in both directions. If the panel is flat, the straight edge will touch both corners and the center of the panel in both directions.

If the panel is warped:

3. Set a large hand plane or electric hand planer to take a medium cut.

4. Plane diagonally from one high corner to the other.

5. Continue making diagonal cuts in that direction.

6. Check the diagonal from the low corners until the straight edge is approximately 1/4 inch above the two low corners.

7. Proceed to the next set of instructions.

If the panel isn't warped or you've leveled it:

8. Plane diagonally in one direction from corner to corner. (image 1)

9. Move to one side of the diagonal cut to plane in the same direction.

10. Move to the side of that cut and continue planing.

11. Continue until you've gone to the corner.

12. Repeat this on the other side of the diagonal.

13. When you've made one pass over the entire panel in one direction, turn and make a pass diagonally from the other two corners. (image 2) You'll be planing across the first set of cuts.

14. After you've gone over the entire panel diagonally in both directions, check the surface diagonally in both directions with a straight edge. At this point, the panel should be reasonably flat with small depressions which you'll clean up later.

15. Set your plane or planer to make a smaller cut.

16. Plane in line with the grain line starting at one edge.

17. Continue making passes till you have reached the other edge. (image 3)

18. As you work along the grain, you'll be taking out grooves left by planing diagonally. You may have to go over the panel several more times to clean up the surface.

19. Look for spots where the plane or planer has torn out or chipped the surface. Tear out or chipping indicates

you've gone against the grain. If so, reverse direction and go over the panel again.

20. If you can't avoid tear out in either direction, the grain is reversing. Make sure your blade is sharp, set it to take a very slight cut and go over the entire panel diagonally.

21. If that doesn't work, use a panel scraper or a power sander.

22. At this point, the panel should be flat and reasonably smooth.

23. Look for any slight tear out and mark it with a pencil.

24. What's left to do on this side will be done with sanding.

Now, it's time to start on side A.

25. Turn the panel over and secure it on your work-station.

26. If you haven't taken much off the surface of side B, the thickness of the panel should be reasonably uniform.

27. If side B was warped, side A will be warped as well. In that case, follow 3 through 21 starting on page 178.

28. If you suspect the panel varies in thickness, a panel caliper can help you determine where and how much it varies.

using a panel caliper

1. Set the ends of the panel on sawhorses so the caliper can reach below it.

2. Work in a 6 to 8 inch grid to create a clear picture of the surface.

3. Place one end of the caliper around the panel.

4. Hold the caliper in one hand slightly to the side of its center, away from the panel.

5. Keep moderate pressure on the jaws around the panel. Pressing too hard may scar the panel and give you an incorrect measurement.

6. Set a small ruler against the open jaw to read the thickness of the panel.

7. Write that measurement at the corresponding spot on the panel.

8. When you've checked the entire panel, find the thinnest and thickest spots and circle them. There may be more than one. These are control points.

9. Look for a set of high spots that run consecutively in a line or curve making a ridge. There may be more than one set.

10. Draw a thick line around the set or sets of high spots.

11. Look for a set of low spots that run consecutively in a line or curve making a valley. Again, there may be more than one set.

12. Draw a thick line around the set or sets of low spots.

13. Move the panel to a work-station that is sturdy enough to withstand the lateral force created when you plane the surface and secure it with bench stops or clamps.

14. Plane along the ridge of high spots.

15. As you work, your plane will begin to hit other high spots and flattened areas will expand.

16. As you continue planing, you should be hitting all the spots with matching measurements at the same time.

At some point, all the measurements will be planed off and the entire panel will be flattened although there may be traces of the lowest spots on the surface. You'll remove those later.

chapter 10

using
these panels
in a project

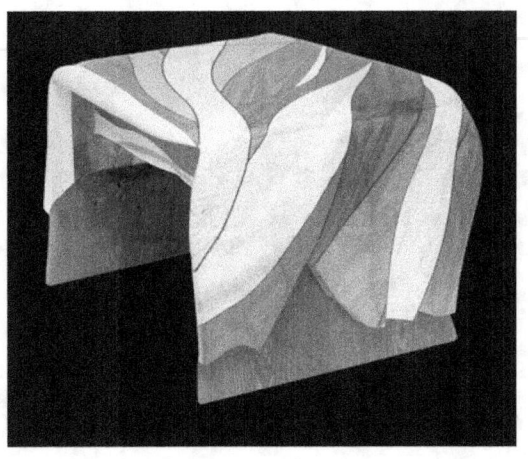

You can use these panels in furniture, doors or cabinets. They can be used as a flat panel or in a frame and panel assembly. But, I believe they make the strongest statement when the lines of the curved joints run through the corners of a piece.

In this chapter, you'll learn how to make a desk with these panels. However, the instructions can also be used to make a cabinet, a bookcase or anything that has flat surfaces joined in a miter.

1. Select a board. It's length should be at least five inches longer than the sum of the two sides plus the top of the desk.

2. Find the mid-point on the board.

3. Mark the board two feet in each direction from the mid-point. This is where the top and sides meet.

4. All curved joints must be near parallel to the edges of the board at both of those points (A & B in image 1) so the lines of the curved joints will match at the miters.

5. Cut and assemble the curved joints.

6. Add boards until the entire length of the panel is wide enough to be cut to the correct width.

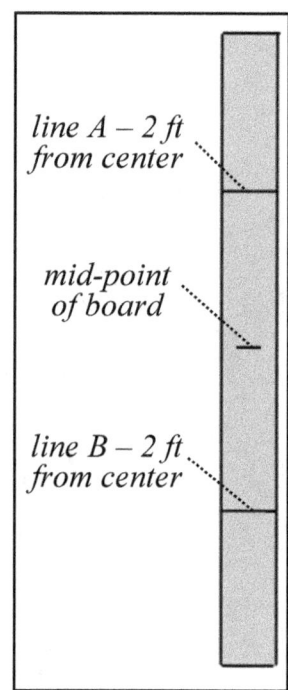

image 1 – bd with layout for miters

7. When the panel is complete, prepare it as described on page 177.

8. Make sure the saw blade is square to the table.

9. Screw plywood to the B side of the panel. The plywood will run against the fence to make one edge of the panel straight.

10. Set the fence to the maximum width that will remove the entire edge.

11. If the cut leaves the edge perfectly straight, prepare to cut the other edge.

12. Set the fence to the maximum width that will remove the entire length of the other edge.

If a panel is more than 8 feet long, use a perfectly straight board that's at least as long as the panel.

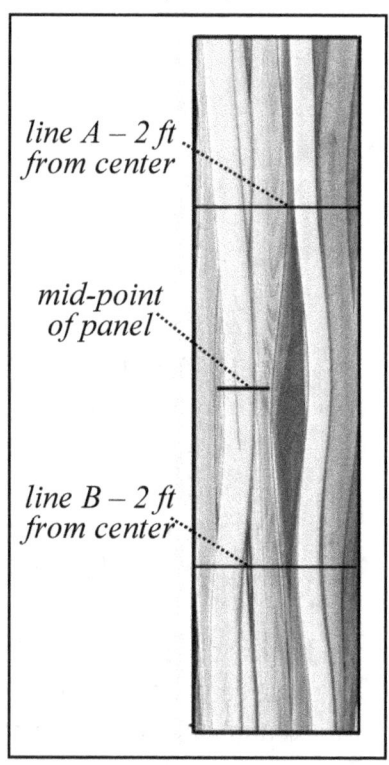

image 2 – panel with layout for sides and top

13. Select the best edge and set the fence to cut the other edge to the final width of the panel.

14. Mark the mid-point of the panel as shown in image 2.

15. From the mid-point, measure 2 feet in both directions. This is where you'll be cutting the miters. (image 2)

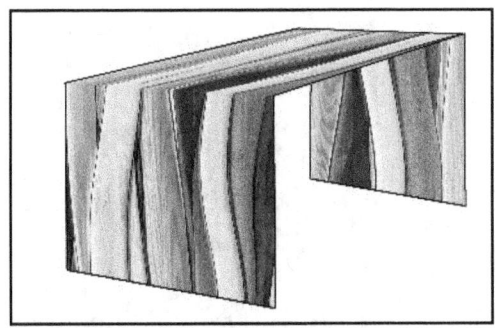

curved joints running through a mitered corner

16. Square those marks across the panel.

You're ready to cut the miters for the top and sides. The panel will be too long to make accurate cuts with the miter gauge of your saw so you'll need a panel sled.

making a mitered joint

For the lines of the curved joints to line up, you must have two conditions. First, the lines of the joints must run reasonably straight where you're going to make the miters. Second, when cutting the miters, you must remove as little of the panel as possible which is the width of one saw kerf.

To perform these operations, you'll need a panel sled for your table saw. Complete instructions for making one are on page 40.

Here's how to make miters that work for curved joinery:

1. Set the blade of your table-saw at 45 degrees.

2. Make a test cut with scraps to check the angle of the blade by cutting miters on each scrap. Set the miters together. Set a square against the joint. It should make a 90 degree angle.

3. Make the cuts on the panel in series starting from one end of the panel.

4. Draw a line at the end of the panel that will work as the base of the piece.

5. The length of the first section will be longer than the height of the piece so you will be able to remove any irregularities in the end.

6. Draw a line across the A side of the panel with a framing square showing the line to be cut. (image 3)

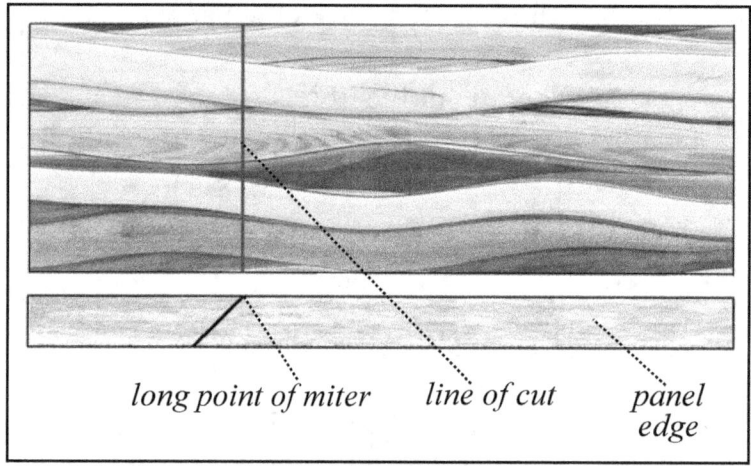

long point of miter   *line of cut*   *panel edge*

image 3 – set up for 1st miter (typical for 3rd miter)

7. Draw a 45 degree line on the edge of the panel facing the blade. (image 3)

8. Set the panel sled on the table-saw.

9. Set the panel on the sled so the blade lines up with the correct side of the mark.

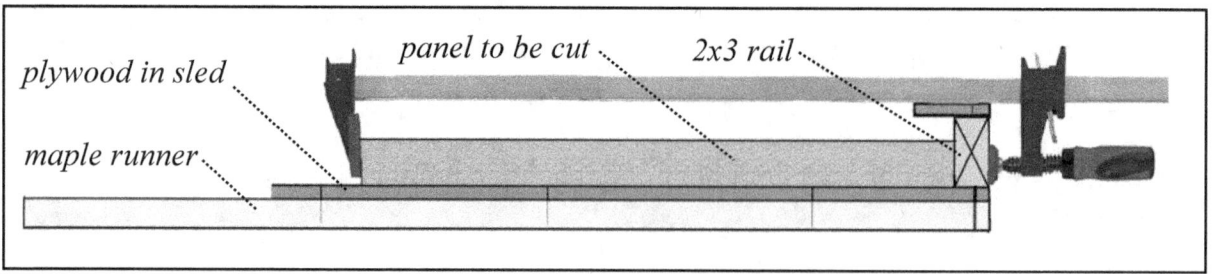

plywood in sled   *panel to be cut*   *2x3 rail*

maple runner

panel clamped to the 2x3 rail on the sled

10. Clamp the panel to the 2x3 rail on the sled.

11. With the saw turned off, move the sled forward till the panel meets the blade.

12. Press down on the panel while checking the alignment of the mark with the blade again.

13. Turn the saw on and move the sled forward slowly and carefully till the blade barely touches the panel.

14. Press down firmly on the panel but keep your hand away from the line of cut.

15. Pull the sled back and turn the saw off.

16. Check that the blade has precisely hit the correct side of the mark. If necessary, adjust and test the position again.

17. With your hand away from the line of cut, press down firmly on the panel and move the sled forward slowly and carefully. Keep the sled moving at a moderate and steady speed throughout the cut. Stopping may scar the edge of the miter and make a poor joint.

18. This is the first miter.

19. Remove the section you just cut (section A – image 4). This is the first side of the cabinet.

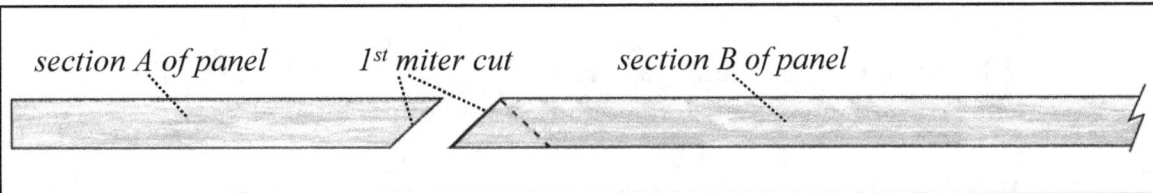

section A of panel   1st miter cut   section B of panel

image 4 - 1st miter (identical for 3rd miter)

20. Turn section B around but do not turn it over. All cuts must be made with the A side up.

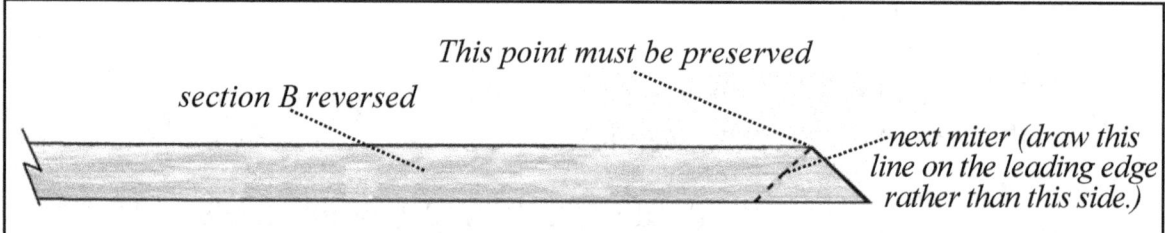

section B reversed

This point must be preserved

next miter (draw this line on the leading edge rather than this side.)

image 5 - set up for 2ⁿᵈ miter (identical set up for 4ᵗʰ miter)

21. Draw a line on the leading edge of the panel at 45 degrees precisely at the edge of the last cut. (image 5)

22. Move the sled forward and line the blade up with the outside of the mark. Your cut must exactly hit the 45 degree line you drew so that you leave the point of the last cut.

23. Clamp the panel to the 2x3 rail.

24. With the saw turned off, move the sled forward till the panel meets the blade.

25. Press down on the panel while checking the alignment of the mark with the blade again.

26. Turn the saw on, press down firmly on the panel and move the sled forward slowly till the blade barely touches the panel.

27. Pull the sled back and turn the saw off.

28. Check that the blade has precisely hit the correct side of the mark. If necessary, adjust and test the position again.

29. With your hand away from the line of cut, press down firmly on the panel and move the sled forward slowly and carefully. Keep the sled moving at a moderate and steady speed

throughout the cut. Stopping may scar the edge of the miter and make a poor joint.

30. This is the second miter. Turn the panel around again.

31. Mark the panel to the length you want for the top.

32. Square the line across the panel with a framing square.

33. Draw a line on the leading edge of the panel at 45 degrees. (identical to image 3)

34. Set the panel on your sled so the blade lines up with the correct side of the mark.

35. Clamp the panel to the 2x3 rail.

36. Move the sled forward and line the blade up with the outside of the mark.

37. Clamp the panel to the 2x3 rail.

38. With the saw turned off, move the sled forward till the panel meets the blade.

39. Press down on the panel and check the alignment of the mark with the blade again.

40. Turn the saw on.

41. Press down firmly on the panel and move the sled forward till the blade barely touches the panel.

42. Pull the sled back and turn the saw off.

43. Check that the blade has precisely hit the correct side of the mark. If necessary, adjust and test the position again.

44. With your hand away from the line of cut, press down firmly on the panel and move the sled forward slowly and carefully. Keep the sled moving at a moderate and steady speed throughout the cut. Stopping may scar the edge of the miter and make a poor joint.

45. This is the third miter and the top of the cabinet. (image 4)

46. Set the top aside.

47. Turn the remainder of the panel around but don't turn it over.

48. Draw a line on the leading edge of the panel at 45 degrees precisely to the point of the last cut. (image 5)

49. Move the sled forward and line the blade up with the outside of the mark. Your cut must exactly hit the 45 degree line you drew so that you leave the point of the last cut.

50. Clamp the panel to the 2x3 rail.

51. With the saw turned off, move the sled forward till the panel meets the blade.

52. Press down on the panel while checking the alignment of the mark with the blade again.

53. Turn the saw on, press down firmly on the panel and move the sled forward slowly till the blade barely touches the panel.

54. Pull the sled back and turn the saw off.

55. Check that the blade has precisely hit the correct side of the mark. If necessary, adjust and test the position again.

56. With your hand away from the line of cut, press down firmly on the panel and move the sled forward slowly and carefully. Keep the sled moving at a moderate and steady

speed throughout the cut. Stopping may scar the edge of the miter and make a poor joint.

57. This is the fourth miter and the second side. It should be long enough that you can remove the rough edge at the end.

58. Remove the sled and set the blade square with the table with a hand square.

59. Replace the sled and set one of the side panels on it.

60. Mark the panel from the long end of the miter to the length you want for the sides.

61. Transfer that mark to side B. (the side with the short end of the miter)

62. Square that mark across side B and set it aside.

63. Set the other side panel on the sled with side A (the long end of the miter) up.

64. Set the first side panel (which you marked) on top of the second one so the long ends of the miters face each other. The line you drew should be visible.

65. Make the long points of both side panels flush. They should be flush along the entire edge of the miters.

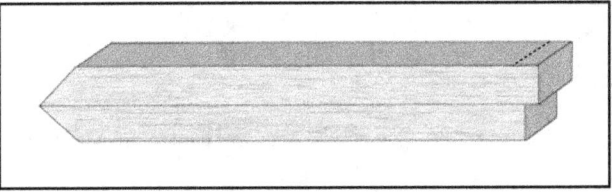

miters set flush with boards ready to cut

66. With an adjustable square, extend that line down the leading edge of both side panels.

67. Move the sled forward and position the panels so the blade is is set to the correct side of the line.

68. Make sure the long points of the panels are still flush with each other.

69. Place a small scrap against the panels and clamp them to the 2x3 rail on the sled.

70. With the saw turned off, move the sled forward till the panel meets the blade to check the alignment of the mark with the blade.

71. With your hand away from the line of cut, press down firmly on the panel.

72. Turn the saw on and move the sled forward slowly and carefully till the blade barely touches the wood.

73. Pull the sled back and turn the saw off.

74. Check that the blade has precisely hit the correct side of the mark. If necessary, adjust and test the position again.

75. With your hand away from the line of cut, press down firmly on the panel and move the sled forward slowly and carefully. Keep the sled moving at a moderate and steady speed throughout the cut.

76. The sides are cut to size. If the piece will have a back panel and/or shelves, cut rabbets and dadoes as you would with standard tops and sides.

assembling mitered joints of panels with curved joints

1. Make a trial assembly of the cabinet to make sure the panels fit properly and the lines in the curved joints line up correctly at the miters.

2. Measure the distance between the side panels below the top.

3. Cut a board or 3/4 inch plywood to match that distance.

4. Assemble the top and sides with the board or plywood between the bottoms of the sides.

5. If the lines of the curved joints line up and the corner joints work, you're ready to glue the panels together.

6. If the miters don't match up perfectly, clean up both sides of the joint with a block plane till they match.

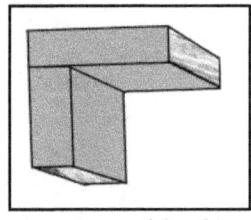

corner block
for miters

7. Make four corner blocks.

8. Lay the top and sides on a table which is absolutely flat and in one plane with the inside of the panels facing up.

9. Apply glue to the miters.

10. When the glue has lost its gloss but isn't dry, apply a second coat of glue to miters.

11. Clamp the sides and the top together with corner blocks on both sides of the mitered joint to keep the joint aligned.

12. Put two clamps on each side pulling the top down and two clamps across the top.

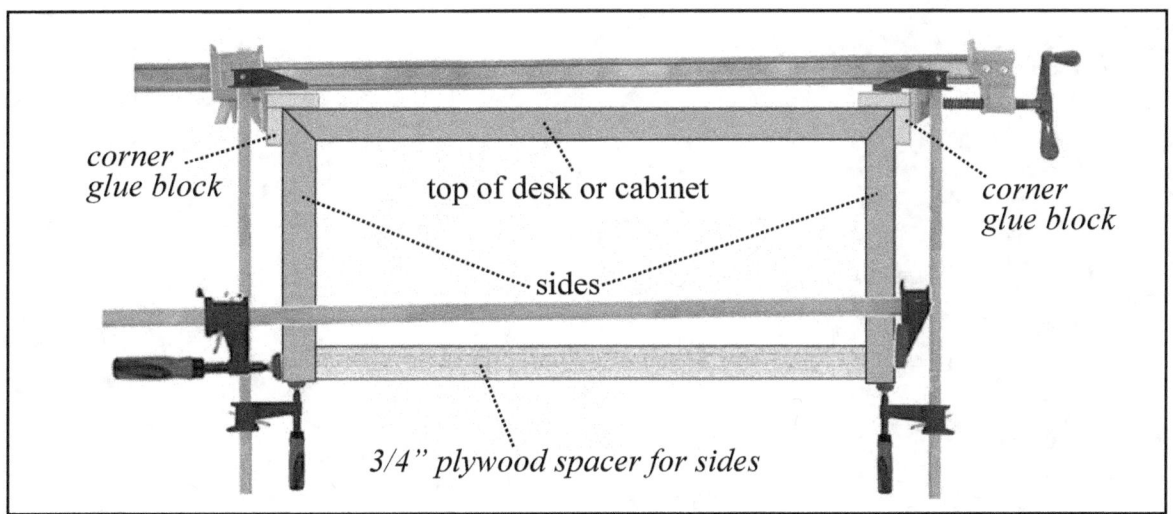

schematic for gluing ides to top

13. Apply enough pressure so every part is in place but not too tight so you can make adjustments.

14. Move the panels at the joints so all lines of the curved joints match. The unit must be sitting flush on the table.

15. Measure the diagonals at the back and front of the assembly.

16. If the diagonals are equal, the unit is square. If not, use pressure to move the unit in the correct direction to make the diagonals equal. Long clamps placed diagonally across the long dimension of the carcass will move the unit to square.

summary of chapter 10

using
these panels
in a project

1.   Select a board. It's length should be at least five inches longer than the sum of the two sides plus the top of the desk.

2. Find the mid-point on the board.

3. Mark the board two feet in each direction from the mid-point. This is where the top and sides meet.

4. All curved joints must be near parallel to the edges of the board at both of those points (A & B in image 1) so the lines of the curved joints will match at the miters.

5. Cut and assemble the curved joints.

6. Add boards until the entire length of the panel is wide enough to be cut to the correct width.

7. When the panel is complete, prepare it as described on page 177.

8. Make sure the saw blade is square to the table.

9. Screw plywood to the B side of the panel. The plywood will run against the fence to make one edge of the panel straight.

10. Set the fence to the maximum width that will remove the entire edge.

11. If the cut leaves the edge perfectly straight, prepare to cut the other edge.

12. Set the fence to the maximum width that will remove the entire length of the other edge.

13. Select the best edge and set the fence to cut the other edge to the final width of the panel.

14. Mark the mid-point of the panel as shown in image 2.

15. From the mid-point, measure 2 feet in both directions. This is where you'll be cutting the miters. (image 2)

16. Square those marks across the panel.

You're ready to cut the miters for the top and sides. The panel will be too long to make accurate cuts with the miter gauge of your saw so you'll need a panel sled.

making a mitered joint

For the lines of the curved joints to line up, you must have two conditions. First, the lines of the joints must run reasonably straight where you're going to make the miters. Second, when cutting the miters, you must remove as little of the panel as possible which is the width of one saw kerf.

Here's how to make miters that work for curved joinery:

1. Set the blade of your table-saw at 45 degrees.

2. Make a test cut with scraps to check the angle of the blade by cutting miters on each scrap. Set the miters together. Set a square against the joint. It should make a 90 degree angle.

3. Make the cuts on the panel in series starting from one end of the panel.

4.Draw a line at the end of the panel that will work as the base of the piece.

5. The length of the first section will be longer than the height of the piece so you will be able to remove any irregularities in the end.

6. Draw a line across the A side of the panel with a framing square showing the line to be cut. (image 3)

7. Draw a 45 degree line on the edge of the panel facing the blade. (image 3)

8. Set the panel sled on the table-saw.

9. Set the panel on the sled so the blade lines up with the correct side of the mark.

10. Clamp the panel to the 2x3 rail on the sled.

11. With the saw turned off, move the sled forward till the panel meets the blade.

12. Press down on the panel while checking the alignment of the mark with the blade again.

13. Turn the saw on and move the sled forward slowly and carefully till the blade barely touches the panel.

14. Press down firmly on the panel but keep your hand away from the line of cut.

15. Pull the sled back and turn the saw off.

16. Check that the blade has precisely hit the correct side of the mark. If necessary, adjust and test the position again.

17. With your hand away from the line of cut, press down firmly on the panel and move the sled forward slowly and carefully. Keep the sled moving at a moderate and steady speed throughout the cut. Stopping may scar the edge of the miter and make a poor joint.

18. This is the first miter. With the cut complete, remove the section you just cut (section A – image 4). This is the first side of the cabinet.

19. Turn section B around but do not turn it over. All cuts must be made with the A side up.

20. Draw a line on the leading edge of the panel at 45 degrees precisely at the edge of the last cut. (image 5)

21. Move the sled forward and line the blade up with the outside of the mark. Your cut must exactly hit the 45 degree line you drew so that you leave the point of the last cut.

22. Clamp the panel to the 2x3 rail.

23. With the saw turned off, move the sled forward till the panel meets the blade.

24. Press down on the panel while checking the alignment of the mark with the blade again.

25. Turn the saw on, press down firmly on the panel and move the sled forward slowly till the blade barely touches the panel.

26. Pull the sled back and turn the saw off.

27. Check that the blade has precisely hit the correct side of the mark. If necessary, adjust and test the position again.

28. With your hand away from the line of cut, press down firmly on the panel and move the sled forward slowly and carefully. Keep the sled moving at a moderate and steady speed throughout the cut. Stopping may scar the edge of the miter and make a poor joint.

29. This is the second miter. Turn the panel around again.

30. Mark the panel to the length you want for the top.

31. Square the line across the panel with a framing square.

32. Draw a line on the leading edge of the panel at 45 degrees. (identical to image 3)

33. Set the panel on your sled so the blade lines up with the correct side of the mark.

34. Clamp the panel to the 2x3 rail.

35. Move the sled forward and line the blade up with the outside of the mark.

36. Clamp the panel to the 2x3 rail.

37. With the saw turned off, move the sled forward till the panel meets the blade.

38. Press down on the panel and check the alignment of the mark with the blade again.

39. Turn the saw on.

40. Press down firmly on the panel and move the sled forward till the blade barely touches the panel.

41. Pull the sled back and turn the saw off.

42. Check that the blade has precisely hit the correct side of the mark. If necessary, adjust and test the position again.

43. With your hand away from the line of cut, press down firmly on the panel and move the sled forward slowly and carefully. Keep the sled moving at a moderate and steady speed throughout the cut. Stopping may scar the edge of the miter and make a poor joint.

44. This is the third miter and the top of the cabinet. (image 4)

45. Set the top aside.

46. Turn the remainder of the panel around but don't turn it over.

47. Draw a line on the leading edge of the panel at 45 degrees precisely to the point of the last cut. (image 5)

48. Move the sled forward and line the blade up with the outside of the mark. Your cut must exactly hit the 45 degree line you drew so that you leave the point of the last cut.

49. Clamp the panel to the 2x3 rail.

50. With the saw turned off, move the sled forward till the panel meets the blade.

51. Press down on the panel while checking the alignment of the mark with the blade again.

52. Turn the saw on, press down firmly on the panel and move the sled forward slowly till the blade barely touches the panel.

53. Pull the sled back and turn the saw off.

54. Check that the blade has precisely hit the correct side of the mark. If necessary, adjust and test the position again.

55. With your hand away from the line of cut, press down firmly on the panel and move the sled forward slowly and carefully. Keep the sled moving at a moderate and steady speed throughout the cut. Stopping may scar the edge of the miter and make a poor joint.

56. This is the fourth miter and the second side. It should be long enough that you can remove the rough edge at the end.

57. Remove the sled and set the blade square with the table with a hand square.

58. Replace the sled and set one of the side panels on it.

59. Mark the panel from the long end of the miter to the length you want for the sides.

60. Transfer that mark to side B. (the side with the short end of the miter)

61. Square that mark across side B and set it aside.

62. Set the other side panel on the sled with side A (the long end of the miter) up.

63. Set the first side panel (which you marked) on top of the second one so the long ends of the miters face each other. The line you drew should be visible.

64. Make the long points of both side panels flush. They should be flush along the entire edge of the miters.

65. With an adjustable square, extend that line down the leading edge of both side panels.

66. Move the sled forward and position the panels so the blade is is set to the correct side of the line.

67. Make sure the long points of the panels are still flush with each other.

68. Place a small scrap against the panels and clamp them to the 2x3 rail on the sled.

69. With the saw turned off, move the sled forward till the panel meets the blade to check the alignment of the mark with the blade.

70. With your hand away from the line of cut, press down firmly on the panel.

71. Turn the saw on and move the sled forward slowly and carefully till the blade barely touches the wood.

72. Pull the sled back and turn the saw off.

73. Check that the blade has precisely hit the correct side of the mark. If necessary, adjust and test the position again.

74. With your hand away from the line of cut, press down firmly on the panel and move the sled forward slowly and

carefully. Keep the sled moving at a moderate and steady speed throughout the cut.

75. The sides are cut to size. If the piece will have a back panel and/or shelves, cut rabbets and dadoes as you would with standard tops and sides.

assembling mitered joints of panels with curved joints

1. Make a trial assembly of the cabinet to make sure the panels fit properly and the lines in the curved joints line up correctly at the miters.

2. Measure the distance between the side panels below the top.

3. Cut a board or 3/4 inch plywood to match that distance.

4. Assemble the top and sides with the board or plywood between the bottoms of the sides.

5. If the lines of the curved joints line up and the corner joints work, you're ready to glue the panels together.

6. If the miters don't match up perfectly, clean up both sides of the joint with a block plane till they match.

7. Make four corner blocks.

8. Lay the top and sides on a table which is absolutely flat and in one plane with the inside of the panels facing up.

9. Apply glue to the miters.

10. When the glue has lost its gloss but isn't dry, apply a second coat of glue to miters.

11. Clamp the sides and the top together with corner blocks on both sides of the mitered joint to keep the joint aligned.

12. Put two clamps on each side pulling the top down and two clamps across the top.

13. Apply enough pressure so every part is in place but not too tight so you can make adjustments.

14. Move the panels at the joints so all lines of the curved joints match. The unit must be sitting flush on the table.

15. Measure the diagonals at the back and front of the assembly.

16. If the diagonals are equal, the unit is square. If not, use pressure to move the unit in the correct direction to make the diagonals equal. Long clamps placed diagonally across the long dimension of the carcass will move the unit to square.

chapter 11

curved joints
in three dimensions

In 2016, a musician in Boston asked me to make a snare drum with curved joinery for him. I'd never made a cylinder with curved joints so I had to create a set of procedures for it.

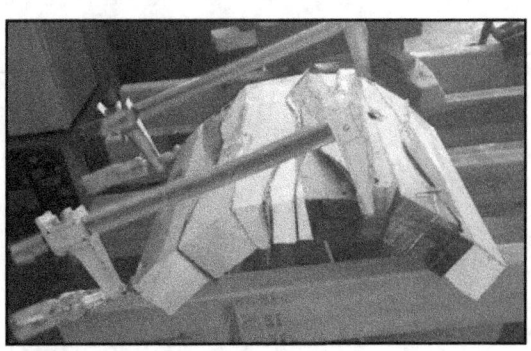

In this chapter, you'll learn how to make a cylinder or similar shape with curved joints.

1. Use boards that are thicker and longer than the finished piece will be. The rough piece will be extremely irregular so you'll have to take off a lot of it to get the finished shape. I built the snare drum from boards that were 2 inches thick and it finished at 9/16th inch.

2. Draw a circle – circle 1 – representing the actual size of the finished piece on 3/4 inch plywood.

3. Draw a circle representing the size of the rough piece (circle 2 in image 1).

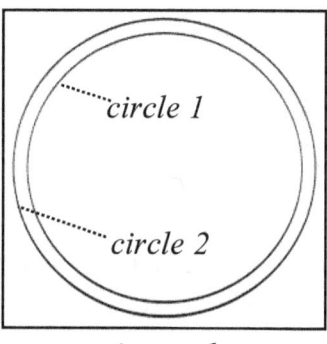

image 1

- The diameter of circle 2 (the template for rough piece) is equal to the diameter of circle 1 (the outline of the finished piece) plus the thickness of a board in the rough piece minus the thickness of one side in the finished piece.

  - If the diameter of circle 1 (the finished piece) is 20 inches and the boards you use are 2 inches thick and the finished piece is 1/2 inch thick, the diameter of circle 2 would be 21½ inches.

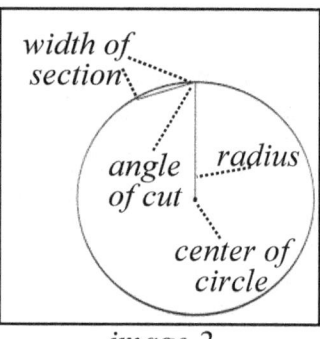

image 2

4. Join the edges of all boards before you use them.

5. Find the center of the circle and draw a radius from it (image 2).

6. Estimate the width of the section you will be making and mark that width from the end of the radius to a point along the perimeter of the circle.

7. Measure the angle between the radius and that line.

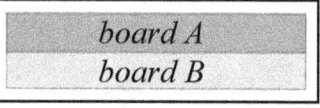

image 3

8. Set the blade of your table-saw to that angle.

9. Rip both edges of a board – board A – with that angle to make it the width you want for the first segment.

10. Cut a second board – board B – with a miter on one edge.

11. Screw board B to board A (image 3).

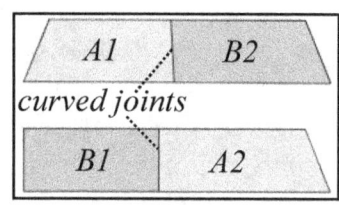

image 4

12. Follow the directions for making a curved joint starting on page 96.

13. The cut must not go off the edges of either board.

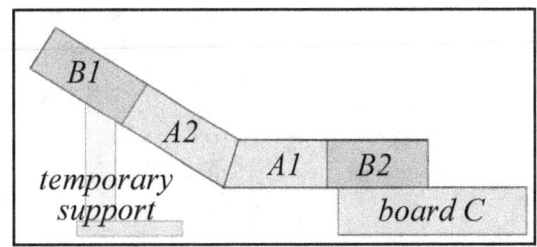

image 5

14. Check the fit and make hash marks.

15. Clamp the two curved joints together – board A1 to B2 and board A2 to B1 (image 4).

16. When the glue has set on the curved joints, join the mitered edges of boards A1 and A2 (image 5).

17. Place a board across the inside of the sections at top and bottom and place clamps from the boards to the ridge of the miter (image 5). This will prevent the miter from opening.

18. Probe the inside and outside of the joint with a sharp knife to make sure the entire surface is in contact. Adjust the tension on the clamps as necessary to create full contact in the joint.

19. When the glue is dry, plane or sand the miters flush on both sides of the miter.

20. Cut another board – board C – with a miter on one edge.

image 6

21. Set board C under one end of the assembly (image 6) and screw them together.

22. Follow the instruction starting on page 96 for making a curved joint. One end of the assembly will be elevated off the table while you cut. You may want to screw a temporary support to the assembly as you cut the curve (image 6).

23. Board C is now C1 and C2. Section B2 is now B2 and B3 (image 7).

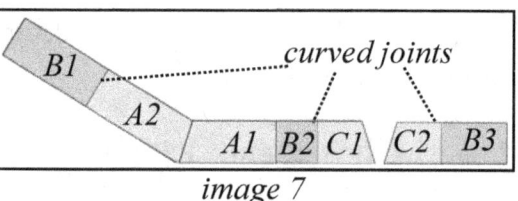
image 7

24. The joint C1-B2 and C2-B3 are curved joints.

25. Check the fit of both joints and make hash marks.

26. Set the blade at the correct angle.

27. Set the fence to cut the edges of C1 and C2 at a bevel for a miter joint (image 8).

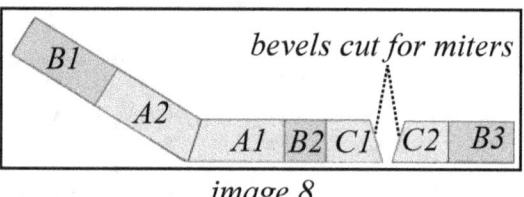
image 8

28. Glue the curved joint.

29. When the glue has set, assemble the miter between C1 and C2 (image 9). You may need to make notches at the ends of the assembly and at the previous miter to accommodate the clamps across the joint.

30. Place a board across the inside of the sections at top and bottom and place clamps from the boards to the ridge of the miter (image 9). This will prevent the miter from opening.

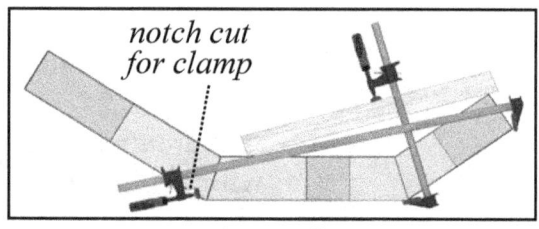
image 9

31. Probe the inside and outside of the joint with a sharp knife to make sure the entire surface is in contact. Adjust the tension on the clamps as necessary to create full contact in the joint.

32. When the glue is dry, plane or sand the miters flush on both sides of the miter.

33. After every joint is glued, set the assembly on the larger circle you drew on the plywood (image 10). The shape of the

assembly should roughly conform to the circle. If it doesn't, adjust the angle of the cut for the next miter to bring the assembly back to the arc.

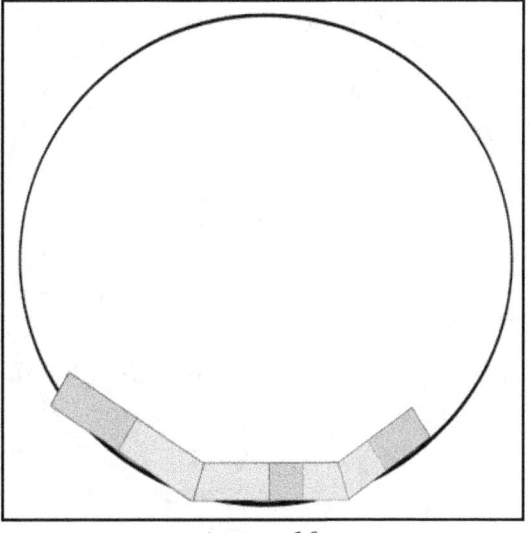

image 10

34. Before ripping the bevel for the next miter, check the side and the edges of the assembly against the plywood with a framing square. They should be roughly square to the plywood.

35. Repeat steps 33 and 35 after each assembly – especially before gluing up miters – so you can adjust the angle of the bevel, if necessary, to bring the assembly back to the arc of the circle.

36. Plan for the point when the assembly will be too big to run through the band-saw so the last board at both ends is cut on an appropriate bevel.

37. Set this section aside.

38. Select a board that closely matches a board at one end of that section.

39. Start from instruction 4 to make the second section of the assembly.

40. After every joint is glued, set the assembly on the larger circle you drew on the plywood to ensure it conforms to the arc and is square to the plywood.

41. If necessary, adjust the angle of your table-saw blade to increase or decrease the miter and bring the assembly back to the arc.

42. When the second assembly is too large to run through the band-saw, make a third assembly.

43. The last board in the second assembly must match the first board in the third assembly.

44. Continue making sections and test them against circle 2.

45. Assemble the first and second sections with matching boards facing each other.

46. Before tightening the clamps, adjust the tilt and alignment of the sections so the sides of the assembly and the faces of the mitered joints are square to the plywood.

47. When the glue has set, add the third section with matching boards facing each other. Before tightening the clamps, check the assembly against the plywood. For the last piece of the cylinder to fit properly, the cylinder must be near square to the plywood.

48. Add sections until the gap between the beginning of the first section and the end of the last section is six to eight inches.

49. Carefully plan the final steps in the assembly.

50. The boards on each end of this last section must match the boards at each end of the assembly.

51. Cut and assemble curved joints in the final section.

52. As you add boards, test the final section in the remaining space until the gap is approximately 1 inch.

53. Glue this section to the assembly.

The width of the last gap may not be uniform.

54. When the glue has set, measure the distance between the four corners of the gap.

55. Cut a board slightly more than the widest of those measurements.

56. Plane one side of the board till it conforms to the measurements. Test it while you work.

57. When the piece fits perfectly, glue and clamp it into the final assembly.

At this point, the cylinder is rough and uneven. To clean it up:

1. Near one end of the cylinder, draw a line square to the line of a miter joint.

2. Continue the line around the cylinder square to each miter.

3. When the line has come all the way around the cylinder, should meet the start of the line. If it doesn't, adjust the line along the circumference till it is reasonably close.

4. Repeat this at the other end of the cylinder.

5. Build a stop to keep the cylinder from turning while you cut it. Cut 2 pieces of plywood cut in a curve and screwed to two 2x4s between them (image 11).

6. Cut both lines on the cylinder.

7. Make both cuts reasonably flat with a belt sander. They don't have to be perfectly flat.

8. Set the cylinder on a sheet of 3/4 inch plywood and scribe the edge.

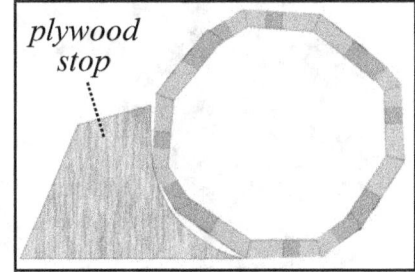

image 11

9. Cut the circle.

10. Make a second plywood circle to match the first.

11. Screw the plywood circles to the top and bottom of the cylinder. Keep the screws away from the inside and outside edges of the cylinder.

12. Find the center points of both circles.

13. Set the head and tail of your lathe on the center points.

14. Turn the cylinder to eliminate irregularities.

15. When you are satisfied with the appearance, remove one of the plywood circles.

16. Screw a faceplate to the plywood.

To make another shape, draw the shape on 3/4 inch plywood and cut the miters to follow the outline of the shape in the same manner described in this chapter.

17. Turn the inside of the cylinder till you are satisfied with the appearance.

18. Sand and finish the cylinder.

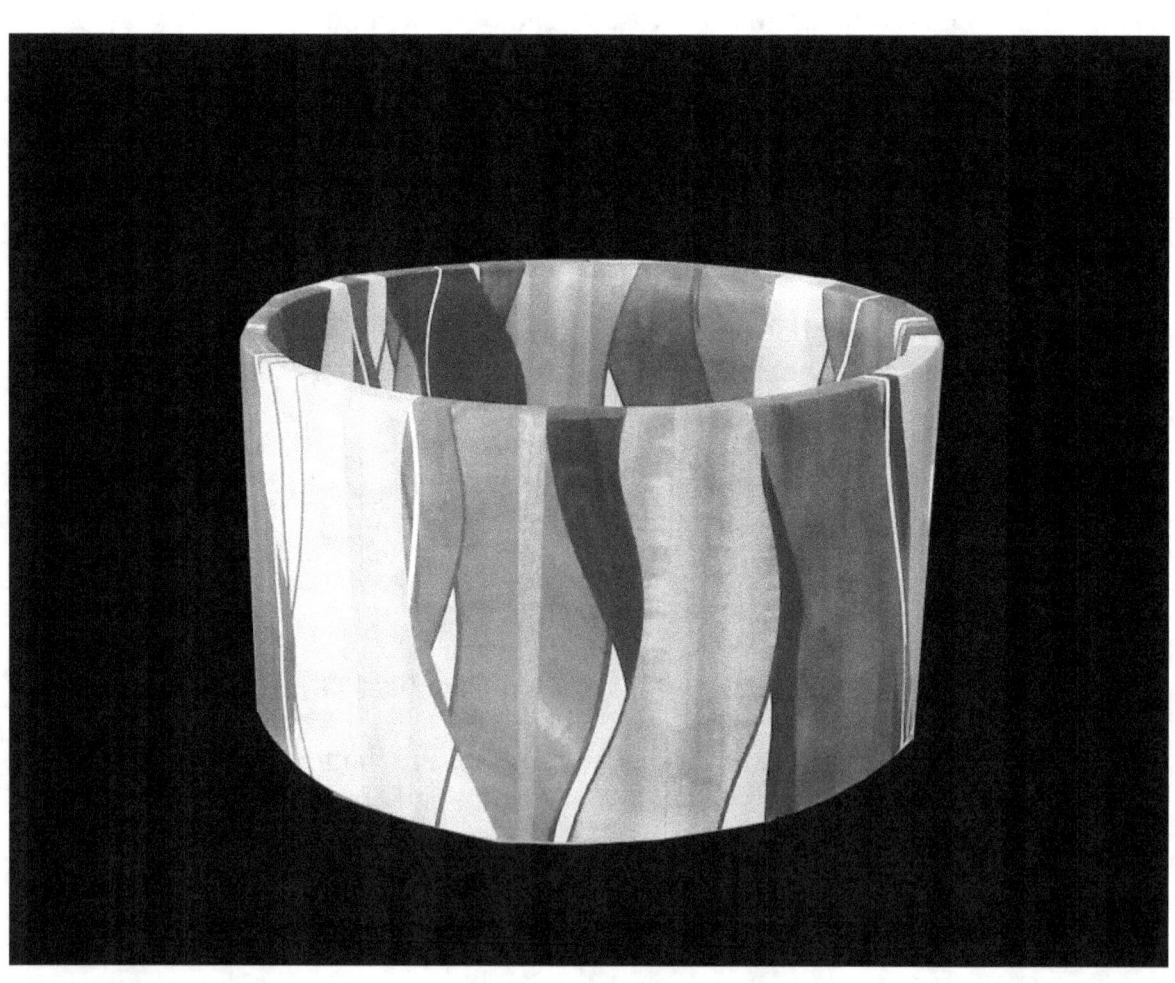

summary of chapter 11

curved joints in three dimensions

your

notes

procedures.

1. Use boards that are thicker and longer than the finished piece will be. The rough piece will be extremely irregular so you'll have to take off a lot of it to get the finished shape. I built the snare drum from boards that were 2 inches thick and it finished at 9/16th inch.

2. Draw a circle – circle 1 – representing the actual size of the finished piece on 3/4 inch plywood.

3. Draw a circle representing the size of the rough piece (circle 2 in image 1).

• The diameter of circle 2 (the template for rough piece) is equal to the diameter of circle 1 (the outline of the finished piece) plus the thickness of a board in the rough piece minus the thickness of one side in the finished piece.

• If the diameter of circle 1 (the finished piece) is 20 inches and the boards you use are 2 inches thick and the finished piece is 1/2 inch thick, the diameter of circle 2 would be 21½ inches.

4. Join the edges of all boards before you use them.

5. Find the center of the circle and draw a radius from it (image 2).

6. Estimate the width of the section you will be making and mark that width from the end of the radius to a point along the perimeter of the circle.

7. Measure the angle between the radius and that line.

8. Set the blade of your table-saw to that angle.

9. Rip both edges of a board – board A – with that angle to make it the width you want for the first segment.

10. Cut a second board – board B – with a miter on one edge.

11. Screw board B to board A (image 3).

12. Follow the directions for making a curved joint starting on page 96.

13. The cut must not go off the edges of either board.

14. Check the fit and make hash marks.

15. Clamp the two curved joints together – board A1 to B2 and board A2 to B1 (image 4).

16. When the glue has set on the curved joints, join the mitered edges of boards A1 and A2 (image 5).

17. Place a board across the inside of the sections at top and bottom and place clamps from the boards to the ridge of the miter (image 5). This will prevent the miter from opening.

18. Probe the inside and outside of the joint with a sharp knife to make sure the entire surface is in contact. Adjust the tension on the clamps as necessary to create full contact in the joint.

19. When the glue is dry, plane or sand the miters flush on both sides of the miter.

20. Cut another board – board C – with a miter on one edge.

21. Set board C under one end of the assembly (image 6) and screw them together.

22. Follow the instruction starting on page 96 for making a curved joint. One end of the assembly will be elevated off the table while you cut. You may want to screw a temporary support to the assembly as you cut the curve (image 6).

23. Board C is now C1 and C2. Section B2 is now B2 and B3 (image 7).

24. The joint C1-B2 and C2-B3 are curved joints.

25. Check the fit of both joints and make hash marks.

26. Set the blade at the correct angle.

27. Set the fence to cut the edges of C1 and C2 at a bevel for a miter joint (image 8).

28. Glue up the curved joint.

29. When the glue has set, glue up the miter between C1 and C2 (image 9). You may need to make notches at the ends of the assembly and at the previous miter to accommodate the clamps across the joint.

30. Place a board across the inside of the sections at top and bottom and place clamps from the boards to the ridge of the miter (image 9). This will prevent the miter from opening.

31. Probe the inside and outside of the joint with a sharp knife to make sure the entire surface is in contact. Adjust the tension on the clamps as necessary to create full contact in the joint.

32. When the glue is dry, plane or sand the miters flush on both sides of the miter.

33. After every joint is glued, set the assembly on the larger circle you drew on the plywood (image 10). The shape of the assembly should roughly conform to the circle. If it

doesn't, adjust the angle of the cut for the next miter to bring the assembly back to the arc.

34. Before ripping the bevel for the next miter, check the side and the edges of the assembly against the plywood with a framing square. They should be roughly square to the plywood.

35. Repeat steps 33 and 35 after each glue up – especially before gluing up miters – so you can adjust the angle of the bevel, if necessary, to bring the assembly back to the arc of the circle.

36. Plan for the point when the assembly will be too big to run through the band-saw so the last board at both ends is cut on an appropriate bevel.

37. Set this section aside.

38. Select a board that closely matches a board at one end of that section.

39. Start from instruction 4 to make the second section of the assembly.

40. After every joint is glued, set the assembly on the larger circle you drew on the plywood to ensure it conforms to the arc and is square to the plywood.

41. If necessary, adjust the angle of your table-saw blade to increase or decrease the miter and bring the assembly back to the arc.

42. When the second assembly is too large to run through the band-saw, make a third assembly.

43. The last board in the second assembly must match the first board in the third assembly.

44. Continue making sections and test them against circle 2.

45. Glue up the first and second sections with matching boards facing each other.

46. Before tightening the clamps, adjust the tilt and alignment of the sections so the sides of the assembly and the faces of the mitered joints are square to the plywood.

47. When the glue has set, add the third section with matching boards facing each other. Before tightening the clamps, check the assembly against the plywood. For the last piece of the cylinder to fit properly, the cylinder must be near square to the plywood.

48. Add sections until the gap between the beginning of the first section and the end of the last section is six to eight inches.

49. Carefully plan the final steps in the assembly.

50. The boards on each end of this last section must match the boards at each end of the assembly.

51. Cut and assemble curved joints in the final section.

52. As you add boards, test the final section in the remaining space until the gap is approximately 1 inch.

53. Glue this section to the assembly.

54. When the glue has set, measure the distance between the four corners of the gap.

55. Cut a board slightly more than the widest of those measurements.

56. Plane one side of the board till it conforms to the measurements. Test it while you work.

57. When the piece fits perfectly, glue and clamp it into the final assembly.

 At this point, the cylinder is rough and uneven. To clean it up:

1. Near one end of the cylinder, draw a line square to the line of a miter joint.

2. Continue the line around the cylinder square to each miter.

3. When the line has come all the way around the cylinder, should meet the start of the line. If it doesn't, adjust the line along the circumference till it is reasonably close.

4. Repeat this at the other end of the cylinder.

5. Build a stop to keep the cylinder from turning while you cut it. Cut 2 pieces of plywood cut in a curve and screwed to two 2x4s between them (image 11).

6. Cut both lines on the cylinder.

7. Make both cuts reasonably flat with a belt sander. They don't have to be perfectly flat.

8. Set the cylinder on a sheet of 3/4 inch plywood and scribe the edge.

9. Cut the circle.

10. Make a second plywood circle to match the first.

11. Screw the plywood circles to the top and bottom of the cylinder. Keep the screws away from the inside and outside edges of the cylinder.

12. Find the center points of both circles.

13. Set the head and tail of your lathe on the center points.

14. Turn the cylinder to eliminate irregularities.

15. When you are satisfied with the appearance, remove one of the plywood circles.

16. Screw a faceplate to the plywood.

17. Turn the inside of the cylinder till you are satisfied with the appearance.

 Sand and finish the cylinder.

chapter 12

filling voids

I don't use commercial fillers. I make my own from the sawdust of the wood I'm filling. I get an exact match to the wood, it's easy to use, it costs nothing and I never run out.

Here's how to make your own fillers:

1. Whenever you're going to sand a board, start with an empty sawdust bag on our sander.

2. After sanding that board and before you start sanding a board of another color, empty the bag into a jar.

I use a lot of sawdust and it's rare that my projects have only
species of wood. So, sometimes, I produce sawdust by
grinding a board. I made a sawdust collector for that operation.

1. Build a plywood cage. (see the image below)

2. Clamp a board in front of the cage.

3. Create sawdust with a mini-grinder. If you don't have a
mini-grinder, use a belt sander.

4. Don't press hard on the grinding pad or belt sander. Too
much pressure will burn or darken the sawdust.

5. Transfer the sawdust to a jar.

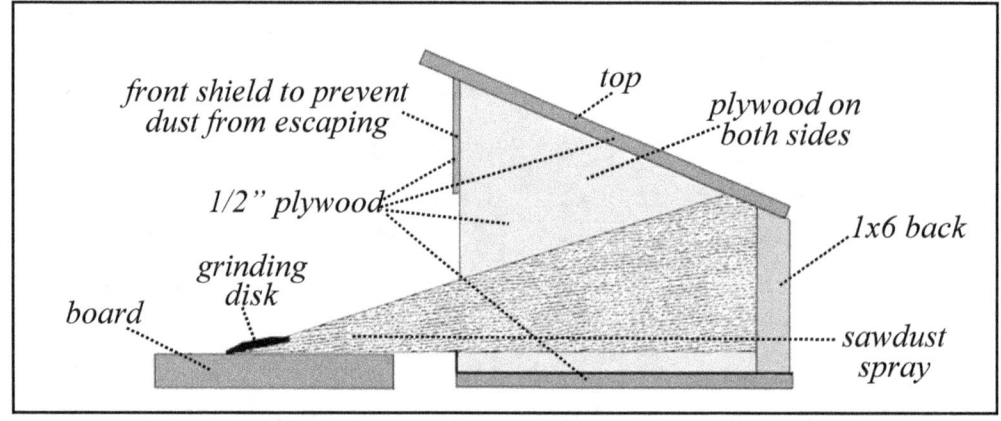

sawdust collector

Getting good results with sawdust fillers requires more time than
with fillers you buy at lumber yards but the results are better.

Sawdust needs a binder. Varnish, shellac or other solvent based
finishes change the color of sawdust and it takes a long time for
them to set up. Filling often takes several steps so it could take
a long time to fill holes and voids.

Aliphatic (yellow) glue, like Titebond, slightly darkens
sawdust but it sets fast. The darkening is rarely noticeable in

woods like oak, African mahogany and walnut but in lighter
woods like maple, birch or hickory, yellow glue can make a
poor match.

White glue won't darken sawdust so it works well in lighter
woods but it takes longer to set up than aliphatic glue (It's
still a a lot faster than solvent based fillers.) so, I use yellow
glue whenever I can.

Epoxy has become the filler of choice for commercial
woodworkers. It picks up the color of the wood around it so
often it's not noticeable. However, even quick setting epoxy
needs to harden for hours or even overnight before the next step.
I can work with my fillers immediately.

Here's how to use sawdust fillers:

1. Lightly sand the area around the void with 120 grit sandpaper
to remove any dirt or loose material.

2. Choose sawdust from your stock which most closely matches
the wood around the void.

3. Prime the void by putting a slight amount of glue into it.

4. Mix sawdust and glue on a smooth, non-porous surface such as
a food container lid or plate to make a loose paste.

5. Add sawdust to the paste till it's thick like bread dough.

6. Press the thick paste into the void with a flat, smooth edged
stick or a plastic blade. Press hard. Pressure promotes bonding
between particles of sawdust in the same way boards are bonded
by clamping them.

7. Add more of the paste and press it but leave a slight dome.

8. Sprinkle sawdust on the dome and press it down with something, hard, smooth and round like a glass bottle. Rolling over the fill will leave it smooth.

A metal putty knife can get a sheen of rust when it gets wet. This will discolor the fill.

9. At this point, if you don't have an exact color match, put a slight amount of white glue around the immediate area of the void and spread it like paint. Use white glue.

10. Sand over the glue with 120 grit paper pushing sawdust into the glue and toward the void. This will produce a paste of the wood you're trying to match.

11. With the white glue sanded off, lightly sand over the area again to move a small amount of sawdust over the paste and roll it in with a smooth, hard, round object.

12. If there's still a depression when the filler is dry, apply white glue around the void and repeat the process. It could take several passes with glue and sanding to satisfactorily fill the void flush to the surface. This step is required with lighter woods like maple,

Pressing sawdust into the surface of the paste creates a high concentration of wood fibers which will take the finish better.

filling a thin crack or small hole

1. Put glue into crack or small hole and spread it around the immediate area like paint.

2. Push the glue toward the crack with a finish sander and 120 grit paper. This will create a thin paste from the wood.

3. Sanding with light pressure allows the paste to sit in the crack. Don't press hard or it will push the paste out of the void.

4. If a power sander drives the paste out of the void, gently hand sand the area to make the paste and push it into the void.

5. When the fill is satisfactory, sand the area around the filled crack using light pressure until the surface is clear of glue. Since the paste comes from the wood around the void, the match should be perfect and the crack should disappear.

If glue gets on the surface of the board you can sand it off later.

If the crack is the result of a bad glue joint, glue will be at the surface of the crack and can't take filler. The glue must be removed.

1. Use your largest chisel and a mallet to score a shallow line along one side of the glue.

2. Score another shallow line on the other side of the glue.

Thin cracks are difficult to fill and may require repeating the process several times.

3. Remove the loose material from the area.

4. Putty the groove as described above.

summary of chapter 12

filling
voids

Here's how to make your own fillers:

1. Whenever you're going to sand a board, start with an empty sawdust bag on our sander.

2. After sanding that board and before you start sanding a board of another color, empty the bag into a jar.

I use a lot of sawdust and it's rare that my projects have only species of wood. So, sometimes, I produce sawdust by grinding a board. I made a sawdust collector for that operation.

1. Build a plywood cage. (see the image below)

2. Clamp a board in front of the cage.

3. Create sawdust with a mini-grinder. If you don't have a mini-grinder, use a belt sander.

4. Don't press hard on the grinding pad or belt sander. Too much pressure will burn or darken the sawdust.

5. Transfer the sawdust to a jar.

Here's how to use sawdust fillers:

1. Lightly sand the area around the void with 120 grit sandpaper to remove any dirt or loose material.

2. Choose sawdust from your stock which most closely matches the wood around the void.

3. Prime the void by putting a slight amount of glue into it.

4. Mix sawdust and glue on a smooth, non-porous surface such as a food container lid or plate to make a loose paste.

5. Add sawdust to the paste till it's thick like bread dough.

6. Press the thick paste into the void with a flat, smooth edged stick or a plastic blade. Press hard. Pressure promotes bonding between particles of sawdust in the same way boards are bonded by clamping them.

7. Add more of the paste and press it but leave a slight dome.

8. Sprinkle sawdust on the dome and press it down with something, hard, smooth and round like a glass bottle. Rolling over the fill will leave it smooth.

9. At this point, if you don't have an exact color match, put a slight amount of white glue around the immediate area of the void and spread it like paint. Use white glue.

10. Sand over the glue with 120 grit paper pushing sawdust into the glue and toward the void. This will produce a paste of the wood you're trying to match.

11. With the white glue sanded off, lightly sand over the area again to move a small amount of sawdust over the paste and roll it in with a smooth, hard, round object.

12. If there's still a depression when the filler is dry, apply white glue around the void and repeat the process. It could take several passes with glue and sanding to satisfactorily

fill the void flush to the surface. This step is required with lighter woods like maple,

filling a thin crack or small hole

1. Put glue into crack or small hole and spread it around the immediate area like paint.

2. Push the glue toward the crack with a finish sander and 120 grit paper. This will create a thin paste from the wood.

3. Sanding with light pressure allows the paste to sit in the crack. Don't press hard or it will push the paste out of the void.

4. Sometimes, the speed of a power sander won't let the paste sit on the void. In that case, hand sanding will give you more control.

5. When the fill is satisfactory, sand the area around the filled crack using light pressure until the surface is clear of glue. Since the paste comes from the wood around the void, the match should be perfect and the crack should disappear.

If the crack is the result of a bad glue joint, glue will be at the surface of the crack and can't take filler. The glue must be removed.

1. Use your largest chisel and a mallet to score a shallow line along one side of the glue.

2. Score another shallow line on the other side of the glue.

3. Remove the loose material from the area.

4. Putty the groove as described above.

How I Came to Love Woodworking

Chapter 13, **edge joints**, *starts on page 241.*

part 3

On my first job as a journeyman carpenter, I was part of a crew framing office buildings and I was good at it. But, after four months, the framing was done and I was laid off. Fortunately, I had amassed five hundred hours so I could find a job on my own and get a dispatch. After a few days driving from site to site, a company hired me to work on a crew framing duplexes in a retirement community. These were similar to the houses I had worked on the year before, so most of the time I knew what I was doing.

I was a hard worker and fast with a hammer, so I earned my boss's respect. If I didn't know something, I was able to hide my lack of experience by copying what the other guys did or guessing what had to be done. While I couldn't fake what I'd never done before, my ability in geometry allowed me to figure out complex structures even if I had never built one like it.

Eventually, the foreman sent the most experienced guys to install cabinets and trim in the first duplex while the rest of us framed the last two buildings. Layoffs weren't far off.

One day, the foreman pulled me aside. I expected bad news. Instead, he told me to go work with the finish crew. I was excited at the chance to learn something I knew very little about. It was as if I was working with artisans from the past. They used hand tools I'd never seen before. They wore heavy aprons with pockets for nail sets, pencils, screws, putty and whatever else they might need. And, everything they did came out perfect.

They coped corners rather than miter them. They scribed the edges of cabinets so they fit cleanly against walls without trim. And they never walked away from a project until it looked right. While they worked with precision, they were very productive because they had little wasted motion.

I wanted to watch them work but, of course, couldn't do that. With no experience in finish carpentry, I couldn't figure out how to match what they were doing. My work was slow and not very good.

After three days, I was sent back to the framing crew. I felt awful. I hated losing the chance to learn finish carpentry the way they did it. A few days later, I walked up to the foreman and asked for another chance. He seemed surprised that I'd ask.

"I'll think about it," he said.

The next day, I was back on the finish crew and for some reason, everything made sense to me. I hung doors, coped joints and set cabinets at least as fast and accurately as anyone. Within a year, I was installing intricate interior finishes for the company's most prized customers. After three years, I decided to start my own construction company. I could build just about anything but knew nothing about business. As usual, I learned the hard way .

My first customer went four months before paying his bill. My first year, I didn't save for taxes and just barely got it together by April 15th. My company grew but my skill at business didn't keep up with it. Although we did a lot of work, I never made much money. Then, in December, 1991, I found that my bookkeeper had embezzled enough money to put me out of business.

After that, I needed a break from construction. I decided to use my background in writing and theater and go into advertising. I wrote and produced radio and TV ads for several small companies in Olympia. Some were jingles. Others were comedy. It was great fun, but I missed working with wood.

In 1995, I began building a small shop behind my house. I dug the footings by hand, poured the concrete and framed the walls in evenings and weekends. A month before it was finished, the president of my synagogue asked if I'd design and build a podium for the temple. It sat on a single point, supported by a metal frame that I fabricated. I surrounded the frame with two inch padauk then carved it into the shape of the Hebrew letter, shin, the first letter in the word, shalom, which means peace. I was excited about wood again.

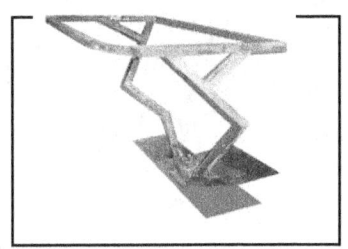
metal frame

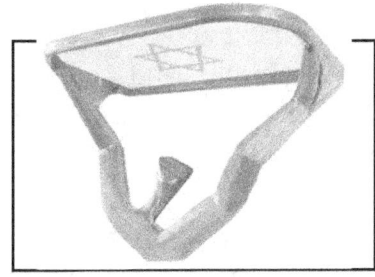
front view

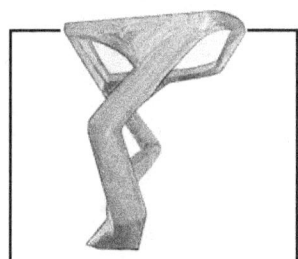
side view

Whenever I wasn't writing ads, I worked in my shop. One day in 1996, I tried something I'd never seen before. I cut cherry and walnut boards at the same time on my band-saw and set the opposite sides against each other. The fit was close but not close enough to work. For weeks, I tried several methods but none of them worked consistently. I needed help.

Being a woodworker is like being part of a club. We gladly help each other and share information. So, I figured if I could find someone who used this technique, I'd save a lot of time and trouble. Unfortunately, nobody knew anything about it and there were no books or magazines on the subject. I wrote to Fine Woodworking but they didn't know anyone who used that technique. If I was going to learn the technique, it would be through trial and error. Being in the shop part time, it took two

years for me to come up with a set of dependable procedures.
I started making simple furniture using the technique but very
few of them sold. I wondered if I had created something
worthwhile or if it was just an interesting detail that had little
value for anyone.

In 2003, I started making free-standing
cabinets and lamps with curved joinery and
sold a few. A woman from a church in
Columbia Heights asked me to make a cross
for their chapel. When I told her I was
Jewish, she said, "I don't care." I spent
hours with their building committee
working on the design. The cross is six
feet tall and four feet wide. It was one of
the most fulfilling and enjoyable
projects I've ever done. But outside of
that project, I had very few sales.

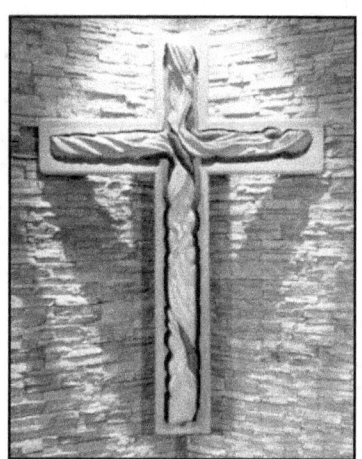

In 2010, I started making bowls. I
made blanks using my techniques
which I turned on my lathe. Several
galleries took them but very few sold.
By 2012, I'd been using my techniques
for sixteen years with little to show for
it. I considered giving it up.

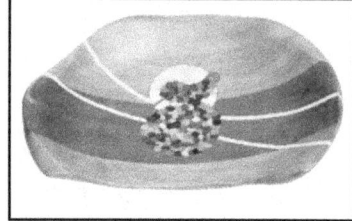

One day, I took several bowls to Vicki Hovde, an art
consultant who worked with hospitals and clinics. She was very
gracious.

"I love these bowls," she said.

My heart filled.

"But I could never sell them."

"Oh," I said.

"Hospitals don't have horizontal surfaces for art. But, if you made a wall hanging in this style, I could sell those."

I made two which she sold to Regions Hospital in St. Paul. As of this writing, my works are in hospitals – including the Mayo Clinic – colleges, corporate offices and hundreds of homes all over the country.

I've been very lucky to do something I love. And more fortunate for the people I've met and learned from. Woodworking has filled my years with a consistent theme of productivity and creativity. I certainly didn't imagine I'd be saying that when I was a kid growing up on the north side of Chicago.

The end.

section three

background information

chapter 13

edge
joints

Years ago, I read a book by Tage Frid, a highly regarded author and woodworker. He wrote that biscuits are not the best way to join boards and showed a better method. That surprised me. Woodworkers on TV and in magazines said biscuits make the strongest and easiest edge joints possible. And, most of the woodworkers I knew, including professional furniture and cabinet-makers, used them. However, after reading his book, I realized they were all wrong.

making strong straight edge joints

1. Unplug your table-saw, run the blade up to full height and use a hand square to make sure the blade is square to the table.

2. Select two boards.

3. Use a joiner or a fence extender to make the edges of the boards straight, smooth and perfectly square to the surface.

4. Use a block plane to create a shallow arc. A four foot board will have 1/16 inch off the center of its edge.

The amount to be removed increases with longer boards.

5. Keep the sole of the plane flat against the edge to keep it square to the face of the board. That allows the edges to be in full contact when the joint is assembled. Periodically check the edge with a hand square.

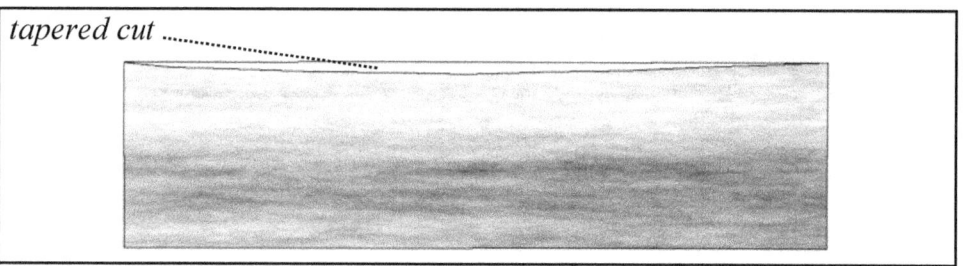

drawing of board with top edge planed in a curve
(depth of the taper is exaggerated)

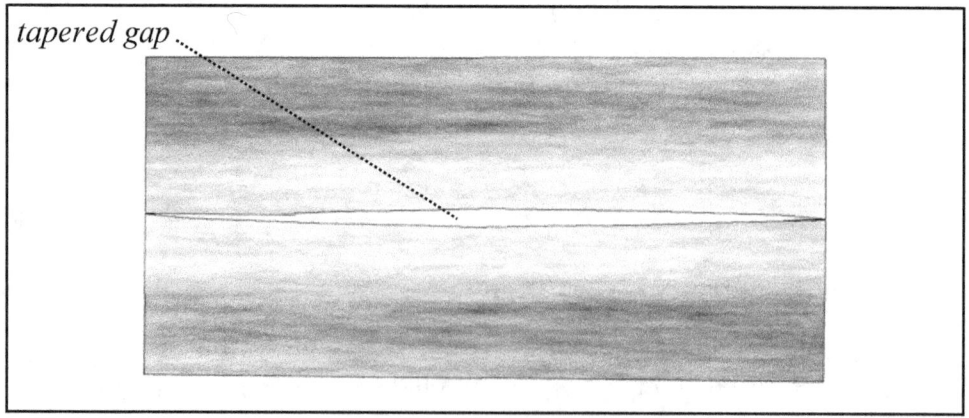

boards with gap before clamping
(width of the gap is exaggerated)

6. Make the first cut at the mid-point of the board and every subsequent cut a little longer until you've gone over the entire length of the board. This will give you a gentle curve.

7. When the two boards are put together, there will be 1/8 to 3/16 inch gap in the center of the joint.

8. Clamping the boards will close the gap and create pressure at the ends of the boards. This reduces the possibility of the ends cracking or splitting.

9. Apply small clamps to secure the boards to the strong backs. This will hold them down ensuring full and even contact of their edges and a flat panel when the clamps are removed.

10. Set clamps across the board and tighten them until the gap is closed but don't put full pressure on the clamps.

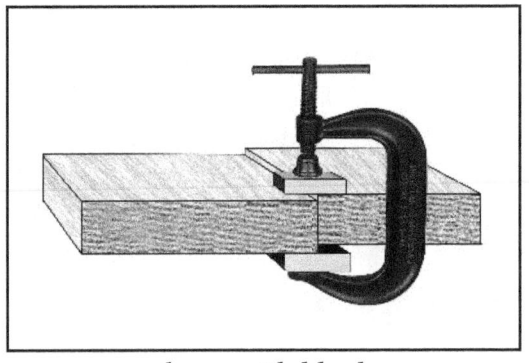

clamp with blocks

11. The surface of the two boards at the joint should be flush. If it isn't, use a rubber mallet to drive the high board down.

12. If that won't do it, put a small clamp on the joint. If there are places along the joint where the surface of the two boards don't line up and your clamps won't reach them, clamp a board across the two boards at that point and drive wedges under or over the boards to force them flush.

13. When the boards are flush, tighten the clamps to full pressure.

summary of chapter 13

edge joints

your

notes

making strong straight edge joints

1. Unplug your table-saw, run the blade up to full height and use a hand square to make sure the blade is square to the table.

2. Select two boards.

3. Use a joiner or a fence extender to make the edges of the boards straight, smooth and perfectly square to the surface.

4. Use a block plane to create a shallow arc. A four foot board will have 1/16 to 3/32 inch off the center of its edge.

5. Keep the sole of the plane flat against the edge to keep it square to the face of the board. That allows the edges to be in full contact when the joint is assembled. Periodically check the edge with a hand square.

6. Make the first cut at the mid-point of the board and every subsequent cut a little longer until you've gone over the entire length of the board. This will give you a gentle arch.

7. When the two boards are put together, there will be 1/8 to 3/16 inch gap in the center of the joint.

8. Clamping the boards will close the gap and create pressure at the ends of the boards. This reduces the possibility of the ends cracking or splitting.

9. Apply small clamps to secure the boards to the strong backs. This will hold them down ensuring full and even contact of their edges and a flat panel when the clamps are removed.

10. Set clamps across the board and tighten them until the gap is closed but don't put full pressure on the clamps.

11. The surface of the two boards at the joint should be flush. If it isn't, use a rubber mallet to drive the high board down.

12. If that won't do it, put a small clamp on the joint. If there are places along the joint where the surface of the two boards don't line up and your clamps won't reach them, clamp a board across the two boards at that point and drive wedges under or over the boards to force them flush.

13. When the boards are flush, tighten the clamps to full pressure.

chapter 14

the

properties

of wood

Lumber comes from a living, growing organism made of cells. No matter how it's used, wood never loses some of the properties of the tree it comes from.

When a tree is cut into logs, the cells begin to lose moisture, but very slowly. When logs are cut into boards, moisture escapes from the cells faster. When the moisture content of the cells drops below fifteen percent, the cells and the boards begin to shrink. Conversely, when a dry board gains moisture and goes above fifteen percent, the cells and the board expand.

Most of the lumber you buy has been kiln dried. After a tree is cut into boards, they go into a kiln where the moisture content is gradually brought down below fifteen percent making them stable and ready for use. If, at some point, the cells gain moisture – which can happen in high humidity – the wood may swell. You must allow for expansion and contraction or you risk the long term viability of your project.

The exact amount of movement in a board depends on the species and whether the board was flat, radial or quarter sawn.

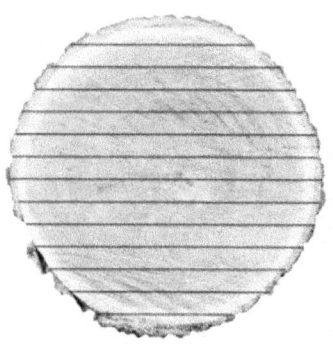

image 1 – flat sawn log

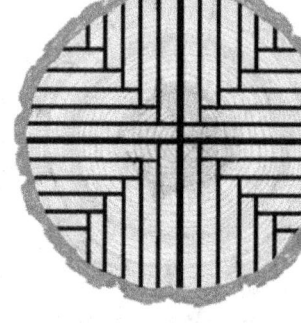

image 2 – quarter-sawn

Boards are called quarter sawn because the log is cut in quarters to allow cutting the boards. (image 2)

If the lines in the end grain of a board run across the width of the board, it was flat sawn. (image 4) If the lines in the end-grain run across the thickness of the board, that board was quarter sawn. (image 3)

Flat sawn boards can be cut with the log in one position. (image 1) But, to cut quarter sawn boards, a log must be repositioned while it's being cut in the mill. (image 2) A log will produce fewer quarter-sawn than flat sawn boards. You can see how all this makes quarter sawn boards much more expensive than flat-sawn boards.

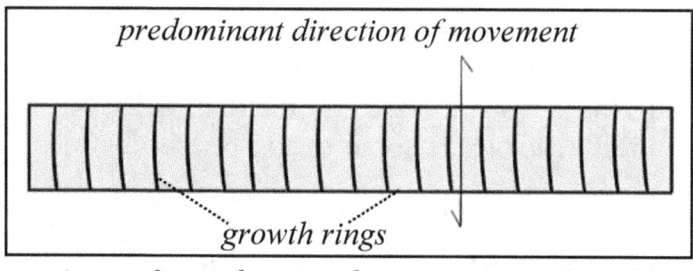

image 3 – end grain of a quarter sawn board

Expansion and contraction is very slight along the length of a board. There is some movement between the lines of grain but most of the movement in a board happens along its grain lines. (images 3, 4 , 5 & 6) That's why a quarter-sawn board is more dimensionally stable than a flat-sawn board. It's also why flat sawn boards can cup.

why boards cup

You may have seen a board with its edges raised so its surface isn't flat. That was caused by different vectors of movement in the board. If you see arcing lines in the end-grain

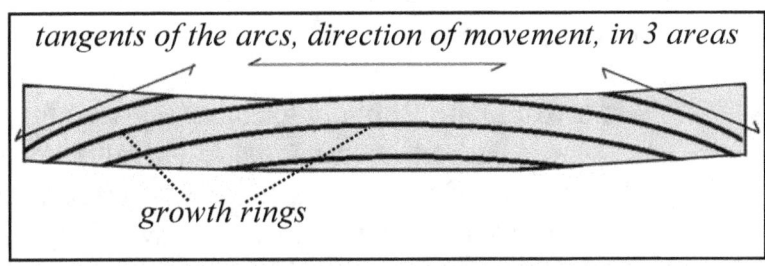
image 4 – cupping in a wide flat sawn board

running across the width of a board, that board was flat-sawn. (image 4) Those arcing lines were part of the rings of a tree. The tangents of the arcs (the direction of the arc at a specific point) are different from the center to the edges of the board.

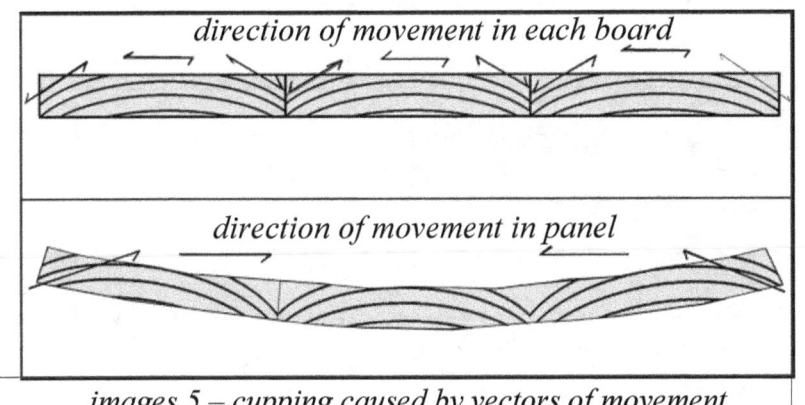
images 5 – cupping caused by vectors of movement

This creates different directions of movement between the center and the edges of the board. The shrinkage along the grain pulls the outside edges of the board up. In narrow boards, cupping is usually so small that it's not noticeable. In wider boards, cupping can be dramatic and can ruin a panel.

Boards that are less than six inches rarely show cupping. However, if you make a panel using narrow boards but the arcs of the boards face the same way, (image 5) that panel will have the same differential of forces as a wide, flat sawn board.

The traditional method to prevent cupping in a panel involves using boards that are no more than six inches wide. The boards are set so that no two adjoining boards have the arcs of their grain facing in the same direction. (image 6)

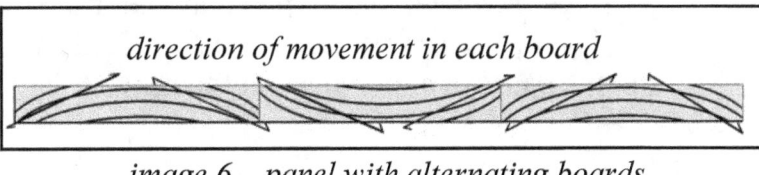
image 6 – panel with alternating boards

Since each board will cup too slightly to be noticeable, the panel will remain flat. However, alternating arcs may create another problem.

The cambium, commonly called sap wood, is the part of a tree inside the bark. It carries water and nutrients from the soil up into the tree. Heart wood is the central part of a tree. Usually, sap wood has a different tone than heart wood so if alternating boards have sapwood, the panel may have strips of a different tone in it. On the other hand, boards with a strong grain pattern may create distinct six inch strips in a panel.

If you want to avoid either of these conditions, you can set all the boards with the grain facing the same way by restraining the cupping with a rail or strong-back attached to the underside of the panel with screws. (image 7) This will also work with wide boards.

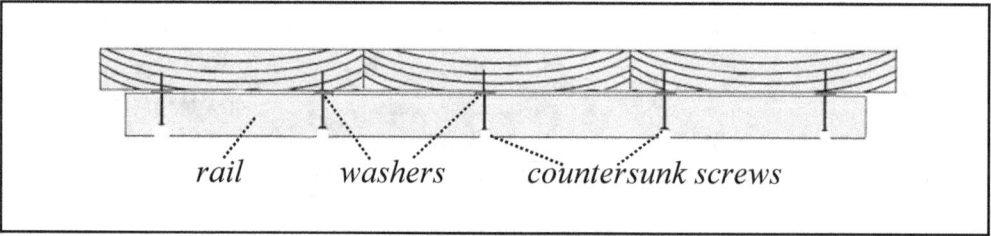

rail   washers   countersunk screws

image 7 – panel with rail

Once a panel has cupped it's difficult to bring it back to flat. However, if you prevent the panel from cupping in the first place, it will maintain its integrity.

Maple requires a thicker rail than mahogany or walnut.

The thickness of the rail required to stabilize the panel depends on the thickness and width of the panel and the species of the boards in the panel.

Since the panel may expand and contract, the rail should have a slot for the screws and metal or plastic washers between it and the panel to allow the panel to move.

why plywood is stable

Plywood consists of thin sheets of wood (veneers) laid one over the other with the direction of their grain running perpendicular to the layer above and below them. The long fibers of each layer restrain the movement across the width of the layers above and below it. This creates a sheet which is dimensionally stable as well as structurally sound in both directions across the sheet.

why wood warps and twists

Trees are made of cells which are arranged in fibers that run up it. The hereditary forces in a tree are vertical, toward the sun. In most cases, those fibers run straight and long up the trunk. But, if something falls against the tree or if it's in a constant struggle against wind, those fibers must resist – exerting force laterally – to survive. With time, the upward and lateral forces find an equilibrium. The competing forces become stored in the fibers and when the tree is cut into logs, the forces remain in balance. However, when the logs are cut into boards, that balance is disturbed, the lateral forces are unleashed and the boards warp.

Sometimes, a board is cut with the competing forces still in balance within it so it's flat when you buy it. However, when you rip it on your table saw, the forces are unleashed. The board may bind the blade, warp or twist. This is the result of a struggle between the forces of a tree's genetics with the forces of its environment.

controlling the effects of changes in humidity

If you apply finish to one side of a panel and leave the other side unfinished, moisture will move in and out of the unfinished side faster than through the finished side. If the humidity changes and one side of a panel gains moisture while the other side does not, the panel may cup because the cells on the unfinished side will have gained moisture and expanded.

End grain gains moisture faster than edge grain so changes in humidity will affect the ends of boards faster causing them to swell and crack the body of the board or shrink and crack the ends of it.

To mitigate the effects of changes in humidity, apply finish to all exposed sides of a panel and to all exposed end grain whether they are seen or not.

Unseen areas are good places to use up old finishes.

chapter 15

how wood goes from tree to shop

When a log is cut into boards, those boards have a very high moisture content. For a board to be usable in furniture and cabinets, it must have a moisture level below fifteen per cent. There are two ways to accomplish that: kiln drying or air drying.

kiln dried lumber

The boards you buy at a lumber yard are kiln dried. That lumber comes from mills which cut the logs into boards then put the boards into huge kilns which bake out the moisture in a controlled process to prevent cracking while bringing the moisture content down below 15 percent. That lumber is ready for use immediately.

air drying lumber

Some woodworkers believe that kiln dried lumber is like bread with a "crust" and that, like bread, the interior and the crust have different properties. They claim that when a kiln dried board is cut it can warp because of this difference. They also claim that air dried lumber finishes better. All that may or may not be true, but one thing is unquestionably true: green wood is far cheaper than kiln dried wood. If you have the space, the time and the effort available to do it, you'll save a lot of money buying green lumber and air-drying it.

It takes one year for every inch of thickness of the boards to air dry lumber. Therefore, you'll have to wait at least one year from the time you buy the wood before you can use it. You'll have to carefully plan and buy today for what you expect to use a year from now so you have enough dry lumber when you need it.

That being said, if you're dedicated to using air dried lumber, here's how to do it:

Find a saw mill that sells green lumber. Most mills have their own kilns and may not sell their green lumber. Smaller mills are more likely to do that. Someone who has a portable mill may be willing to mill logs for you. If you have some land with a tree lot, they may be willing to bring their mill to your lot. You can buy a portable mill and make your own lumber but running a saw mill is an extremely dangerous operation so make sure to research how to use the equipment before you start. If you buy a mill, you'll be maintaining equipment, cutting, trimming, storing, moving and milling logs as well as air drying the lumber so you'll be spending a lot of time not making furniture.

When storing green lumber, the ends must be sealed. Coat the ends of the boards with a sealant that won't penetrate too deep into the wood. Old paint works well. Sealing the ends of boards slows the rate of moisture migration to approximately the same as at the edges of the boards. If you don't coat the ends, moisture will escape faster from the end grain than from the edges causing the ends of a board to shrink faster than the rest of it. That difference in shrinkage will cause the ends to crack several inches into the board. If you have an eight foot board, and lose six inches at each end, you've lost twelve per cent of your investment.

After painting the ends, stack the lumber under cover starting at least four inches off the ground. Put one inch strips of wood between each layer of boards so air can flow around them. That allows them to dry and prevents mold. It's best to keep it in an open shed for the first few months so the wood dries slowly and then move it inside for the last few months. Although wood takes one year for every inch of thickness to reach a moisture level below fifteen percent, extremely high humidity will slow the process and extremely high humidity will speed it up. It's a good idea to use a moisture gauge to know when the boards are ready to be used.

Once the boards have reached moisture stability, you can treat them the same as kiln dried lumber.

final

notes

Nature has made wood extraordinarily beautiful, versatile and complex. We are fortunate to be able to explore what it offers.

Woodworking is seductive. I love the tools, the designs, the planning and the implementation. I love seeing stacks of hardwoods at a lumber yard, the smell of cherry when I cut it, of oak being sanded and the fragrance of maple sawdust on my hands at the end of the day. I love discovering hidden figures in boards when I oil them and the feel of wood after I've sanded it. I love the work, but most of all, I love the feelings I get when I'm doing it.

If you'd like to take a class in these techniques or if you'd like me to give a talk to a group or organization, contact me at *cubsrmarc@msn.com.*

If you have any comments on my book or my art, I'd like to read them.

Good luck in all you do.

Glossary

air dried lumber – a method of drying boards by stacking them so that air flows around them.

aliphatic (yellow) glue – a modified form of white glue which has a faster set up time and greater moisture resistance.

biscuits – a short spline set into a pocket within a joint.

caliper –measures the thickness of an object.

coped joints – junction of two boards with one cut to fit the contour of the other.

cupping – bowing of a board across its grain.

curved joint – two boards joined along a curve.

edge grain – the surface at the sides of a board in line with the direction of the grain.

end grain – the surface at the ends of a board created when cutting across the grain.

feathers on the edge of a cut – random long fibers of a board which are loose but still attached after the edge is cut.

flat-sawn – board cut tangentially from a log.

Forstner – name of a company that produces a specific type drill bit.

green lumber – boards that have a high moisture content, usually shortly after the tree was milled.

hash marks – marks used to align two boards along a joint.

hole saw – a circular tool with teeth around its circumference; used to make large diameter holes.

joiner – a stationary tool which straightens and smooths the edge of a board.

joining – gluing two boards together.

journeyman – someone who has gotten credentials, usually from a labor union, as a skilled trades person.

kerf – the space left after cutting a board with a saw blade.

kiln – an oven for drying lumber in controlled conditions.

mallet – a hammer-like tool, normally with a wooden or hard rubber head.

mini-grinder – a smaller and lighter weight version of an auto body grinder.

modified tung oil – tung oil which has been chemically altered by adding plasticizers.

pilot hole – a hole drilled with a drill bit for a screw.

pipe clamp – a length of pipe (usually 2 - 7 feet long) with jaws attached.

plug cutter – a bit (usually with four cutting spurs) used with a drill or drill press to make pegs.

quarter-sawn – boards milled on a line from the center of a tree towards the outer edge.

scribing – marking a board to precisely match it to another surface.

strong-back – board which is attached to a panel to keep it flat.

trapezoid – a four sided figure with two parallel sides.

veneers – thin sheets of wood used in making plywood or laid over wood to make a finished surface.

Waterlox – brand name for modified tung oil.

Index

A

Adding circles to your design.............................. 154, 162

Albany Park,... 49

aligned... 243, 246

alignment........................ 70, 72, 86-87, 101-103, 112-113

apply finish... 251, 252

arcs.. 250

alternating.. 249

assembly 31, 34, 36, 65, 70, 72, 82, 86-88, 97-98, 101, 103-104, 108-109, 111, 114

axes... 57

B

blade 15-17, 32, 65-66, 82-83, 98-99, 109, 125-127, 136-138, 146-148, 156-157

80 tooth.. 68, 84

boards 69, 70, 72, 73, 85, 86, 88, 96-97, 99-104, 107-108, 110-115, 117, 123-124, 126, 135-138, 243, 246, 248-250

Boards.. 99, 110

bow.. 104, 114

Brotherhood Tavern on Capital Way............................... 120

business agent... 120

C

cabinet.................. 104, 114, 190, 191, 194, 196, 201-203, 206

caliper... 34

Carpenters Local Union 1148... 120

Chicago.. 49

clamp. 32, 35, 70-71, 86, 97, 102, 108, 112, 128, 139, 243, 246

Clamp 70, 86, 101, 111, 124, 125, 127, 130, 136, 137, 139, 141, 146, 155

clamps............. 63, 69-72, 85-88, 100-104, 110-114, 243, 246

Countersink... 42, 43

cracking and splitting... 243, 246

Creating a pegging pattern............................... 129, 140 cup... 249

cupping... 249

curved joinery... 57

cut radially... 249

D

Douglas fir.. 120

dowels... 121

Draw the line.. 34

drill......................... 35, 96, 107, 127-132, 138-143, 146, 155

Drill.. 41, 43, 96, 107

F

fence. 17, 31-34, 68, 84, 124-126, 136-138, 148, 150, 157, 159

fence extender... 40, 68, 84

fibers... 68, 84, 226, 250

filler.. 226, 227, 230, 231

flat-sawn... 248-249

G

gauge. 32, 130, 131, 141, 142, 146, 149, 150, 155, 157, 159, 255

geometry... 57

Geometry... 50

gloves.. 16

glue 45, 69-72, 84-85, 87, 99-100, 102-103, 110-111, 113, 129, 131, 140, 142, 149-153, 158-162, 224-227, 230-231

Glue.. 31, 124, 136

glue-up table... 99, 110

gluing... 118

grain.... 63, 105, 115, 123-124, 126, 135-137, 179, 185, 248, 250

end... 248

lines of... 248

H

hand plane.. 178, 183

hash mark..... 64, 69-71, 81, 85-87, 100-102, 110, 111, 113

heart wood... 249

Heart wood.. 249
Hole saw.. 131, 142

I

industrial revolution... 8
   inserts..................................... 147, 149-153, 156, 158-162

J

jig........................ 127-128, 130, 138-139, 141, 146, 155-156
   jig for cutting tapers... 163, 171
  joint 58, 64, 69-72, 81, 84-87, 97-104, 108-114, 227, 231,
    241, 243, 246

K

kerf.. 148-149, 151-153, 157-162

L

Leif Eriksson... 121
line 16, 34, 58, 64-65, 70, 81-82, 86, 97-98, 101-103, 108-109,
112-113, 125, 137, 227, 231, 243, 246

M

mahogany.. 63, 250
maple... 8, 46, 226, 231, 250, 257
Mayo Clinic... 236
Minneapolis... 46
mitered joint.. 189, 196, 200, 206
moisture.. 247, 251, 255
motor
one-horse.. 15
movement.. 250

N

Nature.. 257

O

Olympia, Washington... 119
Overlapping curved joints...................................... 104, 114

P

palaces and cathedrals... 8
pegs... 122-126, 135-138
cutting, with a hole saw.. 126, 138
drilling and setting... 128, 140
drilling holes for large.. 130, 141
making, in edge grain... 123, 135
Pegs... 123
pilot hole.. 96, 107
planer.. 40, 47, 179, 184
plug cutters.. 122, 126, 138
plywood 22, 31, 33-34, 40-43, 46, 47, 118, 124-127, 136-138,
146, 155, 250
Plywood... 250
podium.. 234
Position the board.. 129, 140
push stick................................. 14, 17, 125-126, 137, 148, 157

Q

quarter-sawn.. 248

R

rail... 250
rubber mallet.. 243, 246

S

sap wood.. 249
Sap wood.. 249
saw 14, 16, 32, 34, 46, 64-66, 68, 69, 81-82, 84, 98-99, 104,
109-110, 115, 117, 123-128, 130-131, 135-139, 141, 146, 149,
150, 155-157, 159, 235

sawdust 8, 47, 126, 138, 150, 152, 158, 161, 223-226, 229-230, 257

Sawstop.. 16

screw 31, 34, 42-43, 96-98, 104, 107-109, 115, 122, 124, 127, 128, 136, 138, 139

Screw... 36, 97, 108

shims.. 104, 115, 132, 143

shop.. 16-17, 46, 118

strips 40-42, 68, 73, 84, 88, 104, 114, 148, 149, 151, 157-159

overlaying.. 73, 88

T

table 15, 16, 31, 66, 72, 82-84, 87, 99, 103, 104, 109, 114, 117, 118, 125-127, 130, 136-139, 141, 146-147, 155-156

Titebond.. 224

tools... 7-8, 49, 96, 107, 257

tree.. 247, 249

trial assembly.. 196, 206

U

U. S. Bureau of Labor Statistics.. 7

Urbana, Illinois... 117

W

walnut.. 120, 225

Waynesboro, Tennessee.. 118

woodworker.. 7, 13, 117, 235

woodworking...................................... 7, 8, 49, 117

Woodworking.. 46, 57

www.ingramcontent.com/pod-product-compliance
Lightning Source LLC
Chambersburg PA
CBHW080407290526
45791CB00008BA/2186

9780692067475